Why Did the United States Iraq?

This edited volume presents the foremost scholarly thinking on why the United States invaded Iraq in 2003, a pivotal event in both modern US foreign policy and international politics.

In the years since the US invasion of Iraq it has become clear that the threat of weapons of mass destruction was not as urgent as the Bush administration presented it and that Saddam Hussein was not involved with either Al Qaeda or 9/11. Many consider the war a mistake and question why Iraq was invaded. A majority of Americans now believe that the public were deliberately misled by the Bush administration in order to bolster support for the war. Public doubt has been strengthened by the growing number of critical scholarly analyses and in-depth journalistic investigations about the invasion that suggest the administration was not candid about its real reasons for wanting to take action against Iraq.

This volume begins with a survey of private scholarly views about the war's origins, then assesses the current state of debate by organizing the best recent thinking by foreign policy and international relations experts on why the United States invaded Iraq. The book covers a broad range of approaches to explaining the Iraq War – the role of the uncertainty of intelligence, cognitive biases, ideas, Israel, and oil, highlighting areas of both agreement and disagreement.

This volume will be of much interest to students of the Iraq War, US foreign and security policy, strategic studies, Middle Eastern politics, and IR/Security Studies in general.

Jane K. Cramer is an Assistant Professor of Political Science at the University of Oregon. Her research focuses on the causes of national overestimations of security threats, as well as other aspects of the domestic politics behind foreign policymaking, especially the diversionary theory of war.

A. Trevor Thrall is Associate Professor of Government and Politics and directs the Biodefense graduate program at George Mason University. Much of his work focuses on the intersection of war, news, and public opinion. His recent work has investigated presidential threat inflation, public support for missile defense, and how changes in the news media have affected US foreign policy.

Routledge Global Security Studies

Series Editors: Aaron Karp, Regina Karp and Terry Teriff

Why Did the United States Invade Iraq?

Edited by Jane K. Cramer and A. Trevor Thrall

Routledge
Taylor & Francis Group

LONDON AND NEW YORK

First published 2012
by Routledge
2 Park Square, Milton Park, Abingdon, Oxon OX14 4RN

Simultaneously published in the USA and Canada
by Routledge
711 Third Avenue, New York, NY 10017

Routledge is an imprint of the Taylor & Francis Group, an informa business

British Library Cataloguing in Publication Data
A catalogue record for this book is available from the British Library

Library of Congress Cataloging-in-Publication Data
Why did the United States invade Iraq?/[edited by] Jane K. Cramer
and A. Trevor Thrall.
  p. cm.
  Includes bibliographical references and index.
  1. Iraq War, 2003–Causes. 2. Iraq–Strategic aspects. 3. United
States–Foreign relations–2001–2009. I. Cramer, Jane K. II. Thrall,
A. Trevor.
  DS79.757.W49 2011
  956.7044′31–dc22   2011011709

ISBN: 978-0-415-78212-8 (hbk)
ISBN: 978-0-415-78213-5 (pbk)
ISBN: 978-0-203-80456-8 (ebk)

Typeset in Baskerville
by Wearset Ltd, Boldon, Tyne and Wear

Contents

Tables

Contributors

Jane K. Cramer is Assistant Professor of Political Science at the University of Oregon. She focuses on the study of international relations, specializing in international security. Her research examines the multiple causes of national security panics in the United States. She also researches the domestic politics behind American foreign policy, and the diversionary theory of war.

Colin Dueck is Associate Professor of Government and International Politics at George Mason University. His research and teaching interests are in the history and practice of international strategy and diplomacy. His most recent book is *Hard Line: The Republican Party and U.S. Foreign Policy since World War II* (Princeton University Press).

John S. Duffield is Professor of Political Science at Georgia State University. His research interests include international politics, the politics of the European Union, and energy politics. He recently edited a volume entitled *Balance Sheet: The Iraq War and U.S. National Security* (Stanford University Press).

Edward C. Duggan is a Ph.D. candidate in the Department of Political Science at the University of Oregon. His research interests include international relations and the domestic politics of national security.

Andrew Flibbert is Assistant Professor in the Department of Political Science at Trinity College. He teaches and writes about international security and American foreign policy, with a regional specialization in the Middle East and North Africa. He has published articles in *Security Studies, Middle East Journal, Political Science Quarterly*, and *PS: Politics and Political Science*, and he is the author of *Commerce in Culture: States and Markets in the World Film Trade*.

Robert Jervis is the Adlai E. Stevenson Professor of International Affairs at Columbia University. Specializing in international politics in general and security policy, decision-making, and theories of conflict and cooperation in particular, his most recent book is *System Effects: Complexity in Political and Social Life* (Princeton University Press).

Michael T. Klare is the Five College Professor of Peace and World Security Studies, based at Hampshire College in Amherst, Massachusetts. Widely published on US defense policy, the arms trade, and international security affairs, his most recent book is *Rising Powers, Shrinking Planet: The New Geopolitics of Energy* (Holt Paperbacks).

Michael Lind is Policy Director of New America's Economic Growth Program. He is a co-founder of the New America Foundation, along with Ted Halstead and Sherle Schwenninger, and was the first New America fellow. With Ted Halstead he is co-author of *The Radical Center: The Future of American Politics* (Doubleday)

Jane M. O. Sharp is Visiting Senior Research Fellow in the Department of War Studies at King's College London. Her research interests include international arms control, Balkan security, and Russian attitudes toward arms control. She is at work on a book about Russia, the West, and the Balkans for the US Institute of Peace.

Jerome Slater is University Research Scholar at the State University of New York at Buffalo. His main research interests include US foreign policy in the Middle East and the Israeli–Palestinian conflict. He is at work on a book on US policy and the Arab–Israeli conflict, 1948–present.

A. Trevor Thrall is Associate Professor of Government and Politics at George Mason University where he directs the Graduate Program in Biodefense. His research focuses on the intersection of war, the news media, and public opinion. He is co-editor most recently of *U.S. Foreign Policy and the Politics of Fear: Threat Inflation since 9/11* (Routledge).

Acknowledgments

Like life, an edited volume requires contributions and support from many people. In addition to the unstinting support from our families and friends, we need to thank the Department of Political Science at the University of Oregon, the Social Sciences Department at the University of Michigan – Dearborn, and the Department of Public and International Affairs at George Mason University for providing necessary funding and every form of logistical support. We would also like to thank the contributors to this volume, all of whom have been wonderfully responsive to our repeated requests despite short deadlines and without whom there would be no book. Finally, we thank Paradigm Publishers and Cambridge University Press for permission to reprint portions of material previously published in their books and journals.

Jane K. Cramer
A. Trevor Thrall

1 Introduction

Why did the United States invade Iraq?

Jane K. Cramer and A. Trevor Thrall

On March 22, 2003, President George W. Bush told the United States that "Our mission is clear, to disarm Iraq of weapons of mass destruction, to end Saddam's support of terrorism, and to free the Iraqi people." In the first year after the invasion of Iraq, evidence showed that Saddam Hussein had no weapons of mass destruction (WMDs), nor was there any intelligence to support the claims Saddam Hussein was connected with Al Qaeda or the 9/11 hijackers. These revelations led the majority of Americans to believe that invading Iraq was a mistake and that they had been misled before the war.[1] Revealing documents like the *Downing Street Memo* seemed to confirm for many observers that the Bush administration had intentionally misled the public. Indeed, the secret British memo stated that "military action was now seen as inevitable" by US administration leaders and that the "intelligence and facts were being fixed around the policy" in Washington in July 2002, well before President Bush presented the possibility of invading Iraq to Congress and the UN in September 2002, and long before Bush declared publicly that he reluctantly made the decision to invade in March 2003 (Danner 2006).

In the years since the invasion, the debate over why the United States invaded Iraq has not abated, but it has progressed. This volume is aimed at bringing together the leading arguments to date about why the United States invaded Iraq. Like other scholars, we began studying the run-up to the Iraq War as it happened in 2002. We first focused on discerning how war came about politically—we tried to unravel and explain the intersection of events, intelligence failure, presidential leadership, threat manipulation, congressional acquiescence and international resistance and cooperation—in short, the process and politics of threat inflation that led the United States as a whole to go to war (Thrall and Cramer 2009).

In the spring of 2006, the debate over why the Bush administration *chose* to push for war came into sharp focus. Two leading realist scholars, John J. Mearsheimer and Stephen M. Walt, came out publicly arguing that Bush administration leaders had been convinced after 9/11 to invade Iraq by the now famous neoconservative advisers within the administration including Paul Wolfowitz, Richard Perle, Scooter Libby and others. Mearsheimer and Walt argued the neoconservatives successfully led the broader "Israel Lobby" to press for regime change in Iraq within the administration, with Congress, and the public (Mearsheimer and Walt 2007). They further proposed few other experts would *openly* support their claims about the importance of the Israel lobby for fear of being labeled anti-Semitic, even though they believed many experts privately agreed with them.[2] Our own impression at the time was that Mearsheimer and Walt were correct on this latter point, but we could only guess at the breadth of support for this Israel lobby thesis.

In addition to the Israel lobby argument, informal conversations with many of our colleagues who study foreign policy and international relations indicated that there were many other significant hypotheses experts would not raise publicly for fear of damaging their professional reputations and being labeled conspiracy theorists. For example, we noticed that many international relations experts linked the US invasion of Iraq with geopolitical interests in oil while only a very few US scholars were publicly examining this important realist hypothesis. We also heard many scholars quietly propose that private US corporate interests in oil-related or war-related profits were the likely primary motives behind the war. These colleagues seemed to focus much less on the neoconservative advisers and much more on the leading role of Vice President Cheney. At the same time, we heard many other interesting permutations of explanations for the invasion, and yet these rich hypotheses were not being publicly analyzed.

After noticing the disconnect between vibrant private scholarly discussions and restrained public analysis, we decided in the fall of 2006 to launch an online survey of scholars and other foreign policy experts with the purpose of exploring the question: why *did* the United States invade Iraq? This survey had three purposes. First, we saw this survey as hypothesis-generating, a way to reveal the large number of complex and interesting hypotheses about the main drivers—actors and motives—behind the war. Second, we also hoped to investigate the tendency among our colleagues to publicly and professionally support and analyze "safe" hypotheses, while often privately supporting "conspiracy" type hypotheses. In particular, we noticed many scholars publicly taking politicians at their word, or at least giving politicians the benefit of the doubt, while privately being more cynical and questioning the sincerity of politicians' rhetoric, and believing politicians are likely motivated by factors they do not discuss openly. Third, we saw this survey as providing an historical "snapshot" of scholarly thinking at the time, which would prove interesting to compare with future understandings of this war.

In this introduction we offer the rich findings of this 2006 survey as the starting point for this volume. By presenting the various intricate hypotheses generated in considerable detail here it becomes clear how complex it is to analyze the multiple possible motives behind the invasion. For example, the survey found more than 63 percent of our expert respondents believed oil was a highly important factor for Vice President Cheney who was ranked by 93 percent of our respondents as the most important decision-maker behind the decision to invade Iraq. Thus, privately, a strong majority of experts revealed to us they believed that oil was an important factor in the decision for war even though decision-makers repeatedly flatly denied the oil motive, and almost all scholars publicly summarily dismissed the "oil hypothesis" without analysis. Further, our survey found the neoconservatives were overwhelmingly ranked as the second most influential (84 percent) decision-makers behind the decision to invade (above Rumsfeld and Bush), and the neoconservatives were privately viewed by more than a majority of our respondents as highly motivated by "Defending Israel/Israeli interests"—in sharp contrast with other key leaders. We believe this finding largely confirmed the views of Mearsheimer and Walt at the time: many experts privately agreed with them that Israeli interests had a significant influence on the decision to invade. It should be remembered that Mearsheimer and Walt were widely condemned and rarely defended for attempting to discuss this theory at the time, even though our results show that many experts privately agreed with them in significant respects. Thus, supported by survey evidence that expert opinion privately gives more weight to such "conspiratorial" hypotheses, this volume seeks to make the debate over them more public.

In the end, we argue the results of this survey help to demonstrate that real progress has been made in this debate. We still do not know why the United States invaded Iraq, just as the debate continues about the causes of World War I, for example. But this volume demonstrates that through careful analysis much can be known about why the United States invaded, even without being able to get inside the minds of the top decision-makers. Final and complete answers will never be possible, but we believe that after reading what experts were thinking in 2006 and then comparing it with the arguments and analyses in the rest of this volume, it becomes quite clear that close analysis of this question has led to an evolution in thinking on this question of "why did the U.S. invade Iraq?" We believe the survey demonstrates an interesting "first draft" of history, very much focused on the centrality of the neoconservative advisers. Most of the chapters in this volume have largely moved on from this focus on the neoconservatives to a "second draft" of history, much more concerned with understanding the top leaders of Cheney, Rumsfeld and Bush, including their strong desires to invade Iraq prior to 9/11.

The broad expert consensus of 2006: US dominance was central (not WMD, terrorism or 9/11)

The level of broad expert agreement we found on key issues in 2006 surprised us. Not only is it rare to find so much agreement about controversial foreign policies, but we thought it was striking to find experts very broadly agreed that the Bush administration's stated justifications for war were not in fact the most important motivations for the invasion. The majority of experts surveyed did not believe that WMD were a central motive and saw little to no connection between the Iraq War and the war on terrorism or the events of 9/11. As one respondent put it, "[T]he gap between the Administration's publicly stated reasons for the war and the real reasons behind this decision is the widest ever as well in the history of American wars."

The survey findings reveal these agreements in several ways. The online survey began with and centered on four open-ended questions which allowed respondents unlimited space to respond.[3] The survey also included three more multiple-choice type questions about the administration's decision-making process, which also allowed additional space to comment in open-ended fashion. The first question on the survey began with President Bush's quotation that opened this chapter in which he stated his declared reasons for invasion, and then it simply asked respondents, "As of today, over three years later, why do you think the US invaded Iraq?" While the tabulation of the open-ended responses in Table 1.1 does not adequately capture the rich debate revealed by this question which we discuss at length below, it nonetheless reveals that respondents were about twice as likely to identify broader foreign policy goals as the reason for the war than they were to mention the threat of Iraqi WMD, or the need to

Table 1.1 Factors behind the decision to invade Iraq

Reasons for US invasion of Iraq	Number of mentions	% of respondents mentioning
Reshape/influence democracy in Middle East	112	50.45
Oil interests	62	27.93
Iraqi WMD threat	60	27.03
Oust Saddam/save Iraqi people	52	23.42
Israel security/interests	30	13.51
Exert/enhance US power/hegemony	30	13.51
Neoconservative ideology	30	13.51
Terrorism	30	13.51
Easy victory	23	10.36
Bush's psychology	21	9.46
Unfinished business	18	8.11
US domestic politics	17	7.66
General democracy promotion	12	5.41
9/11 worldview change	11	4.95
General economic interests	5	2.25

Question: on March 22, 2003, at the very beginning of the US invasion of Iraq, President Bush told Americans that: "Our mission is clear, to disarm Iraq of weapons of mass destruction, to end Saddam's support of terrorism, and to free the Iraqi people." As of today, over three years later, why do you think the United States invaded Iraq?

depose Saddam. Further, the specific threat of terrorism or any connection to 9/11 were even much less likely to be mentioned by our respondents, except in the negative. On the other hand, oil interests, though never discussed by the administration, ranked as the second most often mentioned factor. These broad findings are only suggestive, and we elaborate below at length, but these findings are striking considering both President Bush and our question wording specifically listed disarming Iraq's WMD, ending Saddam's support for terrorism, and freeing the Iraqi people as the reasons for the war, and yet our respondents chose not to echo these reasons but largely to provide wholly different reasons.

Second, as Table 1.2 more specifically shows, the vast majority of respondents did not believe that the administration truly believed that Iraq represented an urgent WMD threat. A simple count of these open-ended responses makes it appear that about 45 percent believed there was some type of WMD threat—either short term or long term. However, a simple count understates the level of doubt about this motive as a real reason for war because even those respondents who granted that the administration *might* have believed there was possibly some type of threat, many respondents qualified their arguments to explain that Iraqi WMD were likely not the real motivation to invade.

Finally, respondents also doubted the other pillar of justification for war—Iraq as the central front in the war on terror. In fact, for our respondents the war on terrorism appears to be much less credible than the role of WMD. As Table 1.1 indicates, terrorism was just the eighth most mentioned factor. Further, very few believed that 9/11 played a significant independent role motivating administration officials toward invading Iraq. Our third question tried to determine if experts believed 9/11 actually played an important "triggering" role by changing the way the administration viewed the threat from Iraq. Instead, as Table 1.3 illustrates, most respondents chose to argue that 9/11's importance lay

Table 1.2 Private administration beliefs about Iraqi WMD

Key leaders' private views	*% responding*
Potential long-term US threat	22.28
Serious/urgent threat to United States	22.28
No threat, pretext for war	21.74
Iraqi WMD not a threat	19.57
Iraq had WMD, respondent gave no threat analysis	5.43
Mixed views on WMD	5.43
Do not know	2.17
Potential regional threat	1.09
Total	100.00

Question: how do you think key leaders in the Bush administration privately viewed the threat from Iraq's weapons of mass destruction in 2002 and early 2003?

Table 1.3 The role of 9/11

Role of 9/11 in decision to invade	% responding
Critical: 9/11 changed how leaders viewed the threat from Iraq	28.9
Critical: 9/11 provided a window of opportunity for the administration to do something it already wanted to do	85.1
Not critical: United States would have invaded anyway	6.7

Note
Percentages add up to more than 100% due to multiple responses.
Question: what role do you think 9/11 played in the decision to invade Iraq? Check all that apply.

primarily in providing a "window of opportunity" for pro-war forces to make their case and for the administration to take aggressive action without fear of public censure.

To those who study these issues closely the fact that experts did not believe the Bush administration may seem rather unsurprising, even if the consensus was extremely broad. What many experts fail to appreciate, however, is the stark contrast between expert views and those of the general public. Though most experts had abandoned the official Bush administration justifications and had constructed alternative explanations for the Iraq War, the public, even if skeptical, was at the time of this survey (and remains) far more divided and far more wedded to the Bush administration's justifications for war. In fact, as Table 1.4 indicates, despite near consensus among experts about the irrelevance of these factors, roughly half of the public at the same point still believed Saddam Hussein was connected to 9/11, that Iraq had WMD before the war, and that Iraq was part of the war on terrorism.

It is important to note that mass opinion on these issues had changed only slightly since 2003 despite a great deal of evidence to the contrary— we think most likely because experts failed to thoroughly debate this issue openly. To this day, even as the Iraq War drags on in new form, and

Table 1.4 American public beliefs about the war in Iraq

Belief	% believing	Poll and date
Saddam Hussein was connected to the 9/11 terror attacks	46	Zogby, September 2006
Iraq had weapons of mass destruction before the war began	54	NBC News/ *Wall Street Journal,* January 2005
Iraq is part of the war on terrorism	48	Gallup/ *USA Today,* September 2006

official opinion polls no longer bother to ask about the reasons for this war, in brief surveys of our freshman college students, more than 85 percent very hesitantly state they believe the war was likely launched at least in significant measure because of an administration belief in a WMD threat or because of Saddam's connections with terrorists. This suggests that the lack of expert debate will have lasting consequences on public understanding (and potentially on public support for future wars) as the Iraq War fades into history.

Expert explanations for the war: neoconservative ideology and the assertion of US dominance

The most consistent statement to emerge from our data about what *did* happen was the importance respondents attached to neoconservative ideology and the grand strategic vision it promoted. Indeed, this was the thread running through a great number of the responses to all of our open-ended questions. Roughly 40 percent of responses to the survey's first question ("Why did the US invade Iraq?") identified the neoconservative ideology as the main motivation for the collective decision to go to war with Iraq, with numerous respondents explaining it in some detail. Many others hinted at it indirectly.

One respondent explained it very fully, unprompted, like this:

> Leading figures within the Bush Administration, linked with the Project for a New American Century and sincerely believing that American unilateral hegemony in the international system was (a) pragmatically necessary for the health of the international system, (b) in America's national interest, and (c) morally justified because of the relative "goodness" of the American way of life, decided that the United States needed to act as a far more energetic and effective world hegemon than had been the case under either the George H.W. Bush or the Bill Clinton Administration. Iraq was, in my opinion, chosen as a supposedly easy target for what has been called the "demonstration effect" of American leadership, military strength and moral superiority (through free enterprise and democratization). The alleged presence of WMD was merely a pretense for the assertion of a new supposedly benign American imperial role. The fact that this whole policy was misconceived, mishandled and counterproductive, should not hide the fact that it was part of a clear and systematic world view held by those leaders and that they consciously decided to use Iraq as the first step of a wider design intended to eventually enable the United States to act unilaterally anywhere around the world with relative impunity.

The consistent drumbeat about the importance of neoconservative ideology in the open-ended questions was loudly amplified in responses to our matrix of influential factors. As Table 1.5 indicates, of the thirteen factors we had respondents rank for each key decision-maker, "Assert US dominance in the 'New American Century'" clearly emerged as the most critical factor for all of them. Even for Cheney, Rumsfeld, and Bush, not typically identified as neoconservatives themselves, this factor led the others in perceived importance. The open-ended responses suggest that respondents saw this ideational factor as the core of the collective decision-making process—the glue that held the administration's leaders and their various agendas together. The widespread consensus about the importance of this ideational factor over material interests or other motivations is striking, especially since the importance of ideational factors is notoriously difficult to establish and most often highly contested.

What jumps out from many of the responses is that experts in 2006 widely perceived that administration officials sincerely held this ideology. It was this vision that guided the leaders and helped them see what they were doing as in the "national interest;" it was not simply rhetoric to cover for narrower or hidden interests. A few characterized these beliefs as a product of "blowback," with several respondents commenting: "The

Table 1.5 What factors influenced the decision-makers?

% responding the factor had high importance to decision-maker				
Factor	Bush	Cheney	Rumsfeld	Neocons
Assert US dominance in a New American Century	**53**	**70**	**64**	**77**
Finishing 1991 Gulf War	**52**	45	39	**53**
Removing Saddam Hussein's threat to Mideast stability	45	44	42	**56**
Individual ego/asserting personal power	44	46	44	30
Iraq's WMD program	42	35	31	23
Protecting oil supplies	40	42	36	29
Control Iraqi oil/promote US corporate oil interests	38	**56**	34	22
GOP electoral advantage	36	38	19	21
Iraq's Al Qaeda links	25	21	12	13
Defending Israel/Israeli interests	25	24	16	**53**
Promote Middle East democracy	22	10	5	**50**
Freeing the Iraqi people from Saddam Hussein	19	8	7	27
Punish Iraq's violations of UN resolutions	9	7	6	7

Question: how important were the following factors in convincing US decision-makers to invade Iraq? Please rank the importance of each factor for each decision maker or group of decision makers. Leave blank if you have no opinion or believe a factor was not applicable to a person/group. (Note: the response scale went from 1 to 10 with 1 being extremely unimportant and 10 being extremely important. Factors were rated as "high importance" if the respondent gave them an 8, 9 or 10.)

neocons have a tendency to believe their own propaganda" and "I think it is amazing to hear (watch) Paul Wolfowitz and Dick Cheney swallow their own rhetoric." Nonetheless, this grand strategic thinking was seen as the driving force and the unifying motivation for the administration. It was often noted that it was a radical departure from past administrations' strategic thinking that was, by contrast, more multilateral, more status quo and stability oriented and less assertive militarily. For many respondents, in the absence of an urgent WMD or terrorist threat, the invasion only makes sense *if* you understand this grand strategic vision.

Broad agreement about the importance of neoconservative ideology did not equate with uniform explanations of the specific reasons for war. Different respondents characterized the influence of the neoconservative agenda on the decision to go to war very differently. By far the most popular emphases were regional and global strategic goals. As Table 1.1 shows, fully half the respondents noted such goals as key factors or explanations behind the decision to invade Iraq. These quotes reveal some of the variations in this type of reasoning:

> Geopolitical position: (1) to put pressure on Saudi Arabia to prosecute financial war on al Qaeda, (2) to put pressure on Iran, (3) to secure SW Asian route to Central Asia, and (4) to minimize Chinese and Russian position in Central Asia.

> To secure our position in a strategically important region of the world – the Persian Gulf and Middle East. This region is important mostly because of its oil.

> The invasion followed the logic of the Bush Doctrine of Preemptive War. The reason is a deep geopolitical shift of U.S. Grand Strategy from Europe to the Greater Middle East. The aim is both security – preventing terrorism – and oil-intervene in Saudi Arabia if Islamic fundamentalists are to overthrow the current regime.

> 1) To establish a robust strategic military presence in the oil rich Middle east. 2) To be able to surround Iran on both sides with US military forces, and also threaten Syria. 3) To secure Iraq's oil reserves for the US and UK ... 4) To provide a demonstration case and establish a precedent for the Bush doctrine of preventive war.

Other respondents emphasized the goal of a "demonstration effect" that would have beneficial effects; that administration officials believed that when the United States flexes its military muscle—wields a "big stick"—it can make other states, especially "rogue states," behave better. Respondents were clear to distinguish this explanation from the idea that the administration felt that the US needed to wield force in order to balance other powers from a defensive perspective. Instead, respondents emphasized the neoconservative belief that the assertion of US dominance through military force could have transformative effects on the international system.

Cheney's influence and the influence of oil

A second area of broad agreement was the central importance of Vice President Dick Cheney. Cheney was ranked as the most influential decision-maker; 93 percent of respondents thought Cheney was "very influential" in the decision to invade, with President Bush coming in fourth (74 percent) after the neocons (83 percent) and Donald Rumsfeld (79 percent). In part it seems that Bush's demotion reflects our respondents' focus on neocon ideology as the driving intellectual force at work. But it also appears to reflect the feeling on the part of many that Cheney and his allies throughout the administration were the driving bureaucratic force at work.

Cheney's importance is worth extended consideration because of its connection to the second most popular factor behind the decision to invade Iraq: oil. For many respondents the focus on oil seems intertwined with a belief that Cheney was the most important player in moving the country to war. That oil placed second on the list of most often mentioned factors in the open-ended questions was surprising in the sense that the Bush administration never discussed, and even denied, that oil was a part of its reasons for war. And though the consensus on Cheney is in some ways not surprising—Cheney is widely recognized as the most influential vice president in the history of the country—it is nevertheless noteworthy

Table 1.6 Who influenced the decision to invade?

Actor	Very influential (%)
Richard Cheney	93
Neoconservative advisors	83
Donald Rumsfeld	79
George W. Bush	74
Karl Rove	37
Israel lobby	19
Corporate oil lobby	17
Condoleezza Rice	15
US military contractors	12
Joint Chiefs	3
Colin Powell	2
Pro-war Democrats	2

Question: how influential do you think the following people or groups were in the process leading to the decision to invade Iraq?

because experts rarely agree to this degree about anything. No other arguments made about the decision-making process received such widespread endorsement in our survey as the leading role of Cheney.

Thus the question follows: what motivated Cheney? As Table 1.5 notes, 70 percent of respondents ranked "Assert US dominance in the 'New American Century'" as a highly influential factor for Cheney, making this the most agreed upon factor for Cheney, as it was for the other decision-makers. Table 1.5 also shows that "Control Iraq oil/promote US corporate oil interests," ranked as the second most important factor for Cheney followed closely by "Protecting oil supplies and oil price stability." We designed the survey to have two different "oil factors," having discovered in pre-survey interviews that people made a distinction between them. Numerous people stressed that there was a possible "national interest" in protecting oil supplies and maintaining oil price stability, while others stressed that an invasion would not serve a "national interest" in oil (as it would be wiser to do other things than invade Iraq to protect oil supplies and oil price stability), but an invasion, while costly to the nation, would serve "private interests" in actually gaining US control of Iraq's oil and thereby promoting US corporate oil interests.

The most frequent and fully explicated oil arguments in the survey, and perhaps the most interesting in their variety, were the "protect oil supplies" type arguments. More than 14 percent of respondents made this type of argument in some form in the open-ended questions. Very common were arguments about problems with Saudi Arabia:

> Oil. 9/11 made Saudi Arabia look unreliable or unstable in the long run. That is, destabilizing Islamists looked too strong. Given how many in the administration, for a diverse set of reasons, long supported invasion, the post-9/11 analysis of oil brought Bush to their side.

> [T]o grab the oil fields in case the Wahabis took charge in Saudi Arabia.

> 9/11 ... increased pressure for US policymakers to create a strong ally that could provide US bases, act in concert with US interests, and control significant oil reserves in the Middle East. In other words, Iraq might serve as a more reliable replacement for the House of Saud.

> To secure a military position in the region and secure global oil markets, since continued military presence in Saudi Arabia was no longer feasible, and clearly dangerous.

> The most persuasive strategic argument is that the United States sought to create a friendly regime (ideally a democratic one) in oil-rich Iraq in order to lessen its dependence on Saudi Arabia, given the latter country's complicity with terrorism.

> Reluctantly, I've come to believe that the U.S. invaded Iraq principally to safeguard oil supplies from the Middle East.

It is very interesting to note that although a majority of respondents felt that "Control Iraq oil/promote US corporate oil interests" was important for Cheney, only a very small number of respondents actually articulated—and none explained—possible corporate oil interests in their open-ended responses. One of the very few explicit mentions of this factor simply said: "I think Halliburton and others always wanted their oil."

Neoconservatives and the Israel argument

The neoconservatives ranked as second most influential in the decision to invade—ahead of Rumsfeld and even President Bush. Respondents argued that neoconservative ideology played a central role in the decision to invade, but the importance of the neoconservatives also suggests that Israel heavily figured in the decision to invade given the neoconservatives' widely recognized preoccupation with Israeli security. Indeed, respondents ranked "Defending Israel/Israeli interests" as the second most important factor for the neoconservatives in our matrix. In the first open-ended question, Israel was only specifically mentioned by just over 13 percent of respondents, less than half as often as oil, but a significant number firmly asserted Israel as important, often folded into arguments about reshaping and democratizing the Middle East.

> [The invasion was motivated by] Neocon ideology which thought they could remake the Middle East in a manner more favorable to the U.S. (and Israeli) interests.

> Bush's neo-con advisors, led by Wolfowitz, had a more complex idea, that US military action could promote wholesale reshaping of the Middle East in a democratic direction. The long term security interest of Israel was part of that package. So was oil.

> I also think that a pro-Israel lobby saw the invasion as a way of getting rid of a threat to Israel.

> Some Christian religious rightists thought it would make Israel safer, as did some Jewish groups.

> Although I think the originally given reasons [by the administration] are part of the explanation, they do not include an extremely important component, i.e., the neo-cons behind the President who saw regime change in Iraq as a beginning for the creation of a democratic Middle East from which a "benign" spillover would emanate to other

Arab states as well as Iran. Democracy's advance in this region would, in turn, help ameliorate the Arab world's relations with Israel; and the American neo-con vision of a muscular Wilsonian world would begin to take shape.

The widespread agreement in 2006 about the influence of the neoconservatives was not surprising, but the ranking of the neoconservatives as significantly more influential than President Bush and strongly interested in Israel's security is notable, as mentioned above, in that it revealed significant private expert support for arguments along the lines of the "Israel Lobby" thesis. From our view today we believe that while there was significant support for Israel lobby-type arguments in 2006 and beyond, this support seems to have significantly faded. As a number of the chapters in this volume argue in one way or another, it is not that Israel was not important to many neoconservatives, it is more that assessments of the importance of the top leaders of Cheney, Rumsfeld and Bush has increased, especially as it has become clear that the top leaders likely very much wanted to invade Iraq *prior* to 9/11 and were thus not likely persuaded by neoconservatives *after* 9/11 to invade. Instead, it appears the top leaders did not have a way to build support for this project before 9/11, and 9/11 created an opportunity.

Debate and disagreement

Despite significant levels of agreement in some areas, the survey also revealed many debates surrounding the administration's decision-making process in detail. Three sharp disagreements recurred: respondents voiced polarized opinions about the administration's internal views of the Iraqi WMD threat, the precise role of 9/11, and whether or not the decision-making process was a "perfect storm" of mutually supporting factors leading to war or whether the invasion was primarily motivated by a single overriding interest.

Administration views of WMD: pretext for war or sincere fear?

As noted above, most respondents to our survey did not believe that the administration's public claims about Iraqi WMD were sincere (see Table 1.2). Instead, most argued that the administration was cynical and knowingly misled the public while it privately believed that Iraq was not a threat at the time. Additionally, many argued that administration officials might have believed there was some possible long-term concern about WMD but that WMD was definitely not the primary motive. Others sharply disagreed and explained at length how the administration did sincerely believe Iraq was a serious security threat (typically a long-term threat), even if leaders knowingly exaggerated the threat to the public.

On the skeptical side, many respondents reasoned the administration was insincere because it deliberately suppressed important evidence that Iraq did not have WMD while repeatedly putting forward false evidence that it did, and because they believed US leaders were committed to invading independent of the WMD evidence.

> I think they were totally cynical and knew that Iraq was bottled up and posed no real threat whatever. They never had any hard evidence of WMD and ruthlessly pressured US intelligence agencies to go along with their preferred, but wildly inaccurate, view of the world.

> Perhaps the administration really believed Saddam had a sizable arsenal of WMD's, but the Vice President and political appointees so suppressed the counter-evidence that I feel they must have known the truth.

> I think they knew that the WMDs were either small-scale or nearly non-existent. They also probably understood that Iraq was a long way from nuclear weapons. Considering they knowingly ran false stories (such as uranium from Niger) and suppressed other intelligence, I can't see that they believed the WMDs were an actual threat.

> By 2002 the Bush administration was committed to invade Iraq with or without (as was the case) compelling evidence that Iraq had an active program for obtaining and hiding weapons of mass destruction. The cabal around the White House was determined to attack Iraq irrespective of the empirical findings of the UN inspectors or any other independent (individual, or multilateral, state-based or non-governmental) source.

> There were inspectors in the country, and if WMDs were the issue, we would have given them time to do their work.

> [The WMD threat] was merely an excuse. If they worried about WMD, they would have prepared the troops for such attacks and deployed adequate weapons teams to find and disarm them—but the administration and military did not do so.

> They had to know these weapons did not exist—otherwise they would have never dared to attack.

However, a significant minority of respondents expressed strenuous disagreement with these predominant views. One repeated argument contended the Bush administration believed in their own assessments over evidence presented by intelligence agencies and inspectors because of profound arrogance:

I think that the Bush team knew it had no evidence that Saddam had WMD or WMD programs. But the Bush team (the neocons and the three persuadees [Bush, Cheney, Rumsfeld]) believed Saddam did in fact possess these weapons and programs. They believed this because (1) It was plausible. Saddam had sought WMD, and had possessed it in the past. (2) The Bush team are a cultish group with contempt for everyone outside their group. Hence they have contempt for the IAEA and for U.S. intelligence, hence they did not believe evidence from these agencies that Saddam had no WMD weapons or programs. The Bush team was certain that it would find WMD in Iraq after the invasion. Some members of that team still believe that the WMD did exist and was spirited out of Iraq after the war.

I think that they believed it despite what more knowledgeable people told them. There was an extremely arrogant self confidence in the administration at that time.

They may have thought that Saddam did really have WMDs, but they—as happens in some police cases—had to fix the evidence.

From a slightly different theoretical perspective, other respondents argued the administration believed in their own assessments not because of arrogance but because of psychological biases:

I believe they considered the threat real and severe and the momentum to invade built before the evidence was clear. It was a classic case of groupthink. Cheney and Rumsfeld became the mindguards, silencing dissent – even dissent from the intelligence community.

Some members of the Administration clearly were convinced there were WMD in Iraq and that Saddam Hussein had ties to terrorists; this may have been due to biases—motivated and unmotivated—in information processing. Cognitive closure was reached early on, and so "new" evidence was read through the lens of already being sure there were WMD and terrorist ties.

They persuaded themselves it had to be true since that truth would win domestic and international support for the Bush policy. It was a case of self-delusion.

One repeated variant of the argument that the leaders sincerely believed the WMD threat is the hypothesis that lower ranking officials may have somewhat misled key leaders: "I think Bush, Cheney and others heard what they wanted to hear about WMD. Either they were duped or deliberately overstated the case (maybe a bit of both)." A wholly different view of how the invasion was primarily about WMD and a possible terrorist threat emphasized Cheney's famous "1% doctrine" which holds that the United States could no longer tolerate even improbable threats after 9/11. This argument posited that there was a known serious potential threat from the Iraq regime and that attacking Iraq would eliminate this threat. Most often these respondents recognized that the Bush administration exaggerated or dissembled about Iraq's capabilities at the time, but they contend the invasion was in fact aimed at addressing the publicly discussed threats of WMD and terrorism:

> I suspect that the general logic of what drove the Administration to undertake this disastrous adventure was the following: (1) we cannot afford to take any risk whatsoever that another 9/11 will occur on our watch; (2) Iraq almost certainly has stockpiles of chemical and biological weapons and very well may have active chemical and biological programs in place; (3) the sanctions regime is likely to break down in the near future, above all because of opposition from Russia and France; (4) Iraq's WMD programs are likely to get ramped up once the sanctions regime breaks down, at which point Iraq may well restart its nuclear program; (5) whatever WMD Iraq has may fall into the hands of terrorists, either by regime design, by accident, or by theft; (6) even if it is years away from a nuclear device, the US eventually will have to intervene militarily to stop Saddam from proceeding with a nuclear program; (7) the Middle East is a horribly dysfunctional breeding ground for terrorism, and invading Iraq and democratizing it is the best option available for beginning the process of democratizing and stabilizing the region and eliminating the conditions under which terrorist organizations and militant Islamism thrive; (8) 9/11 and the success of the Afghan campaign mean that this is the time to invade politically—better to do it now if we are going to invade at all—and finally, (9) the military campaign will be a success with little bloodshed, the regime will collapse quickly and easily, the Iraq people will welcome the invaders, and the US will be able to put in place a new, more-or-less democratic and pro-US regime in a relatively short period of time.

> To disarm Iraq of WMD and to show states that support terrorists in one way or another that we mean business.

Overall it is striking how many respondents gave detailed explanations for how the administration could have fully believed in a serious WMD threat despite the abundant evidence leaders highly inflated the evidence of the threat to the public.

The role of 9/11: catalyst vs. window of opportunity

Over 85 percent of the experts we consulted agreed that 9/11 was critical to the decision to invade Iraq in that "the events of 9/11 provided a window of opportunity for the administration to do something they already wanted to do." However, respondents were allowed to select as many characterizations of 9/11 as they deemed applied (see Table 1.3) and nearly 29 percent of respondents selected 9/11 as critical in that "the events of 9/11 changed how leaders viewed the threat from Iraq." Respondents were asked to explain their views in open-ended format.

We found sharp disputes here as to whether or not 9/11 changed only the public mood, or if it also changed the thinking of Bush administration leaders about risk, credibility or led to war through Afghanistan or because of Saudi Arabia. The most common argument about the importance of 9/11 was the description of how those events changed public opinion and softened the potential resistance to military action in Iraq:

> [9/11] got American people to go along with presidential action that might otherwise be questioned.

> 9/11 made the public subject to fear so they could be manipulated.

> 9/11 provided the ability to mobilize Democrats and popular support – intervention would have otherwise lacked popular support.

> It rescued the Bush presidency from a period in which it was floundering, losing popularity and failing to organize itself adequately to conduct successful domestic and foreign policies.

Though it was widely agreed that 9/11 created a permissive public mood, quite a few respondents stressed that 9/11 simply allowed the Bush administration to pursue plans it already had in mind:

> It served as a galvanizing event to scare the American people and give license to the government to pursue nefarious plans drawn up years earlier.

> Without 9/11 Bush would have done a major air power campaign against Iraq at some point. 9/11 allowed him to go in on the ground.

Other respondents disagreed and argued 9/11 did not simply create a political opportunity; instead they stressed how 9/11 significantly changed the strategic thinking of the top leaders:

9/11 made the Administration extraordinarily risk averse about any-thing that might be seen as having contributed to another major ter-rorist attack on US soil.

9/11 reframed the risk presented by Iraq. What had seemed accept-able before 9/11 appeared unacceptable afterwards.

For Bush, 9/11 changed his view. For the neocons, it provided the window of opportunity.

After 9/11 Bush felt "called" to the war on terrorism.

Similarly, other experts argued the administration needed to act after 9/11 in order to restore American credibility or simply to "do something" in response to 9/11:

[The US invaded Iraq] to restore American credibility after the September 11 attacks through a quick and decisive victory.

[The US invaded Iraq in order to] appear to "do something" about the "terrorists," even though there was no link

Still other respondents did not think 9/11 directly led to the invasion of Iraq, but instead linked 9/11 to the invasion of Iraq through Afghanistan, and especially through optimism about a quick and decisive war:

My personal view is that 9/11 led to the invasion of Afghanistan, which in turn motivated the invasion of Iraq by inducing excessive optimism about what can be achieved through the use of force.

9/11 did change how they viewed the world, and they wanted to invade Iraq anyway but couldn't have done it without 9/11. Afghani-stan may also have been important: they thought that war was easy and figured the next one would be too.

Reasoning from a different angle, many experts emphasized that the main contribution of 9/11 to the invasion of Iraq was its impact on the US rela-tionship with Saudi Arabia. Many of the experts argued the invasion of Iraq was a necessary result of the fact that the old strategy of working with Saudi Arabia would no longer work after 9/11:

[The US invaded to] allow the US to withdraw its troops from Saudi Arabia, which was the #1 grievance listed by Al Qaeda. Those US troops were there to protect Saudi Arabia from Iraq; as soon as the US invaded Iraq, the troops in Saudi Arabia were removed.

One of Al Qaeda's rallying cries was to get the Crusaders away from the two holy mosques in Saudi Arabia. The road out of Saudi Arabia was through Baghdad because that was the reason we had stationed 10,000 plus airmen, etc. in Saudi Arabia. The invasion of Iraq was in March. We left Saudi Arabia in August 2003. Not an airman still there.

[The US invaded Iraq] to grab the oil fields in case the Wahabis took charge in Saudi Arabia.

[Among other reasons, the US invaded Iraq] to embark on a new policy that would still guarantee the flow of oil while distancing ourselves from Saudi Arabia.

Controlling Iraqi oil would make the US less dependent on Saudi Arabia and so free the US for other initiatives.

Thus, though the survey found little disagreement that 9/11 created the political opportunity for the administration to act there was considerable disagreement about whether the events of 9/11 significantly changed the administration's thinking or if the administration was already set on invading Iraq.

Oil and Israel: a perfect storm?

The aggregate results of our survey make it clear that many experts believed that numerous interests came together, creating something of a "perfect storm" in favor of war. Indeed, in the open-ended responses many listed both oil and enhancing security for Israel as part of a longer list of multiple factors. This is an interesting argument since historically pro-Arab oil interests usually directly counter the policies favored by Israel; in other words the oil lobby and the Israel lobby do not work together. In this case, many experts think they did. As one respondent combined several of the most popular unstated factors quite frankly: "[The US invaded because of] the two things the VP and Secretary of Defense said were NOT the reasons: oil and Israel." Others simply listed factors together: "Oil, Israel, bases" and "American hegemony/empire, 2. Oil, 3. Israel, 4. Democracy."

However, despite most experts combining these multiple reasons, another oft-repeated point of contention was the many arguments that stressed the invasion was definitely not the result of a "perfect storm." It was striking how many respondents emphasized one set of factors while simply excluding or even sharply denying other factors—most common was emphasizing oil and not mentioning Israel at all:

The US invaded Iraq because of interests in oil, and providing huge profits to Bush's cronies.

For strategic interests, primarily access to oil.

I think it had to do with geopolitics in a number of ways. First, the Bush people wanted a stable oil source and a military presence in the Middle East. Second they wanted to become the hegemonic power in the world.

To control [Iraq's] oil and the Persian Gulf oil in general.

From the opposite view, there were a significant number of respondents that basically marginalized oil, with many of these strongly arguing for the primacy of enhancing Israel's security:

The fundamental question was securing stability and safety for Israel and solidifying our influence in the area. Oil was an issue, but primarily as it affected power.

Motive #1: to strengthen Israel's strategic position. This was an important motivation for the neoconservatives. It was foreshadowed in the "Clean Break" memo that Perle, Feith and Wurmser sent incoming Israeli prime minister Benjamin Netanyahu in 1996, calling for Israeli efforts to oust Saddam's regime and other Mideast regimes. The neoconservatives believe, with the Israeli Likud, that peace with the Arabs is not possible for the foreseeable future. (I think they are wrong about this, but they believe it.) The neoconservatives therefore believe that Israel faces a long conflict, of many decades, with the Arabs. They think Israeli strategy should therefore focus on weakening Israel's Arab enemies, building up Israel's internal strength, and bringing powerful allies into the fight on Israel's side. The prime threat to Israel comes from its eastern front: Syria, Iraq, and Iran. (The southern front has been secured by peace with Egypt.) Israel is strengthened if any of the three hostile eastern front regimes (Saddam, Assad, and the Iranian mullocracy) are destroyed or diminished or policed by American power.... So: A U.S. smashing of Saddam has many strategic benefits to Israel.... [On the other hand, interests in keeping oil prices low or securing oil profits] – these considerations did not play a role in leading the U.S. to war. There was some thought that a friendly regime in Iraq would bring into being a second swing oil producer, and this would reduce Saudi influence, and so let the U.S. coerce the Saudi regime to stop spreading hate that spawns terror (as noted above). But there was no concern for the price or ownership of oil per se. This is a pernicious myth.

Though the vast majority of experts readily combined interests in both oil and Israel as major motives behind the US invasion, a significant minority emphasized one set of issues over the other, and even insisted the other interests were not influential in this war. This is a point of lively debate and one that deserves more attention.

The debate today

These 2006 survey results provide a useful backdrop for this volume. These results show that within the first three years of the war the vast majority of experts had largely dismissed the administration's publicly stated motives that the war was to stop WMD and terrorism, even though the public largely still believed these were the primary motives for the war at this time. Instead, most scholars essentially agreed that other reasons, such as the neoconservative ideology of spreading democracy and asserting "benign hegemony" or unstated motives such as interests in defending Israel or securing oil were the main drivers behind the war.

Nonetheless, despite the emerging, private scholarly consensus about the hollowness of the Bush administration's stated reasons for the war, academic defenders of the Bush administration's sincerity remain, contending that the leaders were focused on the WMD threat and either were too arrogant to believe the intelligence community, or psychologically too committed to their beliefs about the threat from Saddam Hussein to alter their views when discrepant intelligence information surfaced. Professor Robert Jervis, who took part in officially investigating the intelligence failure before the Iraq War, fully developed this perspective in his book *Why Intelligence Fails: Lessons from the Iranian Revolution and the Iraq War* (2010). He argues the WMD threat was indeed very important to the Bush administration's Iraq War decision, stressing the potent combination of uncertainty of intelligence and psychological biases when explaining the Bush administration's misperceptions. This book received considerable attention and prompted heated debate. In this volume, Jervis weighs in on both the profound difficulties of answering the question we posed of "Why did the US invade Iraq?" and he provides his views on this question. To be clear, while his view that the Iraq War was motivated by fears of WMD may still be a minority position among scholars at this time, this view is strongly echoed by other scholars within this volume—scholars who have also studied this question closely. Many find that even though the Bush administration clearly exaggerated the threat to the public, it does not mean leaders were wholly insincere or that the security threat was not a primary motive for the war.

The most agreed upon factor our survey identified was the importance of neoconservative ideology. This was true in both the first open-ended question and in the later multiple-choice question. While neoconservative ideology is singled out as playing a very important role in the war decision, the precise wording and primary goals of this ideology are contested. This ideology generally includes reshaping the Middle East through spreading democracy, known as "muscular Wilsonianism," and/or asserting US dominance, also often known as "benign hegemony," however contradictory it may be to both promote democracy and assert dominance. Two scholars, Colin Dueck and Andrew Flibbert, who have written different detailed accounts of how neoconservative ideology shaped the war decision, agreed to contribute to this volume. Each of them has provided a chapter explaining in rich detail the ideas that guided policy-makers, and how these ideas became consequential for the invasion of Iraq.

While neoconservative ideology was deemed important, the survey also revealed that a majority of experts viewed Israel's security as a highly important motive for the neoconservatives, who were in turn viewed as very influential to the decision by 83 percent of respondents. These findings prompted us to ask Michael Lind, a former neoconservative who had written extensively during the first few years of the war about the role of the neoconservatives in the Iraq War decision, to update his arguments about the neoconservatives, their ideology and their alleged interests in Israel's security. Lind has provided a highly evolved and provocative chapter for this volume. Additionally, we asked Jerome Slater to revisit the debate about the neoconservatives and the role of the Israel lobby in the Iraq War decision. Slater (2009) has written one of the most balanced and comprehensive reviews of Mearsheimer and Walt's book *The Israel Lobby and U.S. Foreign Policy*, to which Mearsheimer and Walt had responded. In this volume, Slater updates his views of the current debate on the Israel lobby hypothesis, and his views of why the Iraq War decision happened overall.

Oil was the other factor the survey identified as highly important for the Iraq War decision, yet surprisingly few scholars have investigated this hypothesis. Two of the most prominent and compelling scholars who have explored how oil may have motivated the invasion of Iraq agreed to contribute to the debate here. Michael Klare presents his version of how the geopolitics of oil best explains this war. He notes that the United States since FDR has defended and insured the flow of oil from the Gulf. This policy was made open and explicit with the Carter Doctrine. It has been maintained by all presidents, and the Bush administration ascribed to this policy and greatly advanced the Carter Doctrine policies of protecting oil resources with military forces not only in Iraq but also in many other regions in this same period. Thus Klare argues the Iraq invasion cannot be viewed in isolation, but should be viewed as one case of many military adventures aimed at maintaining access to oil resources. Similarly, but from a different angle, John Duffield explains many of the specific reasons oil and security interests combined to make it appear very risky and costly for the United States to leave Saddam Hussein in power in 2003, and possibly very beneficial, even cheap and easy, to remove him.

Most of the contributors to this volume recognize how important the released British documents, such as the famous *Downing Street Memos*, have been to coming to understand the US decision-making process concerning the Iraq War. Most interesting is the fact that Britain has been seriously investigating why its government decided to join the United States in invading Iraq, even though the United States has never held a serious investigation as to why it decided to invade. To better understand Britain, Jane Sharp's chapter provides a rich description of why and how Prime Minister Tony Blair decided to join the United States in waging an internationally and domestically unpopular invasion. Drawing on the treasure trove of documents recently declassified by the Iraq Inquiry chaired by John Chilcot, she explores the extraordinary lengths to which Blair went in manipulating intelligence and re-interpreting international law to secure parliamentary approval for the war.

In the final chapter of this volume, Jane Cramer and Edward Duggan assess key aspects of all of these arguments, pointing out which elements have withstood the test of time and which seem to have diminished. In the end, they attempt to tie together the strongest elements in an effort to propose what they see as the best explanation for the Iraq War decision at this time, subject to further revelations from the principals and future research.

As we noted at the beginning of this chapter, we believe the 2006 survey presented above helps reveal a "first draft" of the history of the Iraq War decision. Our study of this war indicates that, perhaps inevitably, policy-makers themselves had a heavy influence on this early version of history. Thus for example, the first draft of history about the war may have over-emphasized the idealism of the neoconservatives while downplaying the many serious contradictions within alleged neoconservative ideology, and the assertive realist inclinations of the Bush administration leadership. Further, tracking the evolution of expert views on the Iraq war helps demonstrate that "conspiracy" type theories are sometimes just currently unpopular theories destined to become more accepted over time. The lesson, we believe, is that all theories deserve public debate and consideration and we hope this volume contributes to that debate about the Iraq War. In this spirit, we intend this volume to at least in part uphold the obligations of the realist, as E. H. Carr (Carr and Cox 2001: 66) once explained:

> it [is] the business of the diplomat to cloak the interests of his country in the language of universal justice. More recently, Mr. Churchill told the House of Commons that "there must be a moral basis for British rearmament and foreign policy." It is rare, however, for modern statesmen to express themselves with this frankness; and in contemporary British and American politics, the most powerful influence has been wielded by those utopian statesmen who are sincerely convinced that policy is deduced from ethical principles, not ethical principles from policy. The realist is nevertheless obliged to uncover the hollowness of this conviction.

Notes

1 In a survey in March 2006, 57 percent of the public believed that invasion of Iraq was a mistake and 51 percent believed that members of the Bush administration had intentionally misled the public (CNN/USA Today/Gallup poll March 10–12, 2006). These views contrasted sharply with public opinion before the invasion, at which time 86 percent of Americans believed that Iraqi efforts to acquire WMD were a critical threat to the United States (Western 2009).
2 Though the hypothesis has been much debated, the few people who openly supported the Mearsheimer and Walt thesis were subject to intense attacks. For example Tony Judt (2006) wrote an op-ed in the *New York Times* that drew intense criticism and debate, and highly controversial abrupt cancellations of scheduled speaking appearances; see Karni (2006).
3 The survey, conducted between November 1 and December 15, 2006, was sent to 864 experts using a list of names of experts compiled by graduate students tasked with finding contact information for as many international relations and US foreign policy experts as they could find in the United States at research universities and think tanks. The online survey resulted in 227 responses for a response rate of 26.3 percent, typical of polling response rates nationally for similar web-based surveys.

References

Carr, E. H. and Cox, M. (2001) "The realist critique," in *The Twenty Years' Crisis, 1919–1939: An Introduction to the Study of International Relations*, Basingstoke: Palgrave.

Danner, M. (2006) *The Secret Way to War: The Downing Street Memo and the Iraq War's Buried History*, New York: New York Review of Books.

Judt, T. (2006) "A lobby: Not a conspiracy," *New York Times*, April 19, p. A21.

Karni, A. (2006) "Another Judt appearance abruptly canceled," *New York Sun*, October 5.

Mearsheimer, J. J. and Walt, S. M. (2007) *The Israel Lobby and U.S. Foreign Policy*, New York: Farrar, Straus and Giroux.

Mearsheimer, J. J. and Walt, S. M. (2009) "Is it love or the lobby? Explaining America's special relationship with Israel," *Security Studies* 18: 58–78.

Slater, J. (2009) "The two books of Mearsheimer and Walt," *Security Studies* 18: 4–57.

Thrall, A. Trevor and Cramer, Jane K. (eds.) (2009) *American Foreign Policy and the Politics of Fear: Threat Inflation since 9/11*, New York: Routledge.

Western, J. (2009) "The war over Iraq: Selling war to the American public," in Thrall, A. T. and Cramer, J. K. (eds.) *American Foreign Policy and the Politics of Fear: Threat Inflation Since 9/11*, New York: Routledge.

2 Explaining the war in Iraq

Robert Jervis

Everyone who explains the US action [in invading Iraq in March 2003] ...
is sure that his analysis is the correct one; more modest answers—such as
that great powers usually take major decisions for several reasons, or that,
lacking reliable documentary or autobiographical evidence, we remain
ignorant—cut little ice in discussions.

(Halliday 2009: 627)

The search for the causes of the Iraq War confronts several obstacles,
some particular to this case and others generic. Although we should not
be surprised at the lack of agreement here because there rarely is consensus about wars or other major human phenomena, we should still try to do
the best we can, and the exploration can produce some forms of knowledge even if the destination remains contested. Before turning to the
case, I want to note some confounding factors, six conceptual and one
empirical.

Conceptual problems

To start with, how the Iraq War ended, or rather progressed, inevitably
influences our analysis of the motives and calculations that produced it.[1]
Would we be puzzling over the case if it had proceeded as Bush and his
colleagues had expected? If the war had not only been swift but uncovered
stockpiles of weapons of mass destruction (WMD), perhaps supplemented
by evidence of Saddam's ties to terrorists, and had the occupation gone
smoothly and resulted in the quick establishment of a stable and at least
semi-democratic government, we would be asking, not why Bush and the
coalition went to war, but why so many people were skeptical. Had the
coalition's military attack proved to be a bloody slog, we would be searching for reasons for the invasion, but the investigation would proceed along
quite different lines than the ones we are now pursuing. Yet these counterfactual histories, although of some interest, cannot be used in the way we
ordinarily do to probe the efficacy of suggested independent variables.

Rather, I mention them for the very reason that while they cannot help us think about the causes at work, they show that they do exercise such an influence. Success usually seems much easier to explain than failure. Even those who are not proponents of rational choice theory generally believe that actors behave in a way that will benefit them. If I see someone bend down and pick up a $20 bill on the street I may feel annoyed that I had not grabbed it first, but I do not search for an explanation. But if the person picks up a leaf or comes up empty-handed, I will be puzzled. So it is not surprising that there is much more scholarly literature and public discussion on the Iraq War than on the Gulf War. While it is obvious that how a war turns out cannot explain why a country embarked on it, thinking about what drove the Bush administration's behavior is inevitably influenced (contaminated?) by what later ensued.

A second and related difficulty is that our evaluation of the policy influences our explanation of it. Some people who view the invasion as appropriate, or at least appropriate given the information available at the time, would say that this behavior (although perhaps not the failure to plan for post-war reconstruction) was self-explanatory in the sense of being what any state would have done in this situation—i.e. it responded to a threat by ending it. In this view, it is the failure of George H. W. Bush and Bill Clinton to remove Saddam that calls for explanation, just as the historiography of the 1930s focuses on the failure of Britain and France to move against Nazi Germany. For those who approved the war but saw a special role for President Bush, this line of argument is incorrect. His two predecessors behaved badly but normally; most states and leaders would not have faced the challenges but instead would have compromised and temporized, just as they did. To explain the war, these observers would turn to Bush's special beliefs, characteristics, and leadership skills. They would then agree with the approach I will use in the next section of this chapter, although they would put a positive rather than a negative valence on the description.

As the previous paragraph implies, many forms of explanation for this and other wars turn on what decision-makers believed, and this is one avenue I will explore. But discussions of this kind, my own included, rarely confront the unfortunate fact that modern psychology has confirmed what Freud argued and novelists have always known—even the most honest self-reports are often misleading even when they are not self-serving. The fundamental problem is not that people are trying to fool others, or even trying to fool themselves, but that so much of our cognitive processing is unconscious and therefore inaccessible to us. While we usually can explicate why we formed the impressions that we have, hold to the beliefs that we do, and act as we do, the factors and chains of reasoning that we point to often were not the ones that operated. We are not better at explaining our own behavior than we are at explaining the behavior of others. We are "strangers to ourselves," to take the title of Timothy Wilson's book that summarizes the relevant research (Wilson 2002). Scholars are well aware of the unfortunate fact that what we read in records of government deliberations and even personal diaries are not only incomplete, but may not reveal what people really believe because claims and arguments are made in order to persuade others. They also try to dig beneath even honestly-expressed beliefs to uncover and understand the assumptions that are so taken for granted by all the participants that they are not articulated, which is perhaps even more difficult (Joll 1972; Autesserre 2010). But we are less aware of the deeper problem that people may not know what is moving them, something that does not yield to the standard if problematic methods we use to cope with the more familiar obstacles to understanding.

A fourth generic difficulty also springs from the first one in that while it is failed policies that call out for the most attention, many schools of theorizing about international politics have trouble explaining failures. This is particularly true of Realism, which in most of its variants argues that leaders seek to further the national interest and are at least fairly rational in doing so. Of course there is room to dispute what the national interest is, and paths to reach it can be blocked by lack of accurate information or clever moves by others. Nevertheless, states are not supposed to do really foolish things. The war in Iraq then poses a problem for Realists. Most of them felt that the war in Iraq was a mistake because Saddam could have been deterred even if he got nuclear weapons and the occupation was likely to prove long and difficult. (See, for example, "War with Iraq is <u>Not</u> in America's National Interest," *New York Times*, September 26, 2002.) Realism could readily explain why the war was a bad idea, but by the same token has trouble explaining why the United States sought it. Most Realist theories of foreign policy are then simultaneously descriptive and prescriptive, and this means that when states behave foolishly the theories as well as the nation suffers (Jervis 2008; Oren 2009).

The fifth conceptual problem is that our explanations for this and other wars are usually couched in terms of what led the actors to believe that they had to fight. But desire is not sufficient, even when paired with capability. Decision-makers may favor war, but not be able to find a plausible occasion that will allow them to bring along their country and perhaps necessary allies. As we will see, even if we can establish why Bush felt that he had to overthrow Saddam, we still need to know how he was able to find or build a path to war.

The final general conundrum is that this war, like many others and a large proportion of other important events, seems under-determined before the fact but over-determined after it (Kurth 1973). Until the last minute, few wars seem inevitable. Indeed, if all the actors expect it to occur, at least some of them might behave differently in order to avoid it (Gartzke 1999). In the case of Iraq, I believe that many people were uncertain whether the United States would go to war until around January 2003.

But after the United States attacked, the decision seemed obvious, not necessarily in the sense of serving the national interest, but in the sense of being supported by multiple imperatives that in retrospect made the decision seem like the only one possible, given the values and perceptions of the administration. As we will see, ironically the effect of this apparent over-determination is to make the war harder rather than easier to explain.

One empirical problem, while not unique to the Iraq case, probably is particularly extreme in it. The quote with which I began this chapter said that explaining the decision might have to await the opening of the relevant documents. Obviously, documents are not a panacea, and we still argue about the origins of World War I despite our ability to read all of the available documents (and I doubt if the problems would disappear even if the Germans had not systematically weeded their files at the end of the war) (Herwig 1987). But in the Iraq case the files are going to be particularly barren. Apparently there were no high-level meetings to discuss whether the United States should go to war, and I very much doubt that the key players like National Security Advisor Rice, Secretary of Defense Rumsfeld, or Vice President Cheney put their thoughts down on paper. I am sure the records will be interesting, but they are not likely to help a great deal.

Beliefs and calculations supporting the war

In focusing on the beliefs of Bush and his most important colleagues, I am assuming that a large part of the explanation for the war is that they were in power. We have here an example of the "butterfly effect"—i.e. were it not for the infamous butterfly ballot in Palm Beach county, Al Gore would have been president and even if his greater concern with terrorism had not prevented the attacks of 9/11, I think it is unlikely that he would have decided to invade Iraq. Put in terms of international politics theory, I believe that Waltz's first image or level of analysis that focuses on individuals is central to this story, although later I will talk about second and third image factors (Jervis 2010; Roberts 1996).[2]

As Director of the Policy Planning Staff, Richard Haass was closer to the action than any later observers can be. It is then significant that he reports: "I will go to my grave not fully understanding why" Bush went to war (Haass 2009). The problem, however, is not that there were insufficient justifications for the war, but that there was a surplus of them. The decision seems over-determined and it is extremely difficult to tell what factors were driving. Of course it is possible that Bush and his colleagues did believe several things, each of which on its own would have been sufficient to have led them to favor overthrowing Saddam. Sometimes people can be simultaneously shot, stabbed, and bludgeoned in a true example of overkill. But there is no reason to think these cases are common. When we talk about multiple causes, as Halliday did in the quote above, what we usually mean is that several factors contributed to the outcome (often in a way that makes parsing the exact contributions among them difficult) and that even if each one were not necessary, neither was each sufficient on its own.

In the Iraq case, the proponents of the war articulated more reasons than were necessary to lead them to their conclusion, and I do not think this is only because different people had different motives. Proponents claim to have perceived the pre-war situation as one embodying both very high threat and significant opportunity, and, furthermore, that both threat and opportunity had significant and distinct sub-components. It would have been quite possible for the proponents of the war to have seen a high threat but also expected the war to have been very costly and to lack the compensating advantages of spreading democracy to Iraq, let alone to the wider region. But perceiving such value trade-offs is painful, and people therefore try to avoid them. In this case as in many others, beliefs are shaped by what psychologists call "motivational biases" in which the need to see the world in a certain way leads to beliefs which, even if they portray a menacing world, ease the person's political and psychological burdens (Jervis 1976, 2006). The mother of a soldier serving in Iraq said: "I know my son's there for a reason. And whatever may happen, that's the way it's supposed to be. And if I took it any other way, I'd be in a funny farm" (Abramsky 2004: 11). Bush and his colleagues may not have been this self-aware, but, feeling even greater responsibilities, they too needed to arrange their beliefs so as to retain their equanimity. They apparently believed that: Saddam had a large and growing WMD program; there were close links between his regime and al Qaeda; the war would be quick; political reconstruction would be relatively easy; and liberation would light the path for the rest of the Middle East. This is belief overkill. If a nuclear-armed Iraq could not have been deterred from coercing its neighbors, then this menace was sufficient to have triggered war. If Saddam was harboring al Qaeda, this by itself could have led to an invasion, as it did in Afghanistan. Had the prospects for establishing democracy in Iraq been great and likely to trigger positive domino effects throughout the region, then overthrowing Saddam would have been a great opportunity even if there were no pressing danger. It is the excess rather than the paucity of reasons that confuses us (Jervis 2006).

If this is correct, the crucial questions in this context are, first of all, whether this is a true case of multiple sufficient causation and, second, if it is not, which of the beliefs set the others in motion. Neither question can be answered with certainty. Three considerations lead me to doubt that this is true multiple sufficient causation, however. First, there is no reason to believe that such arrangements are common, and no reason to think that this case should be exceptional. Second, since the decision to go to war was highly consequential, people would feel especially great psychological pressures to muster all possible reasons to support their positions. Third, more than the Gulf War and even Vietnam, this was a war of choice. Bush was not pushed into fighting, and the fact that he had freedom of maneuver generated additional psychological pressures on him to believe that there were multiple reasons for him to act and that he actually had little choice.

In order to disentangle excess beliefs and determine which of them were primarily responsible for the policy we can see which were most compatible with what the person believed and did over a prolonged period (Flibbert 2006; May 1975). Although this assumes a degree of consistency that may be problematic, it is noteworthy that Bush and his colleagues consistently held a healthy—or unhealthy—respect for the utility of American force in world politics. Furthermore, they came into office thinking that while force is efficacious, deterrence is flawed. During the Cold War they (except for Bush, who was not deeply involved in these questions) strongly favored nuclear counter-force and missile defense. Their belief that an Iraq armed with nuclear weapons could not be deterred from coercing its neighbors fit with this outlook. Although this still leaves us with the question of the sources of these beliefs (and there is no logical stopping place once we start down that road, important as it is to explore), this at least tells us that the claim that force would work was not developed in order to justify the war.

Which other reasons, then, were the real drivers? Although proof is impossible, important evidence is supplied by the role of the attacks of 9/11. Some have argued that Bush wanted to invade Iraq before this time, but while I think he and his colleagues did have this as an abstract preference, they were not prepared to act on it. If they had been serious, they would have ordered the military to update the war plans as soon as they took power and done more to prepare the country for this move. Assuming, then, that 9/11 was important, I think it indicates that threat rather than opportunity was the prime mover. As Bush frequently acknowledged, indeed stressed, he was shocked by the assault, which greatly increased his feelings of danger and led him to drastically different policies. As he put it in a sentence in his Cincinnati speech that came between two paragraphs about the need to disarm Iraq: "On September 11th, 2001, America felt its vulnerability." Three months later in response to an accusation that he always wanted to invade Iraq, Bush replied:

prior to September 11, we were discussing smart sanctions.... After September 11, the doctrine of containment just doesn't hold any water.... My vision shifted dramatically after September 11, because I now realize the stakes, I realize the world has changed.

("Transcript of Press Conference," *New York Times*,
February 1, 2003)

Secretary of Defense Rumsfeld similarly explained that the United States

> did not act in Iraq because we had discovered dramatic new evidence of Iraq's pursuit of weapons of mass murder. We acted because we saw the existing evidence in a new light, through the prism of our experience on September 11.
>
> (Risen *et al.* 2003)

If 9/11 was not enough to generate great fear, it was followed by reports that a nuclear bomb was planted in Washington and by real anthrax attacks.

There is little reason to doubt that Bush and his colleagues sincerely believed that Saddam had active WMD programs. This was the judgment of American intelligence, and, conventional wisdom notwithstanding, all indications are that it was reached independently of political pressures. Furthermore, the frantic nature of the search for WMD in the aftermath of the invasion and the evident distress of leading members of both the policy and intelligence communities as the results unfolded indicate that they had expected to find these menacing weapons (Jervis 2010).

Whether top officials also believed that there were connections between Saddam and terrorists is much less clear. Here intelligence vigorously dissented and the administration's professed belief was much less plausible, although the fact that Bush's immediate instinct after the 9/11 attacks was to tell his subordinates to look for a connection with Saddam indicates a predisposition to believe this (Clarke 2004). But in contrast to the efforts put into finding WMD after the invasion, the administration did not order searches of captured record and interrogations of Iraqi officials to seek evidence for connections to terrorists.

There is an interesting in-between position here. According to the memoirs of Undersecretary of Defense for Policy Douglas Feith, whose office produced the now infamous intelligence pointing to connections between Saddam and al Qaeda, the views held by leading members of the administration were subtly but significantly different. It was not so much that they believed that such connections actually existed (although they thought that they might) as it was their more general fear of terrorism and the possibility that, if not overthrown, Saddam might share WMD with some terrorists—not necessarily al Qaeda—at some time in the future: "Saddam Hussein was in a class by himself as a mass murderer and initiator of aggressive wars" and "whether or not Iraq was linked to al Qaida" he "might someday soon provide terrorists with WMD" (Feith 2008). In this context it is a minor point that if Feith is correct Bush was fundamentally dishonest with the American people (Jervis 2008 and 2009), but it remains unclear whether Feith's analysis represents what he believed at the time, let alone what Bush believed. Unfortunately, all I can say is that it certainly is plausible.

Were Bush and his colleagues strongly pulled by the perception of opportunity as well as or even instead of being pushed by a sense of fear (Tenet 2007; Immerman 2010; Williams 2005)? My sense is that this was a distinctly secondary factor and that the statements of opportunity were the result of the need to bolster conclusions arrived at on other grounds. Only a few members of the administration, most notably Paul Wolfowitz, had a strong commitment to spreading democracy around the world when they came into office. Indeed Bush had scorned nation-building during the presidential campaign. Most importantly, while it is clear how 9/11 could have led people to change their evaluations of what threats were acceptable, it is hard to see how the attacks could logically lead to changes in beliefs about whether other countries could be made democratic and whether doing so in one country would have great and positive ramifications for the region. The main reason why Dick Cheney as Secretary of Defense in the George H. W. Bush administration opposed marching to Baghdad after liberating Kuwait was his belief that the occupation would be bloody and difficult. Nothing in the intervening years should have led him to change his mind.

Nevertheless, certainty is beyond reach here. In post-invasion discussions with mid-level officials in the administration, I found that those who worked on the questions of threat tended to believe that Bush was moved by considerations of opportunity, and those who worked on issues of democratization believed that he must have been most driven by the threat. Bush, like many Americans, had an instinctive faith in the value of democracy and in its appropriateness for all societies. The need for a new policy in the wake of the terrorist attacks may have brought these views to the surface, and Scott McClellan, Bush's press secretary at the time, believes that the president's main motive was to democratize Iraq and the entire Middle East (McClellan 2008). Bush's religion and personal experiences may have played a role. As early as the morning after the attack, he declared that the United States was engaged "in a monumental struggle of good versus evil" and in his memorial remarks at the National Cathedral two days later said that "our responsibility to history is ... clear: to answer these attacks and rid the world of evil" (Bush 2001a and 2001b). While such a worldview is consistent with the American political tradition (Kennan 1951; Divine 2000; Ninkovich 1994), it also owes something to Bush's outlook as a born-again Christian. There is reason to believe that just as his coming to Christ gave meaning to his previously aimless and dissolute personal life, so the war on terrorism became not only the defining characteristic of his foreign policy, but also his sacred mission. As an associate of the president reports: "I believe the president was sincere, after 9/11, thinking 'This is what I was put on this earth for'" (Harding 2003; see also Woodward 2002, 2004).[3] That Bush did believe in the importance and possibility of making Iraq democratic is further indicated by the fact that he twice vetoed proposals from Rumsfeld and Cheney that he install

Ahmed Chalabi in power and that he jettisoned the original plan for leaving Iraq before extensive democratizing reforms were carried out. But these actions are not inconsistent with the argument that threat was the initial and primary motivator and that the sense of opportunity was a later rationalization, albeit one that Bush himself came to believe in and act on.

Of course Iraq not only failed to become democratic, at least not fully so, but the occupation was much longer and bloodier than expected. It is unclear whether Bush would have gone to war had he foreseen this result, his claims that he would have are unreliable, not because he is seeking to deceive us but because this kind of retrospective self-knowledge is impossible. Unlike the belief that Saddam had active WMD programs, the optimism about post-war reconstruction was a minority view among experts and ran counter to the beliefs expressed by the intelligence community. I strongly suspect that the beliefs of Bush and his colleagues here were another instance in which the need to avoid value trade-offs produced motivated reasoning. They knew that support for the war among allies and American public opinion—and indeed among themselves—would be reduced if it were believed that reconstruction would be extremely difficult. They therefore chose to treat the question casually. Planning for the post-war situation was then scandalously superficial and the intelligence community was not even asked for its views on the political landscape that the United States would confront in the wake of Saddam's overthrow. If the views about the threat from Saddam followed worst-case analysis, the thinking about the post-war situation was based on the best case, and could hardly be dignified by the label of "analysis." I think the best explanation for the latter phenomenon was the former. But a more cognitive element may have been involved as well. Francis Fukuyama argues that his fellow neoconservatives were deeply influenced by the trajectory of the countries of Central and Eastern Europe after the end of the Cold War. If stability and democracy followed the liberation from Soviet control, why shouldn't things turn out as well in Iraq? Unlike Fukuyama, those who favored the war saw no reason to answer this question in the negative, while his own skepticism was rooted in the belief that the happy results were the product of special conditions (Fukuyama 2006).[4]

If I am right that the fundamental cause of the invasion was the perception of unacceptable threat from Saddam triggered by the combination of pre-existing beliefs about his regime and the impact of the terrorist attacks, how are we to explain these? Of course any explanation rooted in perceptions, beliefs, and values is always subject to the challenge of accounting for where these came from, and even though there is no obvious stopping point at least a few things can be said. First, although the parsing of responsibility between a triggering event and previous attitudes is difficult and somewhat arbitrary, here as elsewhere the comparative method is useful. Although 9/11 was a shock to everyone, it was a fundamental surprise only to those who were not deeply steeped in the problem of terrorism. The Clinton administration and many academic experts knew very well that al Qaeda was seeking to attack the United States in a dramatic way, and although they had not anticipated the specific time or method of 9/11, their previous awareness of this danger minimized the extent to which the attacks led to fundamental re-evaluations. Bush and his colleagues, on the other hand, previously believed that terrorism was only a minor threat compared to the menace from great powers such as Russia and China, and their evaluations of the threats they faced changed much more. Their very inability to have imagined anything like 9/11 before it happened made them particularly susceptible to the claim that no danger, even distinctly unlikely, could be disregarded. Here we have Cheney's emblematic "1%" attitude:

> If there's a one percent chance that Pakistani scientists are helping al Qaeda build or develop a nuclear weapon, we have to treat it as a certainty in terms of our response. It's not about our analysis. ... It's about our response.
>
> (Suskind 2006)

This may put us on the right track, but leads to the obvious question of why this danger was taken so much more seriously than others. Why was Iraq the target rather than Iran, Libya, or North Korea? The fact that North Korea had nuclear weapons may explain why in the wake of 9/11 Bush did no more than continue the fruitless policy of increasing pressures on that country without seriously exploring negotiations, but the targeting of Iraq rather than the other two countries that had nuclear ambitions and closer ties to terrorism probably can only be explained by the pre-existing hostility to Iraq growing out of the Gulf War and the succeeding frustrating decade.

For some people, the claim that some eventualities are unlikely enough to be put aside lost plausibility in face of the obvious retort: "What could be less likely than terrorists flying airplanes into the World Trade Center and the Pentagon?" During the Cold War, Bernard Brodie expressed his exasperation with wild suggestions about military actions the USSR might undertake:

> All sorts of notions and propositions are churned out, and often presented for consideration with the prefatory words: "It is conceivable that..." Such words establish their own truth, for the fact that someone has conceived of whatever proposition follows is enough to establish that it is conceivable. Whether it is worth a second thought, however, is another matter.
>
> (Brodie 1978; see also Gaddis 2004)

After 9/11 it was hard to say this about anything; worst-case analysis became hard to dismiss. When a disturbing and unexpected event occurs, it is of course rational to change one's estimates of the likelihood of similar or related events. Thus when Chile's Pinochet took the unprecedented step of assassinating a leading adversary who had fled to the United States to organize against the regime, the United States quickly gave credence to the reports that the Uruguayan dictatorship might try to kill a Congressman who had sponsored a bill to cut off aid to that repressive regime (Dinges 2004). It did not increase its worry about Soviet adventures or a PRC attack on Taiwan. For critics, the reaction of Bush and Cheney was like this; defenders reply that it is hard to say what kind of events the terrorist attacks should lead us to now see as more likely and that it was reasonable to see Saddam as an unacceptable danger.

We can still ask what provoked this fear and animus. A defender of the invasion would argue that Saddam did, and would add that most of this chapter and similar analyses miss the point in seeking to explain the war by examining the beliefs of American leaders rather than the barbaric and threatening behavior of the Iraqi regime. For empirical and perhaps moral analysis, the comparative method is again useful in that this kind of reply carries more weight if all observers reached the same conclusion. This is why whatever views they may have on the diplomacy of the 1930s, few scholars doubt that World War II would have occurred (at least not in Europe) had Adolf Hitler not been bent on expansion and conquest. But while Saddam has few defenders, many observers (myself included) denied that he was a major menace to the United States and its interests. Whether we were right or wrong, the very fact of the disagreement means that we want to explain why Bush and his colleagues saw Saddam as such a threat. In this regard, it is interesting that the Bush administration was picky in how it chose to evaluate and respond to dangers. Most obviously, its members not only were highly skeptical of the evidence indicating that human activities were changing the climate, but would not entertain the argument that even a low probability that this was the case should lead the United States and other countries to take remediating actions. Indeed, they came close to applying a "99% solution" in arguing that nothing needed to be done until there was close to certainty about the phenomenon. The obvious explanation, parallel to that concerning motivated beliefs above, is that the analysis, far from producing the behavior, was a product of the desires for it.

The fact that many observers felt that the threat from Iraq was manageably low and that Saddam could be deterred even if he gained nuclear weapons (Jervis 2003; Mearsheimer and Walt 2003; but also see Pollack 2002) raises the question of how to explain the contrary evaluation of Bush and his colleagues. Differences about the extent to which another state is a threat are common in international politics: witness the debates in Great Britain before World Wars I and II and the debates after 1945 about Soviet capabilities and intentions, as well as current arguments about the threat from terrorism, WMD, or global climate change (Mueller

2006, 2009 versus Reese 2003). It is easier to probe the specific beliefs as I have done earlier than to determine the foundations on which they rest, but two underlying attitudes may be relevant here, although neither will explain why war was waged against Iraq rather than Iran or Libya. Robert Art perceptively noted that one of the functions of force is "swaggering"— i.e. to overawe others and show that the state is willing and able to use force even—or especially—in the absence of grave menaces (Art 1980; Tierney 2010). Saddam was a convenient target, but the message was intended for all terrorist groups and, even more, for countries that might support them. Second, Bush, many members of his administration, and especially Vice President Cheney, came into office committed to expanding the role and prerogatives of the executive branch, feeling that these had been dangerously eroded following Vietnam, Watergate, and the Iran-Contra scandal. The Patriot Act and the refusal to ask Congress to expand the president's ability to utilize wiretaps clearly reveal this desire, and as all political observers including the framers of the American Constitution know very well, nothing expands the power of the president more than a war. This is not to say that the Bush administration manufactured a provocation, but only that the sense of threat may have been in part generated by the knowledge that the favored means for dealing with it would have additional benefits.

As an alternative way to look behind expressed attitudes, we could examine personality characteristics and even argue that many of the leading members of the administration, most obviously Bush, Rumsfeld, and Cheney, were essentially bullies (Etheredge 1978; Friedlander and Cohen 1975). I cannot pursue this line of argument here, but would only note that we would want to see whether opponents and proponents of the war, both in and out of government, and in other countries as well as the United States, could be distinguished by their personalities.

The path to war

The previous discussion seeks to explain why the administration felt that it was necessary to overthrow Saddam. But it does not explain how this was possible.[5] A full discussion of the enabling conditions would call for a paper of its own, even putting aside the requirement for Saddam to act in a way that would permit the war to take place, but flagging a few that we take for granted serves the useful function of reminding us that under other conditions they could have been absent. Most obviously, the United States had a large and extremely well-functioning military, having invested a great deal in advanced technology and training on how to use it. In conjunction with the fact that economic sanctions had prevented Saddam from developing his armed forces, this meant that the United States could be confident that Saddam could be overthrown with few casualties. (Indeed, those who criticize American military adventures believe that the best and perhaps the only way to stop them is to drastically shrink the size and capabilities of the American military) (Preble 2009). Another requirement was the cooperation of the Gulf states, especially Kuwait, Bahrain, and Saudi Arabia. Without this, the invasion simply would not have been possible. Their cooperation and the physical facilities on their territory that the United States was able to use were not accidental, but followed from the extensive programs and diplomacy put in place in the years after the Gulf War (Gause 2010). Furthermore, these countries shared the American perception that Saddam Hussein was a menace to them, which is a useful reminder that the preferences and perceptions of the Bush administration, while not acceptable to many of us, were not unique to it.

Third and related, almost all countries, even those that opposed the war, shared the general American assessment of the state of Iraq's WMD programs. Although Bush might have wanted to go to war even had he known that these programs were defunct on the grounds that they would have been resuscitated when sanctions lapsed in the future, for other countries a hypothetical danger would not have been sufficient. Related to this, I doubt if Bush could have taken the country to war without the active support of the British and the acquiescence of the Democrats. Although any British leader would have done what he or she could have to preserve the "special relationship," the British position owed a great deal to the views of Tony Blair, and particularly to his strong commitment to humanitarian intervention (Blair 1999). The war might also have been impossible if it had met strong opposition within the United States. But, in ways that reciprocally reinforced each other, neither the media nor the Democratic Party vigorously opposed it. The former were generally uncritical (Massing 2004) and most leading Democrats calculated that their interests would be best served by acquiescing in Bush's policy, partly because the image of the Democratic Party as soft on national security had been reinforced by its opposition to the Gulf War.

Most interestingly, even these factors were not sufficient to generate the war. Bush needed a path to the invasion, and as late as the summer of 2002 it was not clear that he could find or make one. It does not appear that the administration had a clear plan, and it is hard to see how Bush could have gone to war without some provocation, trick, or facilitating maneuver. Ironically, it was Secretary of State Colin Powell who came up with the latter, although I doubt if he understood it as such. In his most powerful intervention on Iraq, in the summer of 2002 he convinced Bush to override Cheney's objection and take the case to the UN, arguing, correctly I believe, that only by doing so could the United States muster the domestic and international support it needed. The resolution calling for Saddam to admit the inspectors both shifted the onus of avoiding the war onto Iraqi shoulders and reframed the issue as a test of the UN's ability to live up to its mission. The favorable UN vote also made it easier for Blair to support the war and undercut internationalist opposition in the United

States. Even though Saddam surprised many people by letting the inspectors in and a second resolution proved impossible, Bush was able to go to war on the not entirely implausible grounds that Saddam remained in defiance of multiple UN warnings and resolutions. It would be an exaggeration to say that without the UN Bush could not have gone to war because functional substitutes might have been crafted. But Bush needed a path to war, and Powell's suggestion of a UN resolution provided one.

How nations behave

Standard international politics theories provide some quite different explanations for the war, ones that downplay if not bypass the beliefs of the leaders and focus on enduring patterns of international behavior. Political psychologists may be interested in beliefs for their own sakes, but IR scholars care about how countries behave, and as Waltz's original discussion of the three images of the causes of war indicate, looking at individuals may be a distraction from where the action really is (Waltz 1965; Nelson and Olin 1979). The fact that my discussion here will be brief does not mean that I think this position deserves short shrift. Rather, they are as powerful as they are familiar. Two sets of arguments are salient, one focusing on the international system and the normal behavior of powerful states and the second arguing for the peculiar behavior of the United States. Both agree that focusing on detailed and idiosyncratic beliefs is a red herring.

Realism and the third image

Interestingly enough, both proponents and opponents of the war in Iraq have ignored what is perhaps the most standard IR explanation for American actions. At the start of this chapter I said that this case causes real trouble for Realists because their theory is both descriptive and prescriptive and most of them felt that the war was not necessary and would not produce good results—i.e. that it was not in the national interest. This is true, but another strand of Realism severs description from prescription and stresses that the allure and perils of power are such that states typically overreach. As usual, Churchill put it best: although "this is the reverse of what is healthy and wise... when nations or individuals get strong they are often truculent and bullying. But when they are weak they become better mannered" (Wyatt 1954: 42). Of course this does not explain why the United States intervened in Iraq in 2003 rather than in some other country in some other year. But we do not have to study Bush or even the impact of 9/11 to know that something of this sort was likely.

The basic Realist argument has four strands (Jervis 2005: 92–96). First and most general is the core of the Realist outlook that power is checked most effectively if not only by counter-balancing power. Thucydides puts these words into the mouths of the Athenians in the famous Melian dialogue, and while he disapproves and knows the attitude will bring ruin, he probably agrees with the generalization:

> Our opinion of the gods and our knowledge of men lead us to conclude that it is a general and necessary law of nature to rule wherever one can. This is not a law that we made ourselves, nor were we the first to act upon it when it was made. We found it already in existence, and we shall leave it to exist forever among those who come after us. We are merely acting in accordance with it, and we know that you or anybody else with the same power as ours would be acting in precisely the same way.
>
> (Warner 1954: 363)

It follows from the propensity of states to use the power at their disposal that those who are not subject to external restraints tend to feel few restraints at all. As Edmund Burke put it, in a position endorsed by Hans Morgenthau: "I dread our <u>own</u> power and our <u>own</u> ambition; I dread our being too much dreaded. It is ridiculous to say that we are not men, and that, as men, we shall never wish to aggrandize ourselves" (quoted in Morgenthau 1978: 169–170, emphasis in the original). With this a driving idea, Waltz saw the likelihood of the United States' current behavior from the start of the post-Cold War era:

> The powerful state may, and the United States does, think of itself as acting for the sake of peace, justice, and well-being in the world. But these terms will be defined to the liking of the powerful, which may conflict with the preferences and the interests of others. In international politics, overwhelming power repels and leads others to try to balance against it. With benign intent, the United States has behaved, and until its power is brought into a semblance of balance, will continue to behave in ways that annoy and frighten others.
>
> (Waltz 1991: 69; see also Waltz 1992; Krauthammer 1990–1991)

It is the exception rather than the rule for states to stay on the path of moderation when others do not force them to do so (though for contrasting views see Wendt 1999; Schroeder 1994, 1997).

Second and related, states' definitions of their interests tend to expand as their power does (Zakaria 1992; Tucker 1971; Van Evera 1999; Schroeder 1994, 1997). As states become stronger it becomes worth their while to pursue a whole host of objectives that were out of reach when the state's security was in doubt and all efforts had to be directed to primary objectives. With increases in power and security, states seek what Arnold Wolfers called "milieu goals" (Wolfers 1962; Miller 2010). Seen in this light, the administration's perception that this was a time of great opportunity in the Middle

East was the product not so much of the special circumstances in the region as of the enormous resources at the disposal of the United States.

A third structural explanation for American behavior is that increased relative power brought with it new fears. As major threats disappear, people elevate ones that previously were seen as quite manageable (Mueller 1994; Hartmann 1982), and people now seem to be as worried as they were during the height of the Cold War despite the fact that a terrorist or rogue attack, even with WMD, could cause only a small fraction of World War II's devastation. But there is more to it than psychology. As a dominant state, the United States has acquired an enormous stake in the world order and interests spread throughout the globe. Most countries are primarily concerned with what happens in their neighborhoods; the world is the hegemon's neighborhood, and it is not only hubris that leads it to be concerned with everything that happens anywhere. The result is a fusion of narrow and broad self-interest. At a point when most analysts were worried about the decline of American power, not its excesses, Waltz noted that for the United States:

> like some earlier great powers... the interest of the country in security came to be identified with the maintenance of a certain world order. For countries at the top, this is predictable behavior.... Once a state's interests reach a certain extent, they become self-reinforcing.
>
> (Waltz 1979)

The fourth facet can be seen as a broader conception of the previous point. As Realists stress, even states that find the status quo acceptable have to worry about the future (Copeland 2000; Mearsheimer 2001). Indeed, the more an actor sees the current situation as satisfactory, the more it will expect the future to be worse. Psychology is important here too: prospect theory argues that actors are prone to accept great risks when they believe they will suffer losses unless they act boldly. The adoption of a preventive war doctrine may be a mistake, especially if taken too far, but is not foreign to normal state behavior, and it appeals to states that have a valued position to maintain. However secure states are, only rarely can they be secure enough, and if they are currently very powerful they will feel strong impulses to act now to prevent a deterioration that could allow others to harm them in the future. From this perspective we can re-examine the common supposition that the war in Iraq was unusual in its objective of warding off a danger that would not emerge for a number of years. While standard readings of most of twentieth-century history portrayed such behavior as uncommon, Realism correctly leads us to expect states to strike out in anticipation of future dangers when they are either desperate or see an opportunity (Copeland 2000; Gaddis 2004). The great power of the United States in fact makes a preventive strategy more attractive. Not only does it have the ability to carry it out, but the unusual security that it has gained makes it particularly sensitive to the likelihood that its position will deteriorate, and makes it more willing to tolerate risks to ward off this potential loss.

The influence of the external environment is shown by a smaller-scale analysis of recent American foreign policy. Bush's policy not only in Iraq but more generally changed in its last three years or so. The use and threat of force, the seeking of lofty goals (most obviously democratization), and the refusal to negotiate with unpleasant regimes receded, being modified if not replaced by greater flexibility and pragmatism. Obama's policies have much more in common with those of the late Bush years than they do with his rhetoric on the campaign trail. Neither of these developments would surprise a Realist, who would argue that Bush was finally forced to yield to a recalcitrant environment, and that on assuming office Obama similarly found that he had less maneuvering room than he had expected.

The United States and the second image

An alternative line of argument draws on Waltz's second image. It shares with Realism a downplaying of the beliefs and values of individuals, but it focuses not on the external environment, but on the particular character-istics of individual countries or political regimes. To explain the Iraq War, one might turn to nineteenth-century thinkers who believed that demo-cracies were particularly energetic, undisciplined, and short-sighted, a description that many observers feel is quite appropriate to the case under consideration. Even though contrary views about democracies are now more popular, it is not hard to build on older foundations to argue that mass opinion is easily moved by emotion and the need for immediate grat-ification and that democratic leaders not only share many of these senti-ments, but have incentives to seek short-run popularity even at the expense of the national interest. Democratic regimes may also be particu-larly prone to self-righteousness and the pursuit of the chimera of com-plete solutions rather than settling for the adjustment of conflicting interests and principles.

A different domestic focus is prevalent now, especially among histor-ians. This attributes the war in Iraq and most other facets of American behavior to the peculiar if not unique American social and political system. One variant stresses the unusual aspect of American society dating to its having been founded by a "middle class fragment," which leads it to misunderstand the internal dynamics of most countries (Hartz 1955; Mor-genthau 1946; Wolfers 1962; Schroeder unpublished manusript). In Iraq, this produced an overestimate of the threat posed by Saddam's strange regime and an even more striking underestimate of the challenge of post-war reconstruction. Since democracy is the natural order in societies—i.e., the outcome that will occur unless special circumstances intervene (Toulmin 1961)—Iraq would become at least a fledgling democracy once the tyrannical top layer of the government was removed. The nature of this error was encapsulated in a story from the first stages of the war told by the leader of a group of American soldiers who were taken prisoner:

> "The Iraqis had a hard time understanding something," Williams recalled. "Shoshana is Panamanian. Edgar is Hispanic. Joe is Philippine, and Patrick is from Kansas. The Iraqis could not conceive how we could all have been in the same army and not fight one another. One Iraqi said to me, 'You no fighting each other? Why?' "
>
> (Gordon and Trainor 2006)

Overlapping somewhat with this are the more economically-oriented views epitomized by William Appleman Williams that I think it is fair to say constitute the mainstream of American diplomatic history (Williams 1959). Although this "Wisconsin school" is not entirely unified, its members stress the heavy role played by economic interests and institutions in American foreign policy. Ranging from crude if not conspiratorial Marxism to more complex and subtle arguments that seek to link economic forces with domestic institutions and culture, this perspective argues that what we see in Iraq is neither unique to Bush nor general to all countries. Rather, it is particularly American in its need to dominate as much of the world as possible (especially areas with economic significance), coupled with the belief that all societies should be remade in the American image and would welcome our attempt to do so.

To fully rehearse the pros and cons of this school of thought is beyond the scope of this chapter, but two points of method should be noted even though (unfortunately?) they point in opposite directions. First, most proponents of this school neglect comparisons to other countries and so find it easy to attribute brutal American behavior to the American domestic system. Methodologically, this is invalid, and there is much to the Realist riposte that what members of the Wisconsin school see as not only reprehensible but as particularly American is in fact the way great powers typically behave. While arguing that American leaders and the mass public are prone to have a parochial outlook, this scholarship is limited by its own parochialism. But a second use of comparisons, while not entirely inconsistent with Realism, gives more support to those who attribute the war in Iraq to the nature of the American system. This is the continuity in American policy since World War II, if not earlier. Many "traditional" scholars like myself argued that much American behavior during the Cold War, including overthrowing left-wing governments, supporting oppressive but conservative regimes, seeking military advantage over the USSR, and fighting in peripheral areas such as Vietnam, could be explained as the behavior of any state caught in a struggle for worldwide power. There was great explanatory power in standard IR concepts such as the security dilemma, strategic interaction, and the struggle for advantage. Evidence for the utility of this perspective can be found in the striking parallels between Soviet and American international behavior despite the enormous domestic differences and the parallels between the Cold War and previous international struggles, going all the way back to the Peloponnesian War. So far, so good for Realism. But the post-Cold War era, especially after 9/11, calls this picture into question (Chollet and Goldgeier 2008; Brands 2008). I argued above that Realism expects states that face few external restraints to expand until they run into painful obstacles. There is a great deal to this, but I also find value in the riposte that the war in Iraq is more than this. The combination of unwarranted fear and reckless optimism, the crusading ideology, the expectation that others will see the purity of our motives, are hard to explain in terms of a reaction to the international environment. To the extent that American behavior has changed relatively little since the end of the Cold War, the search for domestic sources becomes more appealing. In this view, the explanation for the war in Iraq lies not in George W. Bush, the rise of terrorism, or Saddam's behavior, but in a general American project to remake the world.

Summary

To a large extent, the explanations we give for the war in Iraq will be strongly influenced not only by our views about whether the war was justified, but by our general outlooks and theories about politics. We should not expect people with very different views, established long before the war, to explain it the same way. Roger Hilsman recounts the story of President Kennedy's response to the wildly different reports of two observers who had just come back from a joint trip to Vietnam: "You did visit the same country, didn't you?" (Hilsman 1967). In a very real sense they didn't. While it would be too much to say they merely visited their own minds, they could make sense of what they saw in Vietnam only by utilizing the (different) intellectual frameworks that they brought with them. So just as contemporary proponents and opponents of the war in Iraq (who of course did not form unified and uniform camps) differed in their views about what was happening in the world and what the consequences of alternative course were likely to be, so later analysts will differ—and largely along lines that reflect both the original debate and current political issues (Combs 1983; Ward-Perkins 2005; Schwartz 1991).

In the end, I think that while the generalizations provided by Realism and studies of the nature of the American domestic system point in the right direction, policy-making involves individuals making choices. Not all of them would have chosen war, and to understand what happened we need to deeply and critically enter into the hopes and fears of those who took the country into war. While I am under no illusions that I have provided a coherent answer to why the United States invaded Iraq, I am comforted in my indecision by the knowledge that the debate about the causes of the war will outlive me. So I come back to the point I made at the start that historical explanations are fraught with difficulty and can never be definitive. But here as in much of the rest of scholarship, the journey has more value than the destination.

Notes

1 Throughout I will focus on the United States as the causal agent. Of course it takes (at least) two to have a war, and indeed Saddam's behavior presents more than its share of puzzles. But for the purposes of this chapter I will take for granted his refusal to comply with American and UN demands. For a discussion of the causes of the Iran–Iraq War that notes how the explanation changes when we shift our focus from one of the participants to the other, see Gause (2010: 58–60).
2 I have discussed the broader beliefs behind the Bush Doctrine in Jervis (2005: Ch. 4). For a good study of the sources of beliefs in historical explanation, see Roberts (1996: Ch. 10). I will not discuss the neoconservative world view or ideology because although a significant number of second-level players in the administration were members of this camp, Bush, Rumsfeld, and Cheney were not and I see no reason to believe that they were manipulated or even persuaded by their subordinates.
3 For a range of perceptive analyses, see Bruni (2001) and Erickson (2004: 28–33). Haass (2009: 236) talks of Bush being "attracted to what was bold." Another ruler who believed that God was guiding him and would save his empire from over-extension was Spain's Philip II: see Parker (1998 and 2002).
4 If the Bush administration believed that not only the overthrow of Saddam but the post-war reconstruction would be achieved easily and cheaply, this gives a different perspective to the search for causes of the policy. For a state to adopt a policy in the face of high expected costs requires that there be causal factors of a large magnitude—i.e., that the expected gains had to be large and/or the costs of alternative policies had to be seen as very great. But if the expected costs of the invasion were in fact seen as low, even weak impulses would be sufficient to produce and explain the action. In a marvelous study, Daniel Headrick (1981) argued that our standard explanations for the timing and occurrence of classical imperialism neglect the crucial fact that late nineteenth century technologies, especially the machine gun, low-draft gunboats, and quinine to combat malaria, drastically lowered the costs of conquering Africa.
5 I am grateful to Philip Zelikow for reminding me of this and pointing me to the final argument in this section. For a general discussion of the role of willingness and opportunity in explaining war, see Most and Starr (1989).

References

Abramsky, S. (2004) "Supporting the Troops, Doubting the War," *The Nation*, October 4.

Art, R. (1980) "To What Ends Military Power?" *International Security*, 4: 3–35.

Autesserre, S. (2010) *The Trouble with Congo: Local Violence and the Failure of International Peacebuilding*, New York: Cambridge University Press.

Blair, T. (1999) "Doctrine of the International Community." A speech made to the Economic Club of Chicago, Hilton Hotel, Chicago, April 24.

Brands, H. (2008) *From Berlin to Baghdad: America's Search for Purpose in the Post-Cold War World*, Lexington: University Press of Kentucky.

Brodie, B. (1978) "The Development of Nuclear Strategy," *International Security*, 2: 65–83.

Bruni, F. (2001) "For President, a Mission and a Role in History," *New York Times*, September 22.

Bush, G. W. (2001a) "Remarks to the Nation," September 12.

Bush, G. W. (2001b) "Speech at the National Cathedral," September 14.

Chollet, D. and Goldgeier, J. (2008) *America Between the Wars From 11/9 to 9/11: The Misunderstood Years between the Fall of the Berlin Wall and the Start of the War on Terror*, New York: Public Affairs.

Clarke, R. (2004) *Against All Enemies: Inside America's War on Terror*, New York: Free Press.

Combs, J. (1983) *American Diplomatic History: Two Centuries of Changing Interpretations*, Berkeley: University of California Press.

Copeland, D. (2000) *The Origins of Major War*, Ithaca, NY: Cornell University Press.

Dinges, J. (2004) *The Condor Years: How Pinochet and His Allies Brought Terrorism to Three Continents*, New York: New Press.

Divine, R. (2000) *Perpetual War for Perpetual Peace*, College Station: Texas A&M University Press.

Etheredge, L. S. (1978) *A World of Men: The Private Sources of American Foreign Policy*, Cambridge, MA: MIT Press.

Erickson, S. (2004) "George Bush and the Treacherous Country," *LA Weekly*, February 13.

Feith, D. (2008) *War and Decision: Inside the Pentagon at the Dawn of the War on Terrorism*, New York: HarperCollins.

Flibbert, A. (2006) "The Road to Baghdad: Ideas and Intellectuals in Explanations of the Iraq War," *Security Studies*, 15: 310–352.

Friedlander, S. and Cohen, R. (1975) "The Personality Correlates of Belligerence in International Conflict: A Comparative Analysis of Historical Case Studies," *Comparative Politics*, 7: 155–186.

Fukuyama, F. (2006) *America at the Crossroads: Democracy, Power, and the Neoconservative Legacy*, New Haven: Yale University Press.

Gaddis, J. L. (2004) *Surprise, Security, and the American Experience*, Cambridge, MA: Harvard University Press.

Gartzke, E. (1999) "War is in the Error Term," *International Organization*, 53: 567–578.

Gause, F. G. (2010) *International Relations of the Persian Gulf*, Cambridge: Cambridge University Press.

Gordon, M. and Trainor, B. (2006) *Cobra II: The Inside Story of the Invasion and Occupation of Iraq*, New York: Pantheon.

Haass, R. (2009) *War of Necessity, War of Choice: A Memoir of Two Iraq Wars*, New York: Simon & Schuster.

Halliday, F. (2009) "The Study of US Foreign Policy in the Middle East," *International History Review*, 31.

Harding, J. (2003) "Conflicting Views From Two Bush Camps," *Financial Times*, March 20.

Hartmann, F. (1982) *The Conservation of Enemies: A Study in Enmity*, Westport: Greenwood Press.

Hartz, L. (1955) *The Liberal Tradition in America*, New York: Harcourt, Brace & Company.

Headrick, D. (1981) *The Tools of Empire: Technology and European Imperialism in the Nineteenth Century*, New York: Oxford University Press.

Herwig, H. (1987) "Clio Deceived: Patriotic Self-Censorship in Germany after the Great War," *International Security*, 12: 262–310.

Hilsman, R. (1967) *To Move a Nation: The Politics of Foreign Policy in the Administration of John F. Kennedy*, Garden City: Doubleday.

Immerman, R. (2010) *Empire for Liberty: A History of American Imperialism from Benjamin Franklin to Paul Wolfowitz*, Princeton: Princeton University Press.

Jervis, R. (1976) *Perception and Misperception in International Politics*, Princeton: Princeton University Press.

Jervis, R. (2003) "The Confrontation between Iraq and the US: Implications for the Theory and Practice of Deterrence," *European Journal of International Relations*, 9: 315–337.

Jervis, R. (2005) *American Foreign Policy in a New Era*, New York: Routledge.

Jervis, R. (2006) "Understanding Beliefs," *Political Psychology*, 27: 641–663.

Jervis, R. (2008) "Bridges, Barriers, and Gaps: The Relationships Between Research and Policy," *Political Psychology*, 29: 572–574.

Jervis, R. (2009) "War, Intelligence, and Honesty," *Political Science Quarterly*, 123: 672–675.

Jervis, R. (2010) *Why Intelligence Fails: Lessons from the Iranian Revolution and the Iraq War*, Ithaca, NY: Cornell University Press.

Joll, J. (1972) "1914: The Unspoken Assumptions," in H. W. Koch (ed.) *The Origins of the First World War*, New York: Macmillan.

Kennan, G. (1951) *American Diplomacy, 1900–1965*, Chicago: University of Chicago Press.

Krauthammer, C. (1990–1991) "The Unipolar Moment," *Foreign Affairs*, 70: 23–33.

Kurth, J. (1973) "U.S. Policies, Latin American Politics, and Praetorian Rule," in Phillippe Schmitter (ed.) *Military Rule in Latin America: Function, Consequences and Perspectives*, Beverly Hills and London: Sage.

McClellan, S. (2008) *What Happened: Inside the Bush White House and Washington's Culture of Deception*, New York: PublicAffairs.

Massing, M. (2004) "Now They Tell Us," *The New York Review of Books*, January 29.

May, E. (1975) *The Making of the Monroe Doctrine*, Cambridge, MA: The Belknap Press of the Harvard University Press.

Mearsheimer, J. (2001) *The Tragedy of Great Power Politics*, New York: W. W. Norton.

Mearsheimer, J. and Walt, S. (2003) "An Unnecessary War," *Foreign Policy*, January/February.

Miller, B. (2010) "Explaining Changes in U.S. Grand Strategy: 9/11, The Rise of Offensive Liberalism, and the War in Iraq," *Security Studies*, 19: 26–65.

Morgenthau, H. (1946) *Scientific Man Versus Power Politics*, Chicago: University of Chicago Press.

Morgenthau, H. (1978) *Politics Among Nations*, 5th edn, revised, New York: Knopf.

Most, B. and Starr, H. (1989) *Inquiry, Logic and International Politics*, Columbia: University of South Carolina Press.

Mueller, J. (1994) "The Catastrophe Quota: Trouble after the Cold War," *Journal of Conflict Resolution*, 38: 355–375.

Mueller, J. (2006) *Overblown: How Politicians and the Terrorism Industry Inflate National Security Threats, and Why We Believe Them*, New York: Free Press.

Mueller, J. (2009) *Atomic Obsession: Nuclear Alarmism from Hiroshima to Al-Qaeda*, New York: Oxford University Press.

Nelson, K. and Olin, S. (1979) *Why War: Ideology, Theory, and History*, Berkeley: University of California Press.

Ninkovich, F. (1994) *Modernity and Power: A History of the Domino Theory in the 20th Century*, Chicago: University of Chicago Press.

Oren, I. (2009) "The Unrealism of Contemporary Realism: The Tension between Realist Theory and Realists' Practices," *Perspectives on Politics*, 7: 283–301.

Parker, G. (1998) *The Grand Strategy of Philip II*, New Haven: Yale University Press.

Parker, G. (2002) *Empire, War, and Faith in Early Modern Europe*, London: Penguin Books.

Pollack, K. (2002) *The Threatening Storm: The Case for Invading Iraq*, New York: Random House.

Preble, C. (2009) *The Power Problem: How American Military Dominance Makes Us Less Safe, Less Prosperous, and Less Free*, Ithaca, NY: Cornell University Press.

Reese, M. (2003) *Our Final Hour: A Scientist's Warning*, New York: Basic Books.

Risen, J., Sanger, D., and Shanker, T. (2003) "In Sketchy Data, Trying to Gauge Iraq Threat," *New York Times*, July 20.

Roberts, C. (1996) *The Logic of Historical Explanation*, University Park: Pennsylvania State University Press.

Schroeder, P. "Reflections on System Effects: War, Peace, and the USA as System Leader," unpublished manuscript.

Schroeder, P. (1994) *The Transformation of European Politics, 1763–1848*, New York: Oxford University Press.

Schroeder, P. (1997) "Does the History of International Politics Go Anywhere?" in David Wetzel and Theodore Hamerow (eds.) *International Politics and German History*, Westport: Praeger.

Schwartz, B. (1991) "Social Change and Collective Memory: The Democratization of George Washington," *American Sociological Review*, 56: 221–236.

Suskind, R. (2006) *The One Percent Doctrine: Deep Inside America's Pursuit of Its Enemies Since 9/11*, New York: Simon & Schuster.

Tenet, G. (2007) *At the Center of the Storm: My Years at the CIA*, New York: Harper Collins.

Tierney, D. (2010) *How We Fight: Crusades, Quagmires, and the American Way of War*, New York: Little Brown.

Toulmin, S. (1961) *Foresight and Understanding: An Inquiry Into the Aims of Science*, New York: Harper & Row.

Tucker, R. (1971) *The Radical Left and American Foreign Policy*, Baltimore: Johns Hopkins University Press.

Van Evera, S. (1999) *Causes of War: Power and the Roots of Conflict*, Ithaca, NY: Cornell University Press.

Waltz, K. (1965) *Man, the State, and War*, New York: Columbia University Press.

Waltz, K. (1979) *Theories of International Politics*, New York: McGraw-Hill.

Waltz, K. (1991) "America as a Model for the World? A Foreign Policy Perspective," *PS: Political Science and Politics*, 24: 667–670.

Waltz, K. (1992) "A Necessary War?" in Harry Kriesler (ed.) *Confrontation in the Gulf*, Berkeley: University of California Institute of International Studies.

Ward-Perkins, B. (2005) *The Fall of Rome and the End of Civilization*, New York: Oxford University Press.

Warner, R. (1954) *The Peloponnesian War* (translation), Harmondsworth: Penguin.

Wendt, G. (1999) *Social Theory of International Politics*, New York: Cambridge University Press.

Williams, M. (2005) "What is the National Interest? The Neoconservative Challenge in IR Theory," *European Journal of International Relations*, 11: 307–338.

Williams, W. A. (1959) *The Tragedy of American Diplomacy*, Cleveland: World Publishing Co.

Wilson, T. (2002) *Strangers to Ourselves: Discovering the Adaptive Unconscious*, Cambridge, MA: Belknap Press of Harvard University Press.

Wolfers, A. (1962) *Discord and Collaboration*, Baltimore: Johns Hopkins University Press.

Woodward, B. (2002) *Bush at War*, New York: Simon & Schuster.

Woodward, B. (2004) *Plan of Attack*, New York: Simon & Schuster.

Wyatt, W. (1954) "Churchill in His Element," *Harper's*, September.

Zakaria, F. (1992) "Realism and Domestic Politics: A Review Essay," *International Security*, 17: 177–198.

3 Ideas, American grand strategy, and the war in Iraq

Colin Dueck

I argue in this chapter that the Iraq War was the result of two shifts in grand strategy, one that took place after the Bush administration took office, the other in the wake of the terrorist attacks of 9/11. The larger question thus becomes: why does grand strategy change? To what extent can strategic adjustments be explained by international structural pressures, as opposed to changes in the mentality of decision-makers? I argue that international structural pressures actually explain very little in these cases, and that a more useful explanatory framework points to the influence of policy ideas in shaping strategic outcomes. I also clarify and identify the exact nature of US strategic adjustment between 2000 and 2004: the first adjustment, under Bush, involving a change from Clinton's liberal internationalism to a more realist approach; and the second, after 9/11, involving a change from a strategy of realism to a strategy of American primacy.

The organization of the chapter is as follows: first, I offer a brief definition of grand strategy. Then I outline a number of alternative grand strategies that American foreign policy-makers might have chosen in recent years. Next, I discuss two theoretically informed potential explanations for US strategic adjustment since 2000: one, based upon the structure of the international system, the other, based upon the importance of policy ideas. Finally, I trace the actual changes in US grand strategy since 2000, identifying the nature of those changes, and showing how various policy ideas carried great weight in shaping strategic outcomes, including the US decision to go to war in Iraq in 2003.

What is grand strategy?

A "grand strategy" is the set of assumptions that govern a state's foreign policy behavior in the face of real or potential armed conflict with other states (Christensen 1996; Kupchan 1994; Nordlinger 1996; Posen 1985; Luttwak 1987). Whenever policy-makers are faced with the task of identifying and reconciling foreign policy goals with limited national resources, in the shadow of armed conflict, they are engaging in grand strategy.

Grand strategies can be expansionist or defensive, confrontational or accommodating (Johnston 1995; Kupchan 1994; Luttwak 1987). Levels and forms of defense spending, foreign aid, alliance behavior, troop deployments and diplomatic activity are all influenced by grand strategic assumptions. Grand strategies are not always well designed, coherent or even intentional in nature – especially in a political system as fragmented and decentralized as that of the United States (Friedberg 1991). But whether implicitly or explicitly, leading officials in every country necessarily have a sense of their country's national interests; of the threats that exist to those interests; and of the resources that can be brought to bear against those threats.

Any state's grand strategy can sometimes change significantly: a process also known as "strategic adjustment" (Trubowitz and Rhodes 1999). In order to measure changes in grand strategy, we need to know the following: is military spending raised or lowered? Are alliance commitments extended or withdrawn? Is foreign aid increased or decreased? Does the state engage in significant new diplomatic initiatives, or does it disengage from existing diplomatic activities? And does the state adopt a more aggressive and confrontational stance toward its adversaries, or does it adopt a less confrontational stance?

This list of questions gives us a concrete set of foreign policy outcomes that vary in a precise and observable manner. Variation in grand strategy will therefore be defined as a significant overall change in levels of military spending, alliance commitments, foreign aid, diplomatic activism and/or foreign policy stands toward potential adversaries. We now know what must be explained, when we ask how and why grand strategy changes. Next we outline a number of grand strategies that the United States might have followed in the years 2000–2003.

Alternative post-Cold War US grand strategies

While there are probably as many alternative grand strategies, in theory, as there are strategists, for our purposes we can simplify the available options into four broad schools of thought (Kohout *et al.* 1995; Nacht 1995; Nau 2002; Posen and Ross 1996–1997). First, there are those who clearly reject the notion of the United States as a world power, with its troops and alliances scattered around the globe, and who favor a withdrawal from strategic commitments incurred as a result of the Cold War. Second, there are those who question the liberal assumptions behind US grand strategy, and who advocate a balance of power strategy, an internationalist strategy, but one shorn of global and liberalizing ambitions. Third, there are those who call for a strategy of American primacy, based upon the energetic assertion of US predominance worldwide, as well as the promotion of an "Americanized" international system. Finally, there are those who share the desire to promote a liberal international order, but who wish to do so primarily through the use of multilateral institutions, rather than military power.

Strategic disengagement

Advocates of strategic disengagement favor a complete withdrawal from political and military commitments made during the Cold War, and a return to the United States' interwar policy of "strategic independence" or "hemispheric defense." The essence of this alternative is that the United States abandons its posture of forward deployment in Europe and Asia, that it withdraw from its Cold War alliances and bring its troops home. While this neo-isolationist alternative is rarely articulated in mainstream political circles today, it does have a certain appeal to both the left wing of the Democratic Party and the right wing of the Republican Party (Wittkopf 1996). Indeed, the two leading third party candidates of the 2000 presidential election – Ralph Nader and Pat Buchanan – could both be said to advocate strategic disengagement (Buchanan 2002). The most thoughtful advocates of strategic disengagement, however, have not come from the political arena, but from a small group of foreign policy commentators such as Eric Nordlinger (1996), Christopher Layne (1997), Ted Galen Carpenter (2002), Daryl Press and Eugene Gholz (Gholz *et al.* 1997).

The direct implications of these arguments is that the United States should withdraw from its European and Asian alliances, bring the vast majority of US forces home from their stations overseas, abstain from military adventures abroad, and reduce military spending (Layne 1997: 112–113). Neo-isolationists agree that defense spending should be cut dramatically – by approximately 50 percent from Cold War levels (Nordlinger 1996: 46; Gholz *et al.* 1997: 13). The only military force that neo-isolationists favor is one capable of protecting core US interests in the western hemisphere, along with a minimal capacity for military intervention abroad. Consequently, under a strategy of disengagement, the United States would not require much more than a million soldiers, sailors, airmen and marines (Ravenal 1990–1991: 15–19). This standing force would be heavily weighted toward naval and air power, and supported by a small nuclear arsenal. Even these reduced forces would leave the United States invulnerable to attack. And with more resources to direct inward, and less risk of military entanglement, the United States would actually be stronger, and more secure, as well as truer to its own democratic traditions (Layne 1997: 124).

Balance of power realism

The second major strategic alternative for the United States since the end of the Cold War has been to abandon what Walter McDougall calls "global meliorism," and to simply support a geopolitical balance between the major powers (McDougall 1997: 211). Henry Kissinger has been the leading advocate of this alternative, but a number of foreign policy commentators with realist inclinations have voiced a similar approach – commentators such as James Schlesinger, Alan Tonelson, James Kurth and Sam Huntington (Huntington 1991; Kissinger 2002; Kurth 1996; Schlesinger 1992–1993). These balance of power advocates seek to preserve US alliance commitments to Europe and Asia, because they view these commitments as an insurance policy that dampens security competition overseas. Unlike other internationalists, however, balance of power advocates define American interests, and the threats to those interests, in essentially realist terms.

In practical terms, this means that the United States would abstain from making the domestic political complexion of other countries a subject of foreign policy (Haass 1995). Humanitarian interventions such as those in Bosnia and Kosovo would be avoided. Russia would no longer be lectured on the need for market reform. China would no longer be hectored on its human rights abuses. The democratization of those two countries would no longer be central to Sino-American and Russo-American relations. Nor would the United States define its international enemies as "rogue states," in need of democratic revolution or conversion. Rather, Washington would protect its vital interests overseas, while recognizing the inevitability of both conflict and diplomacy with countries whose self-defined interests run counter to its own.

By abstaining from interference in peripheral civil wars, and by playing down its pretensions as a moral guide for other nations, realists expect that the United States would be able to avoid costly commitments and controversies in areas of little concrete interest. The United States would thus avoid strategic over-extension. At the same time, however, realists advocate a vigorous defense of American interests, in those areas and on those subjects that *are* deemed vital (Morgenthau 1993: 382–383). So in terms of its core strategic commitments to peace and security in Western Europe, Northeast Asia and the Persian Gulf, balance of power realists would be just as engaged as any other internationalist.

Primacy

The third alternative open to the United States since the end of the Cold War has been to pursue a strategy of primacy. Such a strategy would entail acting aggressively to maintain US political and military predominance in the world, while pre-empting any conceivable challenges to a US-led international order. The goal of this strategy, however, is not only US dominance, but an "Americanized" international order, characterized by an expanding zone of market-oriented democracies: what Robert Kagan and William Kristol call a "benevolent global hegemony" (Kagan and Kristol 2000). While de facto support for a strategy of primacy comes from a wide variety of source, the most pointed and explicit calls for such an approach have come from a group of neoconservative foreign policy commentators, including writers, journalists and former government officials such as Kagan, Kristol, Charles Krauthammer, Richard Perle, Joshua Muravchik, Zalmay Khalilzad, Elliot Abrams and Paul Wolfowitz (Kristol and Kagan 1996; Muravchik 1996; Khalilzad 1995; Wolfowitz 2000).

Primacists are hawkish and hard-line, with a keen appreciation for the role of power, force, conflict and national self-interest in international relations. They share this appreciation with balance of power realists. But they are distinct from such realists in two important ways. First, they are more aggressive in terms of the policies and strategies they advocate (Posen and Ross 1996–1997). Like leading members of the Truman administration, they seek not a "balance" of power, but a preponderance of power on the part of the United States and its close allies. Continued predominance over other potential great powers is their goal (Tyler 1992). Second, primacists are more idealistic than balance of power realists. They genuinely believe that democratic and free market values of the United States can be promoted successfully worldwide. And they believe that this is not only in the interests of the United States – although it certainly is that – but also in the interests of the international community as a whole (Nau 2002: 48–55).

Liberal internationalism

The final alternative open to the United States since the end of the Cold War has been to pursue a strategy of liberal internationalism. Liberal internationalist authors in the post-Cold War era have included former and current officials, as well as scholars, such as Graham Allison (Allison and Treverton 1992), David Callahan (1994), John Ikenberry (1998–1999), Joseph Nye (2002) and John Ruggie (1996). Like primacists, liberal internationalists favor the promotion of an "Americanized" world order, characterized by the spread of democratic governments and open markets. Unlike primacists, however, liberal internationalists believe that a strong set of multilateral institutions – rather than US military predominance – is really the key to creating and sustaining a more friendly and democratic world order.

Liberal internationalists favor the promotion of democracy and human rights, worldwide, and they suggest that the United States do so with greater consistency than has often been the case (Halperin 1993; Nye 2002: 148–153; Smith 1994). Pressure should be applied to allies as well as adversaries, great powers as well as small ones. In the case of both Russia and China, liberals do not view human rights violations as purely internal matters. They view them as necessary and legitimate issues for the United States to raise, in its pursuit of a more progressive world order. Liberals therefore put democratic reform at the top of their foreign policy agenda in relation to Russia and China, as well as other authoritarian or semi-democratic countries. In the long run, liberals do not believe that there can be peace or stability in a world characterized by autocratic or dictatorial regimes. Conversely, in a world dominated by democracies, liberals expect cooperation and non-violence to be the norm (Russett 1992). For the most part, liberals favor peaceful methods of democracy promotion, by relying on tools such as economic sanctions, diplomatic pressure, foreign aid and international organizations. But just as liberals are sometimes willing to consider military intervention abroad for humanitarian reasons, so too are they willing to consider intervention for reasons of democracy promotion.

Liberals are divided amongst themselves over how "hawkish" they should be on questions of national security. But they all agree on the need for multilateralism; they all agree that "soft power" is becoming more important; and they all agree that the nature of international relations has changed dramatically enough in recent years to outmode any sort of traditional balance of power, isolationist or unilateralist approach to the world (Kohout *et al.* 1995: 402–404). These are the central characteristics that set liberal internationalists apart from the other three schools of thought.

Explaining changes in grand strategy

Having briefly outlined the basic strategic alternatives open to the United States, and before investigating the chosen cases in detail, how might we explain any changes in US grand strategy over the years 2000–2003? What theoretical framework might prove most useful in understanding patterns in strategic adjustment during these years? And what sort of predictive implications would each theory have?

Structural realist predictions and international conditions

In structural realist terms, the end of the Cold War was a revolutionary change – the sort of change usually associated with the aftermath of a major war. The central feature of that change was the termination of a previously bipolar international system. It is not entirely obvious what sort of strategic behavior a structural realist would expect, in such circumstances, from the world's only remaining superpower. In the early 1990s, structural realists did not offer clear predictions regarding the probable course of post-Cold War US foreign policy. Instead, they offered predictions regarding systemic outcomes. Authors such as Kenneth Waltz and John Mearsheimer, in particular, predicted that the international system would evolve in a multipolar direction, and that previously quiescent powers such as Germany and Japan would begin to assert themselves on political and strategic, as well as economic matters (Mearsheimer 1990; Waltz 1995). The implicit prescription was that the United States accept the inevitable trend toward multipolarity and scale back somewhat on its global role (Kupchan 2002: 28–29, 62–64). In recent years, Mearsheimer has come out with a much more explicit prediction that the United States will soon disengage strategically from Europe and Northeast Asia (Mearsheimer 2001: 385–400). But Mearsheimer's prediction is based in large part upon a questionable premise: that the "stopping power of water" prevents the United States from being able to aspire to any sort of hegemonic role outside the western hemisphere (Mearsheimer 2001: 114–128, 381–382). His prediction is all the more curious, since he argues elsewhere in the same book that all major powers try consistently to maximize their relative power in the world, at the expense of potential rivals (Mearsheimer 2001: 21–22, 29–40). This hardly seems to lead to the conclusion that the United States will soon disengage strategically from Europe and Northeast Asia.

Kenneth Waltz, for his part, has long insisted that structural realism cannot explain or predict foreign policy behavior (Waltz 1979: 121–122). Yet he seems willing to make implicit predictions regarding the future foreign policies of Germany and Japan, when he suggests that they will soon assert their strategic independence from the United States (Waltz 1995: 53–67). Waltz is actually quite vague as to what sort of grand strategy a realist would expect from the world's only superpower. He states that isolationism is "impossible" for the United States in the current international system. He also obviously believes that the United States would be well served by abandoning its globalist pretensions, and by acting with greater "forbearance" internationally. But then he adds that he "would not bet on it" (Waltz 1995: 77). What we are left with, from Waltz, is the sense that the United States *ought* to avoid isolationist, primacist or liberal internationalist grand strategies, without any *predictive* sense of whether it will actually do so.

The basic problem with both Waltz and Mearsheimer, in terms of their understanding of world politics today, is that neither of them have any place in their theories for a state that truly dominates the international system. Neither allows for the possibility of "unipolarity" or "hegemony," as anything other than: an unattainable state of global empire (for Mearsheimer); or a very fleeting and unstable condition (for Waltz) (Mearsheimer 2001: 40–41, 381–382; Waltz 1995: 52). But this does not necessarily mean that realism itself is invalid. There is in fact a long tradition of realist thought which recognizes that hegemonic international systems have been at least as common, historically, as balance of power systems (Gilpin 1981; Organski 1968; Tammen *et al.* 2000; Watson 1992). The United States is so dominant today, relative to other countries, that balance of power theory may have actually become a hindrance to understanding the current world order (Wohlforth 1999; Brooks and Wohlforth 2002). If we take the current distribution of power in the international system as our starting point, and recognize that American capabilities are unmatched, then we actually reach a somewhat different set of predictions than those offered by Waltz and Mearsheimer. For one thing, we would not necessarily expect to see other states balancing against the United States all that vigorously, since such balancing may simply be beyond their capabilities (Glaser 2003; Mastanduno and Kapstein 1999; Wohlforth 1999: 23–37). More to the point, the prediction in terms of US foreign policy behavior would clearly be to expect no disengagement from the United States' international role. In the words of Michael Mastanduno:

> According to realist logic, any great power should prefer to be a uni-polar power, regardless of whether or not it possesses expansionist ambitions. For the state at the top, unipolarity is preferable to being a great power facing either the concentrated hostility and threat of a bipolar world, or the uncertainty and risk of miscalculation inherent in a multipolar world.
>
> (1997: 134)

Realists believe that the definition of "security" tends to flow from the amount of power that a given state possesses. A country as powerful as the United States can afford to define its interests, and its security, in very broad terms. It can afford to have a low tolerance for external threats (Kagan 2002: 9, 13). There are of course a number of ways in which hege-monic powers can respond to new challenges. They can retreat in the face of danger, or appease potential challengers. But as Robert Gilpin points out, hegemonic powers seldom act in this way unless they have to. Their preference, for the most part, is to weaken potential rivals, in order to "eliminate the source of the problem" (Gilpin 1981: 191–194). Again, this is not a question of whether dominant states *should* act in this way. It is a question of what a structural realist would expect or *predict.* Surely no realist would actually expect any nation to voluntarily relinquish its status as the world's pre-eminent political and military power. On the contrary, from a realist perspective, it seems reasonable to predict that the United States would try to prolong the unipolar moment for as long as possible (Mastanduno 1997: 137). In this sense, realists should not have expected the United States to disengage from Europe and Asia, in the wake of the Soviet Union's collapse.

Still, realists face a puzzle, and a problem, in explaining patterns of US strategic adjustment in this new unipolar era. Given that the United States was not about to retreat into isolationism, given that it was not about to surrender its predominance overseas, that still left three strategic altern-atives. The United States could have pursued a strategy of primacy, a strat-egy of liberal internationalism, or a balance of power strategy. That is, the United States could have acted in precisely the way that structural realists seem to favor, by abandoning Wilsonian ambitions. Yet such a course was generally rejected by US policy-makers. There is simply no basis within conventional realist theory – which looks to international systemic pressures first and foremost – to explain the rejection of a balance of power strategy on the part of the United States. International pressures cannot explain that policy choice. Realists might have expected the rejection of neo-isolationism after the end of the Cold War; they cannot explain the adoption of any distinctly liberal grand strategy on the part of the United States, without leaving realist explanatory categories behind.

Strategic ideas

An alternative, ideational model of strategic adjustment would not deny that international conditions exert real pressure on policy-makers. But it would argue that uncertainty over exactly how to pursue the nation's interests, and the limited time and information available to policy-makers, forces leaders to rely to some extent upon specific mental shortcuts or preconceived beliefs variously described by international relations theorists as "belief systems," "operational codes," "policy paradigms," or simply "policy ideas."[1] These beliefs or assumptions offer policy-makers specific guidance under conditions of uncertainty, and therefore have an independent impact on foreign policy decisions. For our purposes, ideas or beliefs regarding the value and efficacy of particular grand strategies will be called "strategic ideas."

Strategic ideas are theories of grand strategy. Since states are forced by their limited resources to make difficult trade-offs between political, military and economic ends and means, policy-makers necessarily choose between distinct grand strategic alternatives, even when those alternatives are not articulated explicitly. Strategic ideas are the implicit or explicit causal assumptions that underlie such specific alternatives. And when strategic ideas change, strategic behavior changes in the direction prescribed, regardless of international conditions.

Drawing on historical institutionalism, an ideational model of strategic adjustment would suggest that strategic ideas tend to persist – in spite of changing material conditions – until "disproven" by some sort of external shock. These shocks cause existing policies to be questioned regardless of their inherent merits.[2] In the case of grand strategy, the most likely sources of such shock are major wars, international crises, or the development of a dramatic new threat. But a change in the identity of the party holding executive office can also act as a catalyst in changing existing strategic ideas. Consequently, the pattern of strategic adjustment, according to an ideational model, is predicted to be somewhat uneven and episodic.

Once some external shock has opened up a window or opportunity for new strategic ideas, the exact nature of those ideas – and the nature of the one that finally wins out – is crucially influenced by a process of domestic political agenda-setting. However feasible a new idea is, it must be put on the agenda of leading policy-makers before it can have a real impact. In the initial stages of agenda-setting, strategic ideas may come to the attention of policy-makers because of the efforts of interest groups, bureaucratic actors or elected officials. Any number of political actors may play a role in this process (Friedberg 1988; Baumgartner and Jones 1993; Kingdon 1984). In the latter stages of agenda-setting, the process takes on a very different dynamic, and the number of politically relevant actors narrows considerably. Leading executive officials become the key agenda-setters, the crucial link between new ideas and policy outcomes.

An ideas-based approach recognizes that on questions of grand strategy, especially at moments of change and uncertainty, leading state officials have considerable autonomy to react to external pressures in the manner they see fit. I argue that state officials react to such pressures in large part on the basis of their perception of the national interest – perceptions that often differ from one person and one administration to the next, even apart from questions of narrow self-interest. Ultimately, it is through leading state officials that new strategic ideas have a concrete impact on policy outcomes; and it is because of their relative autonomy on questions of national security, that such officials can put these ideas into practice. Contrary to the views of structural theorists, there is a surprising degree of room for creativity on the part of the executive to shape and develop grand strategy. The power of ideas is both a cause and a consequence of that freedom. But once any period of strategic adjustment has passed, and a new strategic idea is implemented with reasonable success, resistance to innovation again comes to the fore. The new strategic idea is locked in and institutionalized, both formally and informally, and the bias toward policy continuity resumes.

In sum: ideas have a role in the making of grand strategy because they help specify national interests amidst conditions of uncertainty. International pressures are to a certain extent indeterminate, and leading state officials are given considerable autonomy to interpret and act upon their conceptions of the national interest; these conceptions necessarily have a major impact on policy outcomes. In times of relative stability and continuity, strategic ideas have an impact primarily through their institutionalization or entrenchment in positions of power, both formal and informal. In the wake of international shocks, ideas still have a great impact, but in a very different way: through the process of agenda-setting. While a variety of political actors can play a role in the early stages of agenda-setting, leading state officials are the key figures in this process. In concrete terms, it is only through the advocacy of such officials that new ideas can have an impact on strategic outcomes. Having outlined an ideational model of strategic adjustment, we now turn to a demonstration of the way in which strategic ideas actually shaped changes in US grand strategy between 2000 and 2003.

Ideas and American strategic adjustment, 2000–2003

Bush's initial approach to US grand strategy

The foreign policy positions taken by Bush during the 2000 presidential campaign flowed from criticisms that had been made of Clinton over the prior eight years, and specifically from the advice that Bush received from leading foreign policy experts within the Republican Party. Bush argued for an increase in military spending, along with the transformation and modernization of the armed forces. He was especially critical of what he called the "open-ended deployments and unclear military missions" of the Clinton era, and promised to be much more careful about sending US forces abroad (Bush 1999). He called for limited cuts in US military presence overseas, suggesting for example that US peacekeepers in Bosnia could be brought home. In a noteworthy series of comments, during the October 2000 presidential debates against Al Gore, Bush underscored his skepticism regarding what he called "nation-building" missions. He suggested that as president, he would not have intervened in either Haiti or Somalia. And he called for clear criterion surrounding the use of force, based upon "vital national interests," rather than humanitarian objectives. As Bush put it, "I would be guarded in my approach. I don't think we can be all things to all people in the world. I think we've got to be very careful when we commit our troops" (Presidential Debates, October 3, 2000 Boston, and October 11, 2000).

More generally, Bush tried to make the case during the 2000 campaign for a more hard-line and unyielding approach toward potential adversaries of the United States. He argued, for example, against any further negotiated "deals" with North Korea. He advocated a somewhat more detached and hard-nosed approach with regards to Russia. He suggested that China be treated as a strategic rival, rather than as a strategic partner. He called for a more concerted effort to engineer the overthrow of Saddam Hussein. He argued unreservedly for the construction of a national missile defense system. And he made clear his concern over any erosion of American sovereignty through potential membership in a variety of new multilateral agreements, such as the International Criminal Court. At the same time, however, Governor Bush insisted that "the United States must be humble ... humble in how we treat nations that are figuring out how to chart their own course." So the tone of his comments during the presidential campaign suggested that Bush would be more hard-line than Clinton, but at the same time more modest in intervening in the internal affairs of other countries. The reason was clear: liberal humanitarian concerns would henceforth take a back seat to considerations of American self-interest. As Bush put it during the second presidential debate, "when it comes to foreign policy, that'll be my guiding question: is it in our nation's interests?" (Presidential Debate, October 11, 2000).

Bush's foreign policy appointments in 2001 were broadly consistent with the tone of his presidential campaign. The leading appointments were Colin Powell as Secretary of State, Donald Rumsfeld as Secretary of Defense, and Condoleezza Rice as National Security Advisor. Vice-President Dick Cheney would also turn out to be a figure of central importance in foreign policy-making under Bush. Other significant appointments included Paul Wolfowitz and Douglas Feith at the Pentagon, Richard Armitage, John Bolton and Richard Haass at State, Elliot Abrams at the National Security Council, John Negroponte at the UN, and Lewis Libby at the Vice-President's office. The most popular interpretation of internal divisions within the Bush administration was to point to Powell as the supposed "multilateralist," against Rumsfeld and Cheney as the leading "unilateralists," on almost every issue of significance (Patrick 2001). There was certainly something to this interpretation, in that Powell was visibly more concerned about preserving good relations with the United States' allies than, for example, Rumsfeld. But the ideological differences between these men were often overstated in the press. In fact, Powell was hardly a devotee of liberal multilateralism. Rather, he was simply a prag-matic Republican internationalist, in the tradition of Bush's own father. Nor were Rumsfeld and Cheney as reflexively opposed to every single international organization or agreement as their critics often suggested. The really interesting division within the administration – a division that seemed to cut through many individuals internally, including the Presid-ent himself – was not between unilateralists and multilateralists, but between a "realist" strategic vision, and a more ambitious and idealistic vision of American global primacy.

Referring back to the beliefs of post-Cold War primacists, recall that these authors suggested that the United States act aggressively to "Amer-icanize" the international system, and to perpetuate US political and milit-ary predominance in the world. Certainly there were intimations of this approach even as Bush took office. In fact, many of his leading foreign policy advisors – including Rumsfeld, Cheney, Wolfowitz, Armitage, Feith, Bolton, Abrams and Libby – had signed on in 1997/1998 to an explicit vision of American primacy laid out by the ubiquitous William Kristol in his "Project for the New American Century." The assumptions of the pri-macist position influenced US grand strategy during the opening months of the Bush administration, on a wide range of issues, from missile defense, to China, to international organizations, to "rogue states." But prior to 9/11, the dominant theme in both the strategic thinking and the actual strategic behavior of the Bush team was not so much "primacy," as "realism."

Initially, Bush and his advisors made their skepticism regarding nation-building and humanitarian intervention abundantly clear. They called for a refocusing of US national security policy on great power politics and concrete national interests. They suggested that the United States play down its pretensions as an international social engineer, and show, in Bush's words, "humility" toward internal political processes in other states. They called on the United States to be more selective in its use of force abroad. They argued for bringing US strategic commitments back into balance with its military capabilities. They did not initiate any massive increase in military spending (Myers and Dao 2001). They toned down their adversarial campaign rhetoric against China. They did not embrace a policy of "rogue state rollback." And they did not actually take aggressive actions against particular rogue states such as Iraq. If we compare these assumptions and positions to the various post-Cold War strategic alternatives outlined earlier, it appears that the initial foreign policy approach of George W. Bush was more "realist" than anything else. Committed and consistent primacists, such as Paul Wolfowitz, were certainly inside the administration, but they were unable at first to reshape US grand strategy in the direction they desired. Figures such as Powell, Rice and Haass, as well as the elder statesmen of the first Bush administration, were clearly skeptical of the primacist position, preferring instead a traditional form of Republican realism (Rice 2000). Cheney and Rumsfeld took hard-line stands on a variety of foreign policy issues, but seemed unwilling or unable to press for a comprehensive strategy of primacy across the board. Above all, the new president showed only limited interest in the sweeping, aggressive agenda of primacist foreign policy advocates. His instincts seemed to be hard-nosed, nationalistic and pragmatic, rather than hugely ambitious or idealistic. As long as Bush was uninterested in a more aggressive approach, Cheney and Rumsfeld would lean toward a somewhat intransigent version of strategic realism. Consequently, that remained the dominant tone of the Bush foreign policy team, up until the terrorist attacks on Washington and New York.

From realism to primacy, 2001–2003

The events of 9/11 obviously acted as an intense shock on both the American public, and on US foreign policy-makers. A dramatic attack on the American homeland stimulated the search for a new strategy that would prevent other such catastrophes. An interesting feature of this process, however, consistent with past cases of strategic adjustment, was that the particular strategy chosen was hardly the only one available. Certainly one might have expected the United States to retaliate against the government of Afghanistan for harboring the terrorists that had planned 9/11. A more aggressive counter-terrorist approach was also clearly in the cards. But beyond these changes, it is not self-evident that the United States was compelled to follow any particular grand strategy. The terrorist attacks simply opened up a window of opportunity for advocates of alternative grand strategies to come forward and make their case. What in fact happened in 2001/2002 was that key foreign policy advocates – first within and beyond the Bush administration, and then including the President himself – took advantage of this window of opportunity to set the agenda, and to build support for a new strategy of American primacy. This new strategy – epitomized by the war against Iraq – was both more aggressive, and in many ways more idealistic, than Bush's previous approach. It tapped into long-standing, classical liberal assumptions within the United States as to how to meet foreign threats. The increased sense of danger also meant that domestic constraints on US grand strategy were somewhat reduced. The overall result was a significant adjustment in the mentality underlying US grand strategy.

The first phase of the "war on terrorism" was the least controversial. The administration's initial response to 9/11 was to demand that Afghanistan's Taliban regime turn over the leading members of Al Qaeda. After the Taliban refused this demand, the Bush administration launched US military action in Afghanistan. This was a significant step because it indicated a new and more aggressive counter-terrorist approach. As Bush put it in his address to a special joint session of Congress, on September 20, 2001: "any nation that continues to harbor or support terrorism will be regarded by the United States as a hostile regime" (Bush 2001). This was already a departure from the more restrained counter-terrorist approach that the United States had followed, for example, under Clinton. Nevertheless, US military action against the Taliban had broad public and congressional backing, as well as extensive international support (Huddy *et al.* 2002). Given that the Taliban had sheltered and supported the authors of the worst terrorist attack in American history, and then refused to hand them over, the administration's response was natural and predictable.

Within the United States, the war in Afghanistan was widely viewed as a major success, and ending as soon as it did, it did not trigger any searching public debate over the basic outlines of American grand strategy. The vast majority of politically significant actors within the United States supported military action against the Taliban. Beyond Afghanistan, however, there was still the question of how the United States would reshape its national security policy in response to 9/11. And on this question, there were a number of broad alternatives available. Indeed, the basic alternatives were really the same as they had been since the end of the Cold War. The United States could respond to 9/11 by completely disengaging from its alliances and military deployments overseas (Layne 2002: 233–248). It could respond by deepening its commitment toward cooperative, multilateral engagement abroad (Ikenberry 2001: 14–34; Nye 2002: 15, 39, 141–163). It could respond by following more of a realist approach, playing down Wilsonian pretensions and ambitions (Harries 2001: 117–120; Kissinger 2002: 74–78; Posen 2001–2002). Or it could respond by adopting an aggressive new strategy of American primacy. The actual response of the Bush administration was to move away from its prior realism, and toward a strategy of American primacy.

Already in his September 20, 2001 speech to Congress, Bush had declared that the United States would fight a protracted war not only against Al Qaeda, but against "every terrorist group of global reach." This goal quickly expanded into an even more all-encompassing "war on terror." Critics pointed out the practical impossibility of declaring war against an entire form of violence (Howard 2002). But the administration's use of sweeping language was deliberate. First, it helped to build public support for the upcoming campaigns in Afghanistan and against Al Qaeda. Equally important, however, it reflected a genuine shift in mentality on the part of the administration, and served to notify the public that a fundamental adjustment in American grand strategy was underway. As even the President's critics admit, Bush was truly shocked by the attacks of 9/11. These attacks triggered a willingness on his part to listen to the advocates of a more aggressive strategic approach, across the board (Hirsh 2002: 18–19; Judis 2003: 12–13). They also triggered a willingness on the part of key foreign policy advisors, such as Dick Cheney and Donald Rumsfeld, to press urgently for such an approach. As Rumsfeld put it, 9/11 created "the kind of opportunities that World War II offered, to refashion the world" (Shanker 2001). The advantage of a vague yet sweeping "war on terror" was precisely that it would allow for the pursuit of a broad new national security agenda, even in areas essentially unrelated to the initial terrorist attacks (Kinsley 2001). The leading example of this phenomenon was in Iraq.

Before 9/11, Bush had been unconvinced of the need for urgent military action against Iraq (Lemann 2003). Certainly, he had criticized Clinton for failing to eject Saddam Hussein from power, but once in office, Bush had backed off from his earlier rhetoric, and essentially maintained a strategy of containment. Given a palpable lack of interest on the part of the President, advocates of "regime change" such as Paul Wolfowitz were simply unable to force the issue. In the days immediately after 9/11, very little actually changed. Wolfowitz and Rumsfeld raised the possibility of invading Iraq, but in the absence of any evidence linking Saddam Hussein to 9/11, most of the cabinet remained unconvinced of the need for immediate action. Dick Cheney joined with Colin Powell in arguing that the administration first tackle Afghanistan, before moving on to Iraq (Woodward 2002). The president agreed, and the issue was temporarily postponed.

The conclusion of the war in Afghanistan by December 2001 finally gave administration hawks the opportunity to put Iraq at the top of the president's agenda. Key presidential advisors and hardliners such as Cheney and Rumsfeld joined longtime true believers in arguing for immediate "regime change" in Iraq. Their reasons were several. First, hawks such as Cheney seem to have been truly convinced that if Saddam Hussein continued to maintain and/or develop weapons of mass destruction, he might use them to threaten American interests in the Middle East. And while the link here to 9/11 was indirect at best, it did seem to provide an opportunity and an incentive to take care of this unfinished business. Second, these same hawks suggested that Iraqi weapons of mass destruction might eventually be provided to anti-American terrorists. The example of 9/11 certainly demonstrated, all too vividly, the potential for catastrophic terrorist attacks on the United States. Arguments centering on counter-terrorism would therefore be used publicly, within the United States, as the leading reason for war against Iraq. In reality, concern over terrorism was only one reason among several, and probably not the most important one, in the decision for war. But even critics of the administration, such as John Judis, admitted that broad concerns about WMD use by Iraq were "not just for public consumption" (Judis 2003: 12–13). They were genuine. And they seem to have weighed heavily with Bush.

A third argument that clearly gained currency, in the wake of 9/11, was the neoconservative idea that a defeated Iraq could be democratized, which would subsequently act as a kind of trigger for democratic changes throughout the region. Again, this argument was probably secondary to more basic geopolitical concerns, in terms of its impact on the decision for war. But it did have an effect on the president (Carothers 2003; Packer 2003). And again, 9/11 was the crucial catalyst, since it appeared to demonstrate that US support for authoritarian regimes in the Middle East had only encouraged Islamic extremism along with terrorist organizations such as Al Qaeda. Finally, the very fact that Al Qaeda had recruited so many of its leading operatives from Saudi Arabia, by playing on resentments against US bases there, only highlighted the undesirability of maintaining an extensive US military presence in the Saudi kingdom over the long term. By invading Iraq and overthrowing Saddam Hussein, the United States would be able to shift its military base within the region, and remove its extensive and unwelcome troop presence from Saudi Arabia. Such were the arguments for war. Many career civil servants in the US military, at the State Department, and in the CIA, were by all accounts skeptical of most of these arguments, skeptical that the costs of war would not outweigh the benefits (Marshall 2002). But at some point early in 2002, in the words of one administration official, Bush "internalized the idea of regime change," and made the decision to confront Iraq (Lemann 2003: 37).

Bush's decision for war against Iraq would have been remarkable, even if it had been an isolated incident, unrelated to any broader strategic vision. But of course this was not the case. The war was justified quite explicitly in terms of a new national security strategy, and was itself only the most visible outcome of this new strategy. In the wake of 9/11, Bush consistently gravitated toward a foreign policy approach that was bold, ambitious and moralistic (Lemann 2002: 177). In his September 20, 2001 address, the president had hinted at a broader, global struggle, beyond the immediate threat of Al Qaeda. In his January 2002 state of the union address, Bush was more specific about the administration's new security priority: "to prevent regimes that sponsor terror from threatening America or our friends and allies with weapons of mass destruction." Three regimes, in particular, were singled out as being part of a supposed "axis of evil": Iran, Iraq and North Korea. Bush indicated a willingness to act pre-emptively: "I will not wait on events, while dangers gather." And he struck a remarkably universalistic and uncompromising tone regarding the role of the United States in the world, saying that "America will lead by defending liberty and justice because they are right and true and unchanging for all people everywhere" (Bush 2002a). Already by January 2002, then, the trend was clear: the "war on terror" would morph into a broader crusade against "rogue states," and indeed into a much more assertive and even Wilsonian grand strategy on the part of the United States.

The new strategy was laid out most fully and explicitly in the new National Security Strategy of the United States of America, released by the White House in September 2002. In that document, the administration began by pointing out that "the United States possesses unprecedented – and unequalled – strength and influence in the world." It renounced any purely "realpolitik" approach, in arguing that "the great strength of this nation must be used to promote a balance of power that favors freedom" (Bush 2002b: 1). American classical liberal values were again described, as they had been on the eve of war against the Taliban, as "nonnegotiable demands" (Bush 2002b: 3). The promotion of free trade and market democracy was held up as a central American interest (Bush 2002b: 17–18). And interestingly, the possibility of traditional great power competition was played down. Instead, other powers were urged to join with the United States in affirming the general trend toward democracy and open markets worldwide. "With Russia," the administration stated, "we are already building a new strategic relationship, based on a central reality of the twenty-first century: the United States and Russia are no longer strategic adversaries" (Bush 2002b: 26–27). And even with China, the new national security strategy emphasized areas of common interest, and hopes for liberalization (Bush 2002b: 27–28). Of course, this broad affirmation of classical liberal assumptions was no doubt used, in part, for reasons of domestic politics and public relations. Liberal arguments are always employed, in the United States, to bolster strategic adjustments of any kind. But the United States had been no less liberal – broadly speaking – in the year 2000, when the nascent Bush team was stressing the need for "realism" in foreign affairs. So the new strategy does seem to have reflected a real shift, on the part of the administration, toward a more deliberately Wilsonian approach.

Within this general affirmation of US interest in the promotion of market democracy overseas, the new national security strategy painted a stark picture of grave threats to US security. The threat of terrorism was naturally the focus, but the specific danger was drawn in a striking and expansive manner. Most crucially, the administration argued that the proliferation of weapons of mass destruction on the part of state sponsors of terrorism necessitated an entirely new security strategy on the part of the United States. Deterrence and containment would no longer work. The United States would henceforth reserve the right to use force, in a preventive and unilateral fashion if necessary, against "rogue states," in order to prevent the possibility of weapons transfers to terrorists (Bush 2002b: 13–15). As stated in the September 2002 document:

> Given the goals of rogue states and terrorists, the United States can no longer rely solely on a reactive posture as we have done in the past. The inability to deter a potential attacker, the immediacy of today's threats, and the magnitude of potential harm that could be caused by our adversaries' choice of weapons, do not permit that option.... We must adapt the concept of imminent threat to the capabilities and objectives of today's adversaries.... As was demonstrated by the losses on September 11, 2001, mass civilian casualties is the specific objective of terrorists and these losses would be exponentially more severe if terrorists acquired and used weapons of mass destruction.... To forestall or prevent such hostile acts by our adversaries, the United States will, if necessary, act preemptively.
>
> (Bush 2002b: 15)

All of the above arguments – regarding preventive military action, as well as a broader Wilsonian vision of world order – were repeated by the president in major addresses at West Point in June 2002, at the United Nations in September of that same year, in Cincinnati that October, in the State of the Union address the following January, and on the eve of war against Iraq in February and March 2003 (Bush 2002c).

Preventive wars are not unknown in American history, but by any standard, to openly embrace the concept of preventive military action as a centerpiece of American grand strategy was a remarkably bold departure. Bush did not suggest that Iraq was the only case in which such action might be required. On the contrary, he argued that an entirely new approach towards national security was called for, across the board. And he actually began to implement this new strategy, piece by piece, in the months after 9/11. Not only was Iraq invaded and occupied in the spring of 2003. The form of the invasion, in itself, was a leading indicator of the administration's new willingness to incur serious costs: a major US force in combat on the ground, involving hundreds of thousands of troops, along with the risk of many American casualties. In the United States, for the first time in almost twenty years, defense spending was increased dramatically: from $334 billion, in fiscal year 2002, to $379 billion, in fiscal year 2003 (O'Hanlon 2002: 14). Supplemental spending on the war and on the reconstruction of Iraq also ran into the tens of billions. And of course, the war on terrorism went on, in states as diverse as Pakistan, Djibouti and the Philippines, rearranging US relations with these countries, while introducing an increased American presence in their affairs at the same time.

Given all of these changes, how should the national security strategy of the Bush administration be characterized? In broad terms, the new strategy aggressively affirms American predominance, rather than any sort of global balance of power. It proposes to liberalize and Americanize the international system, in some cases by force. It embraces the concept of "rogue state rollback." And it calls for energetic action to pre-empt any conceivable threat to US national security. As the administration's own supporters recognize, this is a strategy of American primacy, and a striking shift from Bush's more "realist" approach prior to 9/11.

Naturally, this new strategy has caused intense controversy, just as the war in Iraq caused intense controversy. The administration may have had virtually unanimous domestic support for war against the Taliban, but once they began "phase two," against Iraq, and began to clarify the full scope of their ambitions, important sections of domestic support began to fall away. Most realists and liberal internationalists, along with many isolationists, had supported war in Afghanistan after 9/11. But important elements of all three schools of thought were much more resistant to a preventive war against Saddam Hussein. In fact, it might be said that for the first time since the end of the Cold War, during the debate over Iraq, there was a truly widespread and passionate debate within the United States over the appropriateness of some central aspect of US grand strategy. The remarkably ambitious nature of Bush's grand strategy will undoubtedly continue to invite criticism from various quarters within the United States.

Conclusion

The Bush administration came to power in 2001 determined to tone down the liberal internationalism of the Clinton era, and to bring a new realism to the conduct of American grand strategy. In particular, Bush promised to be more selective with regards to intervention overseas. At first, this new approach held, in spite of divisions within the administration and among its supporters. The terrorist attacks of 9/11 opened a window of opportunity for advocates of a more assertive, and indeed a more "idealistic" grand strategy to come to the fore. The war on Iraq was the most visible manifestation of this new strategy. But a change in mentality took place across the board, as the Bush administration made it clear that it would act energetically to pre-empt threats to US security, and to promote a world order more reflective of American values as well as American interests.

None of these changes were dictated by international structural pressures, per se. Structural pressures did not dictate the new realism of the early Bush administration. And in terms of a strategic response to 9/11, beyond adopting a more vigorous counter-terrorism policy, there were any number of ways that the United States might have reacted. At the same time, there is very little evidence that domestic economic interests pushed or pulled US grand strategy in one direction or another. Critics of the Bush administration, both at home and abroad, were right to see the influence of neoconservatives as fundamental in shaping the new strategy; but they were wrong to see that influence as essentially venal, economic or electoral in motivation. The strategists of American primacy believed in what they were doing. The independent influence of ideas was the crucial, missing element in the story.

In terms of thinking about general patterns of strategic adjustment, the implications are these: the international distribution of power provides, at best, a starting point in accounting for changes in grand strategy. Precisely because the United States is so powerful today, structural pressures may actually be relatively unimportant in explaining US strategic adjustment. The promotion and selection of particular ideas about grand strategy – especially on the part of leading defense and foreign policy officials – seems to be more important than structural pressures in bringing about specific policy changes. Moreover, the recurrence of certain prevailing ideas and assumptions regarding strategic affairs within a given country such as the United States points to the potential existence of nationally distinctive strategic cultures. It can hardly be a coincidence that when Bush and his advisors searched for a way to understand and respond to the events of 9/11, they fell back on classical liberal ideas, just as so many American policy-makers had before them. No leader in the United States is ever entirely free from the influence of liberal ideas regarding the nature of international affairs. Bush's early "realism" was never whole-hearted; it was only a corrective to what had come before. But that particular form of realism regarding strategic affairs seems to have disappeared, at least temporarily. Wilsonian ambitions have returned in earnest, and the advocates of nation-building have had their revenge.

Notes

An earlier version of this chapter was published as "Ideas and Alternatives in American Grand Strategy, 2000–2004," *Review of International Studies,* Volume 30, October 2004, pp. 511–535.

1 To paraphrase Max Weber, political actors may be motivated primarily by interests, rather than ideas, but ideas are "switchmen" that determine the tracks along which those actors pursue their self-interest (Weber 1980). On the role of ideas in foreign policy, see Checkel 1998; Goldstein 1993; Goldstein and Keohane 1993, Jervis 1976; Khong 1992; Lebow and Risse-Kappen 1995; Little and Smith 1988; and McNamara 1998. For a good discussion of the role of uncertainty, as well as ideational factors, in the making of national security doctrine, see Goldman 2001. Note that I use the phrase "ideas" in a narrow sense, referring only to specific policy ideas, in order to distinguish them from other broad, non-material factors such as culture, norms and identity. It is of course entirely possible that specific policy ideas are rooted in broader strategic cultures

or identities. There is an extensive literature on the subject of culture, norms and identity as sources of grand strategy, but in order to limit the scope of my investigation I do not address that literature in this chapter. For a "cultural-cognitive" explanation of changes in US grand strategy, see Rhodes 1999.
2 Goldstein and Keohane suggest that ideas become a powerful constraint once institutionalized. Yee points out that such institutionalization can be informal in nature. Ideas have a constraining influence on policy outcomes simply by shaping policy discourse and by making a number of alternative options literally unthinkable. Leading institutionalist works include DiMaggio and Powell 1991; Steinmo *et al.* 1992.

References

Allison, G. and Treverton, G. (1992) *Rethinking America's Security*, New York: W. W. Norton.

Baumgartner, F. and Jones, B. (1993) *Agendas and Instability in American Politics*, Chicago: University of Chicago Press.

Brooks, S. and Wohlforth, W. (2002) "American Primacy in Perspective," *Foreign Affairs*, 81: 20–33.

Buchanan, P. (2002) *A Republic Not an Empire*, Washington, DC: Regnery Press.

Bush, G. W. (1999) "A Period of Consequences," September 23. Accessed at www.citadel.edu/pao/addresses/pres_bush.html on October 15, 2010.

Bush, G. W. (2001) "Address to a Joint Session of Congress," September 20. Accessed at www.whitehouse.gov/news/releases/2001/09/20010920–8.html on October 15, 2010.

Bush, G. W. (2002a) "State of the Union Address," January 29. Accessed at www.whitehouse.gov/news/releases/2002/01/20020129–11.html on October 15, 2010.

Bush, G. W. (2002b) *The National Security Strategy of the United States of America*, Washington, DC: The White House.

Bush, G. W. (2002c) "Speech at West Point," June 1. Accessed at www.whitehouse.gov/news/releases/2002/06/20020601–3.html on October 15, 2010.

Callahan, D. (1994) *Between Two Worlds: Realism, Idealism, and American Foreign Policy After the Cold War*, New York: HarperCollins.

Carothers, T. (2003) "Promoting Democracy and Fighting Terror," *Foreign Affairs*, 82: 84–97.

Carpenter, T. G. (2002) *Peace and Freedom: Foreign Policy for a Constitutional Republic*, Washington, DC: Cato Institute.

Checkel, J. (1998) *Ideas and International Political Change*, New York: Yale University Press.

Christensen, T. (1996) *Useful Adversaries: Grand Strategy, Domestic Mobilization, and Sino-American Conflict, 1947–1958*, Princeton: Princeton University Press.

DiMaggio, P. and Powell, W. (eds.) (1991) *The New Institutionalism in Organizational Analysis*, Chicago: University of Chicago Press.

Friedberg, A. (1991) "Is the US Capable of Acting Strategically?" *The Washington Quarterly*, 14: 5–23.

Friedberg, A. (1998) *The Weary Titan*, Princeton: Princeton University Press.

Gholz, E., Press, D. and Sapolsky, H. (1997) "Come Home, America: The Strategy of Restraint in the Face of Temptation," *International Security*, 21: 5–48.

Gilpin, R. (1981) *War and Change in World Politics*, New York: Cambridge University Press.

Glaser, C. (2003) "Structural Realism in a More Complex World," *Review of International Studies*, 29: 403–414.

Goldman, E. O. (2001) "New Threats, New Identities, and New Ways of War: The Sources of Change in National Security Doctrine," *Journal of Strategic Studies*, 24: 43–76.

Goldstein, J. (1993) *Ideas, Interests and American Trade Policy*, Ithaca, NY: Cornell University Press.

Goldstein, J. and Keohane, R. (eds.) (1993) *Ideas and Foreign Policy*, Ithaca, NY: Cornell University Press.

Haass, R. (1995) "Paradigm Lost?" *Foreign Affairs*, 74: 43–58.

Halperin, M. (1993) "Guaranteeing Democracy," *Foreign Policy*, 91: 105–122.

Harries, O. (2001) "An End to Nonsense," *National Interest*, 65: 117–120.

Hirsh, M. (2002) "Bush and the World," *Foreign Affairs*, 81: 18–19.

Howard, M. (2002) "What's in a Name? How to Fight Terrorism," *Foreign Affairs*, 81: 8–13.

Huddy, L., Khatib, N. and Capelos, T. (2002) "Trends: Reactions to the Terrorist Attacks of September 11, 2001," *Public Opinion Quarterly*, 66: 485–509.

Huntington, S. (1991) "America's Changing Strategic Interests," *Survival*, 33: 3–17.

Ikenberry, J. (1998/1999) "Institutions, Strategic Restraint, and the Persistence of America's Postwar Order," *International Security*, 23: 43–78.

Ikenberry, J. (2001) "American Grand Strategy in the Age of Terror," *Survival*, 43: 19–34.

Jervis, R. (1976) *Perception and Misperception in International Politics*, Princeton: Princeton University Press.

Johnston, A. I. (1995) *Cultural Realism: Strategic Culture and Grand Strategy in Chinese History*, Princeton: Princeton University Press.

Judis, J. (2003) "Why Iraq?" *The American Prospect*, March 1, pp. 12–14.

Kagan, R. (2002) "Power and Weakness," *Policy Review*, 113: 3–28.

Kagan, R. and Kristol W. (eds.) (2000) *Present Dangers: Crisis and Opportunity in American Foreign and Defense Policy*, San Francisco: Encounter Books.

Khalilzad, Z. (1995) "Losing the Moment? The United States and the World After the Cold War," *Washington Quarterly*, 18: 87–107.

Khong, Y. (1992) *Analogies at War*, Princeton: Princeton University Press.

Kingdon, J. (1984) *Agendas, Alternatives and Public Policies*, Boston: Little, Brown.

Kinsley, M. (2001) "Defining Terrorism," *Washington Post*, October 5.

Kissinger, H. (2002) *Does America Need a Foreign Policy?* New York: Touchstone.

Kohout, J., Lambakis, S. J., Payne, K. B., Rudney, R. S., Stanley, W. A., Victory, B. C. and Vlahos, L. H. (1995) "Alternative Grand Strategy Options for the United States," *Comparative Strategy*, 14: 361–420.

Kristol, W. and Kagan, R. (1996) "Toward a Neo-Reaganite Foreign Policy," *Foreign Affairs*, 75: 18–32.

Kupchan, C. (1994) *Vulnerability of Empire*, Ithaca, NY: Cornell University Press.

Kupchan, C. (2002) *The End of the American Era*, New York: Knopf.

Kurth, J. (1996) "America's Grand Strategy: A Pattern of History," *The National Interest*, 43: 3–19.

Layne, C. (1997) "From Preponderance to Offshore Balancing," *International Security*, 22: 86–124.

Layne, C. (2002) "Offshore Balancing Revisited," *Washington Quarterly*, 25: 233–248.

Lebow, R. N. and Risse-Kappen, T. (eds.) (1995) *International Relations Theory and the End of the Cold War*, New York: Columbia University Press.

Lemann, N. (2002) "Without a Doubt," *The New Yorker*, October 14 and 21.

Lemann, N. (2003) "How It Came to War," *The New Yorker*, March 31, pp. 37–38.

Little, R. and Smith, S. (eds.) (1988) *Belief Systems and International Relations*, New York: Blackwell.

Luttwak, E. (1987) *Strategy: The Logic of War and Peace*, Cambridge, MA: Harvard University Press.

McDougall, W. (1997) *Promised Land, Crusader State*, Boston: Houghton Mifflin.

McNamara, K. (1998) *The Currency of Ideas*, Ithaca, NY: Cornell University Press.

Marshall, J. M. (2002) "Bomb Saddam?" *Washington Monthly*, 34: 19–25.

Mastanduno, M. (1997) "Preserving the Unipolar Moment: Realist Theories and U.S. Grand Strategy After the Cold War," in Brown, M. E., Cote, O. R., Lynn-Jones, S. M. and Miller, S. E. (eds.) *America's Strategic Choices*, Cambridge, MA: MIT Press.

Mastanduno, M. and Kapstein, E. (1999) "Realism and State Strategies After the Cold War," in Kapstein, E. and Mastanduno, M. (eds.) *Unipolar Politics*, New York: Columbia University Press.

Mearsheimer, J. (1990) "Back to the Future: Instability in Europe after the Cold War," *International Security*, 15: 5–56.

Mearsheimer, J. (2001) *The Tragedy of Great Power Politics*, New York: W. W. Norton.

Morgenthau, H. (1993) *Politics Among Nations*, brief edition, New York: McGraw-Hill.

Muravchik, J. (1996) *The Imperative of American Leadership*, Washington, DC: AEI Press.

Myers, S. L. and Dao, J. (2001) "Bush Plans Modest Increase for the Pentagon," *New York Times*, February 1.

Nacht, A. (1995) "U.S. Foreign Policy Strategies," *The Washington Quarterly*, 18: 195–210.

Nau, H. (2002) *At Home Abroad: Identity and Power in American Foreign Policy*, Ithaca, NY: Cornell University Press.

Nordlinger, E. (1996) *Isolationism Reconfigured*, Princeton: Princeton University Press.

Nye, J. (2002) *The Paradox of American Power*, New York: Oxford University Press.

O'Hanlon, M. (2002) *Defense Policy Choices for the Bush Administration*, second edition, Washington, DC: Brookings Institution.

Organski, A. F. K. (1968) *World Politics*, New York: Knopf.

Packer, G. (2003) "Dreaming of Democracy," *New York Times Magazine*, March 2, pp. 46–49.

Patrick, S. (2001) "Don't Fence Me In: The Perils of Going It Alone," *World Policy Journal*, 18: 2–14.

Posen, B. (1985) *The Sources of Military Doctrine: France, Britain and Germany Between the World Wars*, Ithaca, NY: Cornell University Press.

Posen, B. (2001/2002) "The Struggle against Terrorism: Grand Strategy, Strategy, and Tactics," *International Security*, 26: 39–55.

Posen, B. and Ross, A. (1996/1997) "Competing Visions for US Grand Strategy," *International Security*, 21: 5–53.

Ravenal, E. (1990/1991) "The Case for Adjustment," *Foreign Policy*, 81: 15–19.

Rhodes, E. (1999) "Constructing Power: Cultural Transformation and Strategic

Adjustment in the 1890s," in Trubowitz, P. Goldman, E. O. and Rhodes, E. (eds.) *Politics of Strategic Adjustment*, New York: Columbia University Press.

Rice, C. (2000) "Promoting the National Interest," *Foreign Affairs*, 79: 45–62.

Ruggie, J. (1996) *Winning the Peace*, New York: Columbia University Press.

Russett, R. (1992) *Grasping the Democratic Peace*, Princeton: Princeton University Press.

Schlesinger, J. (1992/1993) "Quest for a Post-Cold War Foreign Policy," *Foreign Affairs*, 72: 17–28.

Shanker, T. (2001) "Secretary Rumsfeld Interview," *New York Times*, October 12.

Smith, T. (1994) *America's Mission: The United States and the Worldwide Struggle for Democracy in the Twentieth Century*, Princeton: Princeton University Press.

Steinmo, S., Thelen, K. and Longstreth, F. (eds) (1992) *Structuring Politics*, New York: Cambridge University Press.

Tammen, R. L., Kugler, J., Lemke, D., Alsharabati, C., Efird, B. and Organski, A. F. K. (2000) *Power Transitions*, New York: Chatham House Publishers.

Trubowitz, P. and Rhodes, E. (1999) "Explaining American Strategic Adjustment," in Trubowitz, P. Goldman, E. O. and Rhodes, E. (eds.) *The Politics of Strategic Adjustment: Ideas, Institutions and Interests*, New York: Columbia University Press.

Tyler, P. (1992) "U.S. Strategy Plans for Insuring No Rivals Develop," *New York Times*, March 8.

Waltz, K. (1979) *Theory of International Politics*, New York: McGraw-Hill.

Waltz, K. (1995) "The Emerging Structure of International Politics," in Brown, M. E., Lynn-Jones, S. M. and Miller, S. E. (eds.) *The Perils of Anarchy: Contemporary Realism and International Security*, Cambridge, MA: MIT Press.

Watson, A. (1992) *The Evolution of International Society*, London: Routledge.

Weber, M. (1980) "The Social Psychology of the World Religions," in Mills, C. W. (ed.) *From Max Weber*, New York: Oxford University Press.

Wittkopf, E. (1996) "What Americans Really Think About Foreign Policy," *The Washington Quarterly*, 19: 91.

Wohlforth, W. (1999) "The Stability of a Unipolar World," *International Security*, 24: 5–41.

Wolfowitz, P. (2000) "Remembering the Future," *The National Interest*, 59: 35–45.

Woodward, B. (2002) *Bush At War*, New York: Simon & Schuster.

4 Ideas and entrepreneurs

A constructivist explanation of the Iraq War

Andrew Flibbert

The Bush administration had many options in responding to the terrorist attacks of 9/11, since no single course of action was self-evident or pre-ordained. Alternatives to its "war on terrorism" ranged from conducting limited military strikes against al-Qaeda camps in Afghanistan to address-ing the root causes of terrorism or pursuing terrorist planners principally through legal and political means. Rather than adopting any of these approaches, the administration chose a maximalist strategy that included transforming the structure of the American federal government, engaging in an extraordinary defense buildup, defying international law in the pursuit and treatment of terrorist suspects, and waging two wars. Most con-sequentially, after focusing momentarily on Afghanistan, the administra-tion declared Iraq to be the central front in the war on terrorism. In his January 2002 State of the Union address, President George W. Bush began redirecting national attention from al-Qaeda to a newly defined "axis of evil." Fourteen months later, the commander in chief ordered an unpre-cedented invasion of Iraq, setting in motion the single most important foreign policy initiative of his presidency. Why did the administration make Iraq the centerpiece of its wider anti-terror campaign? Why did it take the United States to war with Iraq in the aftermath of September 11?

The Iraq War was launched with bipartisan congressional approval and substantial domestic support, but it remains puzzling for several reasons. First, no obvious domestic political pressure drove American actions. The administration could have pursued a politically popular war on terrorism without greater US involvement in Iraq, riding continued public support to re-election. Second, after the refusal by the United Nations (UN) Secur-ity Council to sanction military action, the Iraq War threatened to damage relations with European, Arab, and Muslim-majority states. This under-mined the administration's stated goals in the war on terrorism. Third, although the administration argued that overthrowing Saddam Hussein and preventing his regime from obtaining weapons of mass destruction (WMD) was essential to US security, the linkage between the Iraq War and American security was always tenuous and indirect. Long before the war, skeptics questioned the imminence and extent of the Iraqi threat, and the war was, at best, preventive more than pre-emptive. Finally, at least some of the potential domestic and international costs were clear from the outset, with the Defense Secretary himself outlining a long list of what could have gone wrong. Few doubted the capacity of the American military to oust Saddam, but the political risk alone was significant, and failure would have serious consequences for both the Bush presidency and the position of the United States in the world. Equally significant was the economic cost of even a successful venture in a time of mounting budget deficits and economic uncertainty.

This chapter explains the Bush administration's decision to place Iraq at the center of its war on terrorism by driving Saddam Hussein from power. It uses a soft constructivist approach to address this empirical puzzle, arguing that the ideas of a handful of policy intellectuals affected political outcomes in remarkably consequential ways. These ideas helped to define US interests, gave strategic direction to their pursuit, and eventually became embedded in the institutions of the post-9/11 national security structure. They affected administration assessments of every major aspect of the Iraq War, beginning with its necessity and justification. Policy ideas diffused throughout the country to help generate a pro-war ideational community that included a majority of Americans, acquiring enough discursive hegemony to sustain the American march to war from 2001 to 2003. They also influenced the shape of the peace, or lack thereof, in subsequent years.

Although the conventional wisdom now holds that the Bush administration inflated threats to the United States in its drive to war, an approach that takes ideas seriously must ask why US officials sought war in the first place. Did predominantly material factors motivate them, or were their ideational commitments decisive? The focus, then, is less on the political and decision-making processes that led to the war, and more on the underlying preference to take the country to war. In other words, this chapter does not address why the administration got what it wanted, but why it wanted what it got. Why did it want the Iraq War?

Four sets of mutually reinforcing ideas were central to the administration's risk-filled gambit in the Middle East: a belief in the necessity and benevolence of American hegemony, a Manichaean conception of politics, a conviction that regime type is the principal determinant of foreign policy, and great confidence in the efficacy of military force. Together, these ideas had a constitutive effect on the administration's understanding of US interests and policy options. More specifically, they defined the social purpose of American power, framed threats to the United States, determined appropriate solutions to core problems, and prescribed policy instruments to achieve national goals. Ideas are not the sole factors setting the course of US foreign policy, but because they can answer the causally prior question—what were they thinking?—ideas are essential to explaining an otherwise puzzling administration decision.

The argument presented here complements existing constructivist accounts of the origins of war. Constructivism traces war and other outcomes in international relations to ideational phenomena and social processes like norms, identities, and culture. It challenges existing formulations of the national interest by moving beyond the materialist and rationalist premises of the leading theoretical paradigms. For example, scholars have emphasized the role of military doctrines, strategic culture, and ideas about warfare to explain the varied uses of force and changes in grand strategy (e.g. Kier 1997; Johnston 1995; Finnemore 2003; Legro 2005; Katzenstein 1996; Lapid and Kratochwil 1996; Wendt 1999; Dueck 2004). My argument contributes theoretically to this body of research by suggesting how a broader set of ideas, not explicitly military in nature, can define state interests in war. It also advances research in this area by elaborating a causal logic linking ideas to war, tracing how particular ideas define social purpose, frame threats, identify opportunities, and prescribe policy instruments.

In relation to the other major perspectives on the origins of the war, this account is most at odds with arguments emphasizing the power of domestic oil interests or Israel. The latter highlight the potential benefits of an Iraq war for either an industry with close ties to the Bush administration or a regional ally to which key figures in the administration had demonstrated commitments. But the potential benefits of war do not translate automatically into causes. Political leaders can have complex motives and envision side or secondary benefits—helping out friendly industries or allies—without such factors being central causes of any given foreign-policy initiative. To pose the counterfactual: had the oil industry or Israel not expected to benefit from the Iraq War, would the administration still have sought the war? It appears so.

The following account has more in common with, and faces its most serious challenge from, explanations centered on the actions and beliefs of a few core decision-makers in the administration, most notably President Bush, Vice President Cheney, and Defense Secretary Rumsfeld. Both this account and Robert Jervis', for example, share a sense that certain characters loom large in the story. The crucial issue, however, is whether to explain the war in terms of the unfolding choices and individually held beliefs of several key figures, or to broaden the account to include the socially shared ideas weighing on the president and moving decision-makers toward a preference for war. I elect to give great analytical weight to the intersubjective structure that prevailed in the run-up to the war, even if this approach faces epistemological challenges in identifying such ideas without resorting to post hoc rationalization. While hand-waving about ideas-in-the-ether as causes of (the preference for) war may strike some as unconvincing, such methodological problems are a challenge unrelated to the truth of the matter.

The chapter proceeds as follows. The first section briefly describes and critiques a few of the leading alternative explanations for the war, including an approach highlighting presidential decision-making, an emphasis on American economic interests, and realist accounts rooted in the balance of power or threat. A constructivist explanation focused on a set of shared ideas put forth, adopted, and defended in administration circles is presented in the second section, and in the third the evidence is examined in relation to this approach, with details of the origins and impact of four central ideas that appear repeatedly in the principal speeches and public statements of Bush and key administration figures. Finally, the evidence is connected to a larger narrative about Iraq, 9/11, and an ideational explanation for the war.

Alternative explanations

Insurgency, civil war, the failure to find WMD, and revelations of American abuse of Iraqi prisoners all contributed to great popular reservations in the United States about the original decision to invade (Stevenson and Elder 2004; Hersh 2004; Chandrasekaran 2006; Ricks 2006). Such developments were politically harmful to the administration, shifting the Iraq War from central asset to potential liability for the commander in chief. In this sense, the war's rising costs and uncertain benefits confirmed important questions that were present from the outset. It is especially unclear why the Bush administration chose to initiate such a risky venture, how official US understanding of the Iraqi threat evolved, and why this costly and controversial war was even considered a viable option.

Several years after its initiation, the war's origins remain subject to starkly different interpretations. Accounts have focused on intelligence failure, oil interests, the Israel lobby, personal revenge, and American imperialism. Alternative explanations at three levels of analysis—decision-making, domestic politics, and the international system—merit especially careful consideration.

Decision-making psychology

A first-image, psychological explanation for the decision to go to war is plausible, given the personalized nature of relations between decision-makers in the United States and Saddam Hussein's Iraq. Some accounts have focused narrowly on Bush's belief system and worldview, including his strong sense of moral purpose and evangelical Christian outlook, stressing an individual perspective rather than shared ideas or the social milieu. By such logic, the president's worldview colored his perception of an Iraqi threat, leading him to associate Saddam's Iraq with Osama bin Laden's al-Qaeda.

Such an account, however, is both empirically problematic and analytically incomplete: it does not fit well the circumstances of the long march to war from 2001 to 2003, nor does it have theoretical space to accommodate these circumstances. Empirically, there is very little evidence that the president sought or expected to go to war with Iraq bfore 9/11. If Bush had been predisposed to invade Iraq, he would not have selected a national security team—especially Cheney, Rice, and Secretary of State Colin Powell—that originally opposed this undertaking (Rice 2000). Analytically, the president's personal psychology could plausibly account for the outcome if the drive toward war had occurred over a short time period, akin to a snap decision made in an escalating international showdown. This was not the case, nor were small-group constraints on rational decision-making relevant in this instance, given the extended time period over which the events took place (Jervis 1976: 13–31; cf. Yetiv 2005).

Domestic politics

A second set of explanations focuses on domestic interests, which purportedly induced the administration to pursue war with Iraq. Such an explanation is a favorite among critics of the war. One of the most popular variants emphasizes economic causes, especially the role of American oil, defense-industry, and construction interests with close ties to the president, the vice president, and the national security adviser. By this logic, the president and his administration sought to use military force to take control of Iraq's enormous oil assets and to award lucrative reconstruction contracts to companies controlled by their powerful friends and supporters. The war and its aftermath were expected to be financially rewarding and politically beneficial by enhancing the resources available to administration supporters. Some expressions of this approach have a conspiratorial dimension that helps critics understand what otherwise seemed to be a risky and illogical undertaking (Ratner *et al.* 2003; Vidal 2002).

Emphasis on the administration's domestic concerns has an intuitive appeal and substantial theoretical grounding, and it seems plausible in light of the many benefits that the Iraq War may have promised. Yet only the most wishful or conspiratorial thinkers could fail to appreciate the uncertainty of such gains. More fundamentally, the mere potential for war-related benefits does not prove that domestic considerations caused the policy choice. The explanatory power of domestic economic interests is especially suspect, since military hostilities were not necessary to advance business interests that could have been aided in less costly and less risky ways. Bush's background in the oil business told him that war carried great risk for Iraq's dilapidated oil-producing infrastructure, and Saddam's regime was certainly capable of contaminating its oil fields before allowing them to fall into American hands (Woodward 2004: 381; cf. Duffield 2005). If business interests had driven an opportunistic administration's choices, it might just as easily have used 9/11 to negotiate an accommodation with Saddam in exchange for business access to Iraq's oil sector and modest cooperation in the war on terror (Bush and Scowcroft 1998: 305; cf. Klare 2005).

The broader claim that domestic political calculations drove the war decision is harder to refute, but the president's unwavering pre-war public approval ratings suggest that a focus on domestic politics is misplaced. The administration's aggressive promotion of the war was too polarizing and potentially damaging to have been merely a pre-emptive effort to maintain support in the face of prospective political difficulties. Preliminary US military action began with Operation Southern Focus in mid-2002, but that year did not witness a decline in the president's popularity or the emergence of a new national crisis from which the administration might have sought to distract attention (M. Gordon 2003: A1). Bush averaged a 71 percent approval rating in 2002—the strongest year of his presidency—and his public support began to erode only well after the onset of the Iraq War, dropping momentarily to 50 percent in mid-September 2003 and below 50 percent in early 2004 (*Washington Post* 2004). The domestic political context made the Iraq War possible by enhancing the president's popularity at home and giving him a free hand abroad, but it did not provide a clear and unambiguous set of incentives to take the country to war in Iraq.

The balance of power or threat

A final explanation for the war relates to the direct military threat posed by Iraq's development of nuclear, chemical, and biological weapons. In a realist account, administration concerns about potential Iraqi WMD led it to wage a preventive war to thwart a rising Iraqi hegemon seeking to change the regional balance. Realism claims that states cannot safely ignore the balance of power, and analysts need not examine the inner workings of state decision-making, since the outer consequences of such processes are generally predictable (Wolfers 1962: 13–14; Waltz 1979: 102–128; Organski 1968: 272–299). A realist analysis focuses less on Bush's beliefs or his administration's domestic concerns, and more on American and Iraqi relative power. From this perspective, the failure of the UN-sponsored inspection regime left some uncertainty as to whether Iraq continued to possess or pursue WMD. This uncertainty was sufficient to induce the United States to act unilaterally to eliminate the potential threat. Although the likelihood of Iraq's successful development of WMD was unclear, the consequences of proliferation were severe enough to compel state action.

The principal difficulty with this explanation is that the pre-war balance of power favored the United States by an overwhelming margin (Mearsheimer and Walt 2003: 50–59). Relative power considerations did not cause the war through the "automatic" operation of balancing tendencies, because Iraqi power was not increasing enough to justify such a costly, high-risk venture (Claude 1962; IISS 2002). Most estimates of Iraqi military power revealed the hollowness of a direct Iraqi threat, a fact vindicated by Iraq's dismal performance in the war and by the post-war American failure to discover any WMD (Duelfer 2004; Kay 2003; Cirincione *et al.* 2004; Kay 2004). Even Iraqi acquisition of nuclear weapons would not have enabled it to threaten the United States directly or to act with impunity in the region. Other regional military powers like Israel, Turkey, Saudi Arabia, and, to a lesser extent, Iran could have acted in concert with the United States to prevent or contain Iraqi aggression and maintain the status quo.

Even more tellingly, the Bush administration never claimed that war was necessary to redress a direct challenge to the balance of power. The president and his advisers were explicit and emphatic in rejecting traditional balance-of-power concerns, along with the strategies of deterrence and containment (Bush 2002c). The administration's remarkable shift toward Iraq was not caused by mistaken balancing efforts, because the president did not believe that balancing was a productive and responsible way of managing security threats. In fact, the administration had new ideas about the threats facing the United States. These ideas centered on the indirect danger posed by Iraq's WMD programs, specifically the potential for cooperation between an Iraqi "rogue state" and its putative terrorist allies. These ideas came to the fore after 9/11, meriting closer scrutiny as the inspiration for the drive toward war.

A constructivist account

A constructivist approach to foreign policy complements the rationalist and materialist orientations of the leading paradigms and research programs in international relations (Finnemore and Sikkink 2001; Adler 2002; Ruggie 1999). By incorporating normative and ideational factors into a broader theoretical account, a constructivist explanation can focus on how certain ideas are introduced in the foreign policy process, adopted by leading decision-makers, defended from critics in and out of power, and accepted by some portion of the general public (Kubalkova 2001; Hopf 2002; Farrell 2002). The articulators of such ideas play the role of policy entrepreneurs, who market their arguments to a large number of ideational consumers (Keck and Sikkink 1998). In some instances, the ideas come to be shared by enough individuals to redefine state interests and influence state policy. It is difficult to specify beforehand the impending causal significance of a given set of ideas, but the ideational context defines all conceivable courses of action for policy-makers through its constraining and enabling effects. As argued in subsequent sections of this chapter, the act of imagining foreign-policy possibilities precedes state action itself (Blyth 2003; Kier 1997).

In the case of Iraq, relevant ideas have appeared in several written forms, authored by a limited number of policy intellectuals and revealed in a handful of signature phrases. These epigrammatic expressions range from the ubiquitous "war on terrorism," "axis of evil," "rogue states," and "weapons of mass destruction," to more complex formulations like "a balance of power that favors freedom." The ideas encapsulated in these slogans define specific threats to American and international security, and they establish a suitable role for the United States in the world. They reflect a very particular reading of the problems facing the Middle East and an understanding of viable solutions. Their substance matters deeply because, in their absence, invading Iraq would have been all but literally unimaginable; war would not have been deemed an appropriate course of action (March and Olsen 1999).

In the United States, a few simple but powerful ideas persuaded administration principals to graft a war in Iraq onto the broader war on terrorism. Such ideas were not significant merely for their influence on the individual worldviews or perceptions of a handful of decision-makers. Their importance was in their social aspect: they came to be shared by a large number of people lacking other political ties, bonding them together in a pro-war ideational community. For the Iraq War, the relevant people who adopted these ideas were in the Bush administration, the military, Congress, the mainstream national media, the wider foreign-policy elite, and some portion of the many Americans who supported launching the war (Okrent 2004). Congressional deference to presidential authority after September 11 enhanced Bush's power and therefore—as with his early Cold War predecessors, Dwight Eisenhower and John F. Kennedy—elevated the significance of the reigning ideas in his administration (Lindsay 2004: 183–195).

As part of a rapidly shifting national ideational structure, precipitated by the cataclysm of September 11, such ideas gained currency over a short time and shaped both elite and, to a lesser extent, popular discourse. They were not static, uncontested, determinative, or even fully coherent, but they provided the basis for a broad national consensus on the post-September 11 world and its dangers (Blyth 2002; Legro 2005; Legro 2000b; Legro 2000a). Ideational dissenters were unable to break the grip of the emerging hegemonic discourse, because the pro-war ideational community had sufficient numbers and material support by early 2003 to move forward with war plans. These ideas are summarized in Table 4.1 and discussed in greater detail below.

Ideational factors present a serious epistemological challenge to scholars seeking to determine if it is ideas per se that have influenced specific political outcomes, or an underlying but undisclosed material interest. Given the tendency of policy-makers to offer self-serving justifications for their actions, disentangling an operative set of ideas from an animating set of interests is challenging. Material factors may influence the relevance of ideational variables, and the complexity of policy-making environments can obscure the role of salient ideas. In some cases, identifying such ideas is relatively easy: well defined economic policy ideas like Keynesianism or

Table 4.1 The role of ideas in the Iraq War

Idea	Causal role	Policy formulation
Benevolent hegemony	Defining social purpose	"A balance of power that favors freedom"
Manichaean primordialism	Framing threats and problems	"Axis of evil," "Rogue states"
Regime centrality	Identifying opportunities and solutions	"Regime change," "The power of freedom"
Efficacy of force	Prescribing a political instrument	"The essential role of American military strength"

market-oriented liberalism have a coherence that makes them readily discernable and amenable to theorizing (Hall 1989; Blyth 2002; Biersteker 1995). In other instances, isolating key ideas and their impact is more difficult, especially when contradictory ideas collide in the policy-making process (Cardenas 2004). Deeply embedded ideas, moreover, have a taken-for-granted quality that camouflages their actual influence.

Consequently, examining the explanatory power of ideas is consistent with careful attention to other units of analysis. Although power and interest may explain the calculations—rational or not—that state leaders make, ideas can be causally prior in defining the parameters of permissible action. In weighing the significance of ideational factors in the Iraq case, the null hypothesis is that the war would have occurred regardless of the ideas that dominated administration thinking. If policy ideas provided only a post-hoc rationale for public consumption, or an epiphenomenal superstructure for deeper causal imperatives, then they need not be central to an explanation for the war. Rival, non-ideational accounts of the war's outbreak, detailed above, are apparent: one describes how Bush decided almost single-handedly to effect Saddam's downfall; another depicts Cheney and presidential adviser Karl Rove plotting the war for domestic political gain; still another tells a story of rising Iraqi power and its challenge to American interests. Each of these may capture some aspect of a complex truth, but a closer scrutiny of the evidence reveals the value of including an explicit ideational dimension in any account.

Logic and evidence

Although the Iraq War is unusual in the diversity of theories purporting to explain it, the alternative explanations almost invariably smuggle in ideational factors. Accounts based on presidential decision-making, for example, incorporate analysis of Bush's worldview and administration beliefs. Domestic-level explanations describe the changed, post-9/11 national consensus on security matters. Realist notions of the balance of power rest on specific conceptualizations of threat, since Iraqi power alone did not concern US policy-makers. None of these alternatives, however, focuses predominantly on a crucial variable that helps explain the drive to war: a set of policy ideas that made waging the Iraq War seem entirely appropriate to the Bush administration and its supporters.

A review of the evidence suggests that four such ideas were especially significant. These ideas have disparate origins—some dating to the founding of the republic, others representing a newer minority opinion in American political discourse (Huntington 2002; Mead 2001). None was as new as the physical circumstances of the post-Cold War world, in which secular developments in technology—communications, transportation, and weapons proliferation—combined with America's unrivaled military power. Yet in the context of these enabling material changes, the four ideas together propelled the United States toward a military venture in Iraq that may eventually prove to be as consequential and transformative as the events of 9/11.

Since amassing reliable evidence regarding such recent history is difficult, I rely on multiple sources and varied strategies to gather and interpret the data. My claims about the collectively held beliefs of Bush administration officials, for example, must be mostly inferential. Toward this end, I canvass a wide range of primary documents to locate early expressions of official thinking, including evidence that soon-to-be influential policy entrepreneurs held the ideas in question prior to 9/11. This makes it less likely that the ideas were deployed post hoc for the purely instrumental purpose of public mobilization, cloaking some other motive. I also search for revelations in the political memoirs and private statements of the president and high-ranking officials, indicating that they believed their own words. Finally, I look for disconfirming evidence: significant American policy choices related to Iraq that are not consistent with US officials' genuine adherence to the four ideas. Such choices would indicate that official rhetoric about the war was motivated more by the need to assure public mobilization than by the constraints of shared "ways of thinking" (Rice 2004; Rumsfeld 2002; Durkheim 1964). My focus is primarily on official thinking, though I also examine polling data alongside changes in administration rhetoric to show how the ideas influenced public support for the war. More broadly, I trace the logic of each idea and draw links to specific actions, such as intelligence analysis, that fueled the drive to war.

Defining American social purpose: benevolent hegemony

In the wake of 9/11, the Bush administration came to define the underlying social purpose of US power as one of achieving a benevolent American hegemony: "unprecedented—and unequaled—strength and influence in the world ... [which] comes with unparalleled responsibilities, obligations, and opportunity" (White House 2002: 3; Ruggie 1982). The idea itself was not new. It tapped into a longstanding American faith in the virtues of projecting power in times of crisis. It echoed the traditional American pursuit of dominance in selected areas deemed vital to US interests, although it assumed that the security threats of the twenty-first century emanated from nearly every corner of the globe (Leffler 2004; Gaddis 2004). The fusion of dominance and benevolence underpinning the administration's core foreign-policy objectives gained traction after the shock of 9/11 and created new political possibilities for a substantially more aggressive American presence worldwide. The Iraq War was the first major expression of the idea, because US intervention there would determine "what sort of role the United States intends to play in the world in the twenty-first century" (Kaplan and Kristol 2003: vii–viii).

In principle, the drive for hegemony contrasted sharply with the liberal institutionalist view that multilateralism in foreign policy is more efficacious, as well as the classical realist contention that a prudent maintenance of the balance of power would best preserve order, stability, and the national interest. The Bush administration challenged the latter two orthodoxies; its thinking was most notably encapsulated in the syncretic phrase "a balance of power that favors freedom," found in its September 2002 policy planning document, *The National Security Strategy of the United States* (White House 2002; also Bush 2001a). This expression represented a call for global American military dominance, or an imbalance of power—one that "favored" the United States. The word "freedom" here and elsewhere was a metonym for the United States, rather than an abstract political value. In this sense, the administration saw US hegemony as both morally defensible and politically necessary to its vision of the future.

American hegemony, by this logic, assured not only a safer United States, but also a more peaceful world. Power was to be used not just to manage international problems, but to change the world for the better. US military dominance made "the destabilizing arms races of other eras pointless, and limit[ed] rivalries to trade and other pursuits of peace" (Bush 2002c). The United States, unlike any other great power in human history, was deemed capable of playing a dominant but benevolent role in world politics, since US intentions were believed to be irreproachable. The purported absence of American imperial ambition—"America has no empire to extend or utopia to establish"—derived from a sense of American exceptionalism (Bush 2002c; cf. Mailer 2003). The idea's advocates claimed that the United States was capable of benevolent hegemony precisely because it was so different from past world powers. It was entitled to a degree of deference from other states by virtue of its exceptional nature, and it was exempt from the conventional rules of international interaction in light of the leadership role it played. This was especially crucial in a time of great challenge and uncertainty, because an exceptional country in exceptional times merited exceptional treatment by others (Hoffmann 2003; Lipset 1996; Friedman 1999).

The benevolence of US hegemony was implicit in the Bush doctrine's arrogation to the United States of a right to wage not only pre-emptive but preventive war: "America will act against such emerging threats before they are fully formed" (White House 2002: 1). From this standpoint, a hegemonic United States served as keeper of the global order and was entitled to defend its primacy from both latent threats and open acts of defiance. Roused by 9/11 and the possibility of even greater danger from WMD in terrorists' hands, the administration maintained that a traditional strategy of deterrence would not suffice (Bush 2003a; Lieber 2003). The mere possibility of an alliance between "rogue states" like Saddam's Iraq and terrorist groups like al-Qaeda necessitated a far more aggressive strategy. Such a strategy included what was expected to be a short war in Iraq, the linchpin and initial "battle" in a much longer struggle to be shouldered by the leading defender of freedom and democracy (Bush 2003e).

The idea of benevolent hegemony appealed to a wide segment of the American public after 9/11, promising both moral righteousness and physical security. By defining US intentions as benevolent, even the most contentious uses of power—including an assault on a sovereign state— became more palatable. Not all Americans were sanguine about the benefits of US dominance, especially in relation to the costs of possible war-related casualties or unilateral action (Pew 2003; Feaver and Gelpi 2003). Still, nine months after the 9/11 attacks, 71 percent of Americans favored "active" engagement in world affairs—a substantial ten-point rise from the Clinton era—with 68 percent supporting the maintenance of "superior military power worldwide" (CCFR/GMF 2002). With official encouragement, aggressively undertaken after 9/11 and rooted in a vision of the virtues of US global dominance, support for international engagement persisted.

The idea was not merely an instrumental adaptation for purposes of public mobilization. Its main proponents included the neoconservatives in the administration itself, who were linked to an emerging network of think tanks, journals, and foundations (Tanenhaus 2003; Dorrien 2004; Atlas 2003; Halper and Clarke 2004; Ikenberry 2004; Stelzer 2004; Kristol 1995; Norton 2004; Packer 2005). They actively developed the idea in the 1990s, most prominently in a 1996 *Foreign Affairs* article written by William Kristol and Robert Kagan, who claimed that "Americans have come to take the fruits of their hegemonic power for granted" in the absence of "a visible threat to U.S. vital interests or to world peace" (Kristol and Kagan 1996). Kristol and Kagan were confidently prescient that, just as the invasions of South Korea and Afghanistan had convinced the American public of the value of Cold War initiatives like NSC-68 and the Reagan Doctrine, an impending threat would make way for their ideas: "As troubles arise and the need to act becomes clear, those who have laid the foundation for a necessary shift in policy have a chance to lead Americans onto a new course" (1996: 26).

Energized by antipathy toward the Clinton administration, Kristol formed the Project for the New American Century (PNAC) in the spring of 1997 "to promote American global leadership" (PNAC 1997). In early 1998, a group of PNAC members wrote to President Bill Clinton, calling for the removal of Saddam Hussein, because "the security of the world in the first part of the 21st century will be determined largely by how we handle this threat [of Iraqi WMD development]" (PNAC 1998). The eighteen signers of the letter included eleven future Bush administration officials, among them Rumsfeld, Wolfowitz, Richard Armitage (deputy secretary of state), Elliott Abrams (National Security Council director for the Middle East), John Bolton (undersecretary of state), Zalmay Khalilzad (ambassador-at-large for free Iraqis and ambassador to Afghanistan), and Richard Perle (chairman of the Defense Policy Board). Four eventful years later, in early 2002, Kristol himself was confident that the United States was moving rapidly toward war in Iraq as an inherent part of the "logic" of the war on terrorism (Kristol 2002).

Framing the problem: Manichaean primordialism

A second idea animating the drive to war was a tendency to see politics in Manichaean and primordial terms. A longstanding propensity in American encounters with international adversaries, Manichaean primordialism defined the threats facing the United States after 9/11 and provided a normative master key to the Iraq War. The Manichaean idea held that we live in a dualist world of good and evil, with little room for political nuance or moral subtlety. It underpinned the moralizing rhetoric common in administration discourse, echoing Cold War formulations like Ronald Reagan's famous reference to the Soviet Union as an "evil empire." The language of moral and political absolutes was most apparent in administration statements after the president's "axis of evil" declaration in his January 2002 State of the Union address (Frum 2003: 234–238). More than 80 percent of respondents to one poll agreed soon after that speech that the Iraqi government was "evil" (Gallup 2002a). The president's stance won the support of those who lauded his "moral clarity," while eliciting criticism from opponents who claimed its polarizing effects and apolitical nature (Bennett 2003).

Manichaean thinking resonated with many Americans after 9/11, opening a discursive space for a form of "rhetorical coercion" and facilitating the mobilization of support for a military response to the attacks (Krebs 2005: 200). In domestic politics, the administration used Manichaeism to eliminate the political middle ground, arouse wartime patriotism, and counter skepticism about the effectiveness of military action. Internationally, this position was typified by the president's oft-cited warning to other countries after the attacks: "Either you are with us, or you are with the terrorists" (Bush 2001c). Little evidence suggests that the president's invocation of these ideas was merely an instrumental aspect of the effort to mobilize American support for war in Iraq, or a rationalization hiding other motives. Unlike his father during the Gulf War, George W. Bush appeared to believe his own stark depiction of an American battle with the forces of darkness. The president declared shortly after 9/11, "We will rid the world of evil-doers" in "this crusade, this war on terrorism" (AP 2001).

The initial proponents of Manichaeism included a small circle of policy intellectuals, some associated with the neoconservative movement and others influenced by an evangelical Christian outlook that emphasized moral absolutes (Niebuhr 1944; Halper and Clarke 2004). Cheney reportedly favored writers like Victor Davis Hanson, a classicist and military historian, though William Kristol's skeptical conservativism also was influential (Kakutani 2003; Hanson 2002). Wolfowitz gave voice to Manichaean dualism and the primacy of religious identity in his frequent dichotomization of "moderate Muslims" and "extremists" (Wolfowitz 2003b: 8; Wolfowitz 2000a; Frum and Pearl 2003; Satloff 2002; Ledeen 2002; Edsall and Milbank 2003: A1). Perhaps most important, the eminent Orientalist scholar Bernard Lewis had unmatched intellectual influence on administration thinking about the Middle East. Having coined the phrase "clash of civilizations"—later popularized by Samuel Huntington—Lewis briefed the White House and participated in meetings of the Defense Policy Board after 9/11, restating his famously undifferentiated assertions of "Muslim rage," jealousy, and resentment (Waldman 2004: 1; Lewis 1990; Lewis 2002a; Lewis 2002b).

The Manichaean idea shaped the Bush administration's definition of threats to American interests, enhancing its preference for military action despite the limited extent of Iraq's direct military threat. A black-and-white understanding of international politics blurred the distinction between US adversaries like Iraq and al-Qaeda, diminishing their marked political and ideological antagonism. It emphasized the possibility—indeed, the seeming inevitability—of their collaboration in attacks on US interests, warning of an acute new American vulnerability. It enabled decision-makers to imagine a deadly nexus between state and non-state actors: the "axis of evil," which referred not to an alliance between Iraq, Iran, and North Korea, but to potential cooperation between Iraq and groups like al-Qaeda (Woodward 2004: 86–87, 93–95). It had direct political consequences when, on September 12, 2001, the president pressed his counter-terrorism coordinator to look for a link between Iraq and the terrorist attacks (Clarke 2004: 30–33; Hughes 2004: 282–283). Bush reportedly declared at NSC meetings shortly thereafter, "Many believe Saddam is involved.... He probably was behind this in the end" (Woodward 2004: 99, 167; Bush 2002d). A Manichaean view that divided the world into enemies and friends of a free United States was at the heart of administration fears that Iraq would share WMD with its putative terrorist allies, regardless of the danger this would have posed to Baghdad.

Identifying the solution: regime type and foreign policy

A third and highly consequential idea that held sway in administration thinking was the notion that regime type is the principal determinant of a state's foreign policy. This reductionist idea asserts that internal state attributes govern external state action. It played a crucial role in the decision to go to war by identifying the only seemingly appropriate response to the threats discerned by the administration: military intervention to achieve "regime change" (Weinstein 2004: 206; Jervis 2003b; Gaddis 2002; P. Gordon 2003). Although the administration used the phrase "regime change" to denote a simple change in government— deposing a dictator—its thinking centered on regime type in the fuller sense of the phrase: the mode of access to power and participation in political life. According to this understanding of the sources of state action, democracies produce generally benevolent behavior and authoritarian regimes act malevolently. With Iraq, the idea was commonly expressed in the president's repeated insistence on the self-evident benefits to international security of eliminating Saddam Hussein's monstrous authoritarianism. Bush declared:

> The current Iraqi regime has shown the power of tyranny to spread discord and violence in the Middle East. A liberated Iraq can show the power of freedom to transform that vital region by bringing hope and progress into the lives of millions.
>
> (Bush 2002a)

In this sense, the administration committed itself to a generalized version of the idea of the "democratic peace," extending it to include the assertion that democracies are more moderate and cautious than authoritarian regimes. As Richard Haass, director of policy planning at the State Department, declared in December 2002, "A democratic world is a more peaceful world. The pattern of established democracies not going to war with one another is among the most demonstrable findings in the study of international relations" (Haass 2002). That same month, the administration expanded its efforts to characterize the impending military action as intended to advance the prospects for democracy in the Middle East. The president himself expressed an unshakable faith in the transformative power of democracy for regional and global security, maintaining that the attacks of 9/11 had targeted American democracy, personal freedom, and "way of life" (Bush 2001c). Such a perspective was consistent with the administration's classically liberal reading of other facets of politics, especially its optimism about the possibility of human progress, a characteristic that distinguishes it from more traditional American conservatives. It also was an area of ideational convergence among neoconservatives, the more cautious internationalists of Bush's foreign policy team, and even some liberal Democrats in and out of power.

The Iraq problem thus was to be solved by double regime change: ending Saddam's rule and transforming political life there and elsewhere in the Middle East. A future democratic Iraq would never waste its considerable resources on the dangerous weapons programs cited by the administration as threatening to international security. The assumption was that democracy produces ideologically virtuous citizens who are not inclined to dangerous forms of political radicalism or foreign adventure. Bush declared on February 26, 2003 in a speech at the American Enterprise Institute:

> The nation of Iraq, with its proud heritage, abundant resources and skilled and educated people is fully capable of moving toward democracy and living in freedom. The world has a clear interest in the spread of democratic values, because stable and free nations do not breed the ideologies of murder. They encourage the peaceful pursuit of a better life.
>
> (Bush 2003b)

The adoption of this idea did help the administration win support for the Iraq War from those who were uncomfortable with its aggressive unilateralism. Left-leaning and centrist war supporters agreed that a democratic Iraq would be superior to Saddam's tyranny, both for its people and for international security (Packer 2002). The idea itself, however, was exceedingly powerful for Bush and his supporters. As Bush declared before the war, his objectives in the Middle East were nothing less than revolutionary:

> I will seize the opportunity to achieve big goals. There is nothing bigger than to achieve world peace.... There is a human condition that we must worry about.... As we think through Iraq ... it will be for the objective of making the world more peaceful.
>
> (Woodward 2002: 339–340)

Such ambition and fervor suggest that the ideas informing the decision to go to war were much more than cleverly deployed rationalizations cloaking basic material interests. These ideas helped convince the president and many others of the necessity of striking first. They defined a normatively defensible and politically tenable course of action: Iraqi "regime change" via an otherwise unimaginable war to contend with a grave threat to the American homeland.

Prescribing the instrument: the efficacy of military force

A final idea at the heart of the Iraq War was an abiding faith in the efficacy of military force as an instrument of US foreign policy. Reaffirming "the essential role of American military strength," the administration held that force was to be used without undue hesitation, because no other means could take its place in a dangerous world (White House 2002: 20; Kagan 2003; Boot 2002; Kagan and Kristol 2000). Allied and enemy skepticism about American steadfastness had to be eliminated: "Through our willingness to use force in our own defense and in defense of others, the United States demonstrates its resolve to maintain a balance of power that favors freedom" (White House 2002: 20). As the president reportedly declared with regard to a related political problem in the region, "Sometimes a show of strength by one side can really clarify things" (Suskind 2004: 72). Deposing Saddam was deemed essential in itself, but doing so by force served broader interests in the war on terror by signaling a transformed American will to accompany its renewed capacity. The Afghanistan War of late 2001 did not suffice as a demonstration of resolve or a means of dissuading potential enemies from challenging the United States. Afghanistan, after all, lacked good targets, according to Rumsfeld, making Iraq a preferable strategic objective (Clarke 2004: 31).

Rumsfeld was not alone in his thinking. With the ongoing revolution in military affairs, observers in and out of the administration expected American military prowess to be unrivaled in the early twenty-first century, delivering greater firepower and costing fewer US casualties than at any prior moment in history (Rumsfeld 2002). This expectation originated partly from the influential strategic thinker Albert Wohlstetter, a mathematician and RAND analyst, who taught at the University of Chicago from 1964 to 1980, promoted the development of anti-ballistic missile systems, and was awarded the Presidential Medal of Freedom in 1985 (Baylis and Garnett 1991). Wohlstetter had mentored such administration figures as Wolfowitz, Khalilzad, and Perle, even introducing Perle to Iraqi exile and eventual Pentagon favorite Ahmed Chalabi. His most politically active followers had no direct military experience of their own, but they developed an appreciation for the efficacy of force by reflecting on US military involvement in the first Gulf War, Somalia, and in the Balkans against Serbia (Halper and Clarke 2004: 92; Norton 2004: 189, 153; Rosen 2005).

Such confidence in the efficacy of force was linked to a view of Middle East politics as exceptionally brutal and therefore resistant to subtler means of external influence. Middle Easterners themselves were said to respond only to power, requiring shows of force to elicit submission and a form of bandwagoning (Snyder 2003; Jervis 2003b; Daalder and Lindsay 2003). As Reuel Marc Gerecht, a former CIA case officer and then PNAC fellow, declared in December 2001:

> We have no choice but to re-instill in our foes and friends the fear and respect that attaches to any great power.... Only a war against Saddam Hussein will decisively restore the awe that protects American interests abroad and citizens at home.
>
> (Gerecht 2001)

Ironically, this idea was consistent with an observation about human nature frequently attributed to bin Laden: "When people see a strong horse and a weak horse, by nature they will like the strong horse" (DoD 2001). Bin Laden's remark was cited repeatedly by commentator Daniel Pipes and other prominent individuals in the conservative media, most often sourced to the writings of Bernard Lewis and, to a lesser extent, Fouad Ajami (Pipes 2003; Lieber 2003: 21; Hayworth 2003; Ajami 2003; Ajami 2006). With key members of the administration beholden to the idea of the efficacy of force, the policy alternatives to war in Iraq received less-than-equal consideration after 9/11. As former counter-terrorism chief Richard Clarke wrote, "All along it seemed inevitable that we would invade.... It was an idée fixe, a rigid belief, received wisdom, a decision already made and one that no fact or event could derail" (Clarke 2004: 265).

Why Iraq?

The Bush administration's shift toward Iraq emanated from the dominance of four distinct ideas that took root in policy-making circles after a great national trauma. It launched the war because these ideas framed the status quo in Iraq as a serious foreign policy problem, with forcible "regime change" as the only viable solution. The administration's conception of the United States, the benevolent hegemon, envisioned a larger purpose for the United States: using power to advance both noble ideals and US interests. Its belief in the unity of American enemies left it with little alternative to war, given the danger such a reality would pose. The war and its aftermath were expected to be relatively easy, because Manichaean thinking implied that Iraq after Saddam's demise would shift naturally from negative to positive political valence, as "the power of freedom" wrought its effects (Bush 2002a; Cheney 2002; Adelman 2002: A27). These ideas shaped the definition of US interests and the strategic direction of American foreign policy. Nothing else necessitated that the administration's considerable post-9/11 power and authority would translate into an invasion of Iraq.

What gave these ideas such traction in American politics after 9/11, allowing the Bush administration to act on them? Fear, and one of the gravest national security crises in years, with Americans feeling "a greater sense of vulnerability and greater need for alertness than they have at any time in the past three decades" (CCFR/GMF 2002; Robin 2004). In fact, shifting US popular support for going to war in Iraq correlated strongly with oscillating public fears of a new terrorist attack. Support for a possible war reached an all-time high of 74 percent in November 2001, declined to 59 percent in June 2002, rose again to 64 percent on the one-year anniversary of September 11, slipped to 55 percent late the next month, and reached 68 percent in March 2003 at the war's outset (Gallup 2001; Gallup 2002b; Pew 2002a; Pew 2002b; ABC News 2003).

Initially, support for military intervention to depose Saddam related less to the Iraqi threat per se, since the public was equally willing to use force against Sudan and Somalia (Pew/CFR 2002). Over the course of more than a year, however, the focus narrowed as the administration argued for the imminence of an Iraqi threat by connecting Saddam to the danger of terrorism and reinforcing popular misperceptions of cooperation between Iraq and al-Qaeda (Kull *et al.* 2003–2004). The president himself explained "why Iraq is different from other countries or regimes that also have terrible weapons," and declared that "while there are many dangers in the world, the threat from Iraq stands alone—because it gathers the most serious dangers of our age in one place" (Bush 2002e).

Eventually, only war with Iraq made sense. Despite the bellicose rhetoric about all three members of the "axis of evil," war with Iran or North Korea would not have been consistent with the ideas dominating administration thinking. The latter two states were added to the "axis" only as an afterthought, and a full-scale invasion of either was too risky to serve as a demonstration of US hegemonic power and resolve (Woodward 2004: 87). Without an ostensible *casus belli*, Iran was too democratic—even if in a profoundly limited and illiberal sense; key officials like Rice and her deputy, Stephen Hadley, even questioned its suitability for membership in the "axis" (Woodward 2004: 87–88). In its determination to "defend the peace against threats from terrorists and tyrants," the administration's focus on Iraq reflected Straussian ideas of tyranny and regime centrality that were less compatible with a frontal assault on Iran (Bush 2002c; Norton 2004: 141–59). Furthermore, because it was not ethnically Arab, Iran was not a suitable place for remaking the Middle East by installing a friendly Arab democracy in the heart of the region for other states to emulate. As the president declared regarding the democratic prospects of the Arab states, "A new regime in Iraq would serve as a dramatic and inspiring example of freedom for other nations in the region" (Bush 2002a).

North Korea, for its part, was not only too dangerous militarily, but its cultural distance from al-Qaeda mattered too much to an administration that interpreted politics in broadly cultural terms by assuming that shared ethnicity or religion precipitates political cooperation. Even if the "axis of evil" invoked the specter of cooperation between states and non-state actors like al-Qaeda, the administration believed Iraqi cooperation with al-Qaeda to be vastly more likely than an al-Qaeda–North Korea nexus, which was never claimed by any US official (Kang and Cha 2003).

Although the administration viewed Kim Jong Il's regime with grave concern and contempt, it saw North Korea as "a country teetering on the verge of collapse" and therefore vulnerable to non-military leverage (Rumsfeld 2003a; Wolfowitz 2003a). It was willing to confront Pyongyang with threats and economic punishment, but it never signaled an intention to plunge headlong into a direct and all-out military confrontation with North Korea.

The events of 9/11 had enormous influence on an ideational level, not changing the world so much as the administration's understanding of it. As Rumsfeld described in congressional testimony in July 2003:

> The coalition did not act in Iraq because we had discovered dramatic new evidence of Iraq's pursuit of weapons of mass murder. We acted because we saw the existing evidence in a new light, through the prism of our experience on September 11 ... and that experience changed our appreciation of our vulnerability and the risks the U.S. faces from terrorist states and terrorist networks armed with powerful weapons.
>
> (Rumsfeld 2003b)

Rice, for her part, noted in her April 2004 testimony to the 9/11 Commission, "Bold and comprehensive changes are sometimes only possible in the wake of catastrophic events—events which create a new consensus that allows us to transcend old ways of thinking and acting" (Rice 2004).

The 9/11 attacks served as a brutal epiphany by demonstrating that an intensely globalizing world brought new dangers to a lone superpower no longer protected by continental and oceanic isolation. They shaped the administration's grand strategy by providing a unifying purpose and direction that was consistent with its ideological preference for a break with the recent past. Ideational change did not appear out of thin air. New possibilities were opened up by 9/11 for policy entrepreneurs to challenge an outmoded conventional wisdom that had failed to anticipate and counter the threat. For these thinkers, it created what chief Bush speechwriter Michael Gerson called a "plastic, teachable moment," a chance to present their ideas about global dangers and opportunities (Woodward 2004: 85). The administration accepted these ideas, sold them vigorously to the public and foreign policy elite, and achieved their actualization in the drive to oust Saddam.

The intensity of the administration's attachment to its ideas enhanced their significance, but the ideas themselves did not constitute a coherent ideology—neoconservative or otherwise—since together they contained fundamental contradictions that mirrored critical divisions in the administration. While the liberal focus on democracy and authoritarianism accorded moral and analytical centrality to the individual and to personal freedom, the call for US hegemony presumed the normative and empirical primacy of state power and national interest. These two sets of ideas are not easily reconciled, but they reflect the deceptively complex ideological crosscurrents—Straussian, Wilsonian, Hayekian, and Jacksonian, among others—in administration thinking. This same inconsistency manifested itself in the administration's rhetorical commitment to the international "power of freedom" while it prioritized national security over civil liberties at home. If the administration's many and varied justifications for the war seemed like alternative pleadings in a legal defense strategy, this was because the war's necessity and appropriateness had become self-evident to the president and other high-ranking officials (Feith 2008; cf. Jervis 2008–2009). Once this happened, they sought to fix the facts and even the intelligence to suit their objective (cf. Tenet 2007).

Ideational factors nonetheless are paramount analytically because ideas—not ideology—were the glue binding together the administration's Iraq policy. They alone deemed the Iraq War necessary and appropriate to the circumstances, and they alone tell us why the administration wanted a war that seemed reckless to many outside the pro-war ideational community. Nothing in presidential psychology, domestic politics, or systemic imperatives demanded the war or made it comprehensible with remotely similar directness. Non-ideational factors did play an important secondary role. The president's personal attributes were essential, because his evangelical Christian beliefs enhanced his receptivity to Manichaean ideas. The post-9/11 domestic environment was actively conducive to a high-risk venture in foreign policy, allowing the administration to incorporate Iraq into a coherent narrative of threat and opportunity that resonated with a majority of Americans. Unmatched US military power enabled Pentagon planners to contemplate and then launch a distant war that few states in history could have attempted. Potential side benefits to allies (Israel) and industries (oil) may have enhanced the war's appeal to some proponents. Yet without close scrutiny of the substance of administration ideas, the war decision itself is inexplicable.

References

ABC News (2003) "9/11 Two Years Later," September 7, www.abcnews.go.com/images/pdf/931a1911Anniversary.pdf.

Adelman, K. (2002) "Cakewalk in Iraq," *Washington Post*, February 13, A27.

Adler, E. (2002) "Constructivism and International Relations," in *Handbook of International Relations*, ed. Walter Carlsnaes, Thomas Risse, and Beth A. Simmons, London: Sage, 95–118.

Ajami, F. (2003) "A Journey without Maps," *U.S. News and World Report*, May 26.

Ajami, F. (2006) *The Foreigner's Gift: The Americans, The Arabs, and the Iraqis in Iraq*, New York: The Free Press.

Associated Press (2001) "Bush Pledges Crusade against 'Evil-doers,'" September 17.

Atlas, J. (2003) "What It Takes to Be a Neo-Neoconservative," *New York Times*, October 19, sec. 4, p. 12.

Baylis, J. and Garnett, J. (eds.) (1991) *The Makers of Nuclear Strategy*, New York: St. Martin's.

Bennett, W. (2003) *Why We Fight: Moral Clarity and the War on Terrorism*, Washington, DC: Regnery.

Biersteker, T. (1995) "The 'Triumph' of Liberal Ideas in the Developing World," in *Global Change, Regional Response: The New International Context of Development*, ed. Barbara Stallings, Cambridge: Cambridge University Press, 174–196.

Blyth, M. (2002) *Great Transformations: Economic Ideas and Institutional Change in the Twentieth Century*, Cambridge: Cambridge University Press.

Blyth, M. (2003) "Structures Do Not Come with an Instruction Sheet: Interests, Ideas, and Progress in Political Science," *Perspectives on Politics* 1, no. 4 (December): 695–706.

Boot, M. (2002) *The Savage Wars of Peace: Small Wars and the Rise of American Power*, New York: Basic Books.

Bush, G. H. W. and Scowcroft, B. (1998) *A World Transformed*, New York: Alfred A. Knopf.

Bush, G. W. (2001a) "President Bush's Inaugural Address," January 20.

Bush, G. W. (2001b) "Statement by the President in His Address to the Nation," September 11.

Bush, G. W. (2001c) "Address to a Joint Session of Congress and the American People," September 20.

Bush, G. W. (2002a) "Interview of the President by Sir Trevor McDonald of Britain's ITV Television Network," April 4, Weekly Compilation of Presidential Documents.

Bush, G. W. (2002b) "President Outlines War Effort," Virginia Military Institute, April 17.

Bush, G. W. (2002c) "Remarks by the President at 2002 Graduation Exercise of the United States Military Academy," June 1.

Bush, G. W. (2002d) "Remarks by President Bush and President Alvaro Uribe of Colombia in Photo Opportunity," September 25.

Bush, G. W. (2002e) "President Bush Outlines Iraqi Threat," Cincinnati, Ohio, October 7.

Bush, G. W. (2003a) "Remarks by the President and British Prime Minister Tony Blair," January 31.

Bush, G. W. (2003b) "President Discusses the Future of Iraq," February 26.

Bush, G. W. (2003c) "President Discusses Roadmap for Peace in the Middle East," March 14.

Bush, G. W. (2003d) "President Addresses the Nation," March 19.

Bush, G. W. (2003e) "President Bush Announces Major Combat Operations in Iraq Have Ended," May 1.

Bush, G. W. (2003f) "President Bush Discusses Iraq Policy at Whitehall Palace in London," November 19.

Cardenas, S. (2004) "Norm Collision: Explaining the Effects of International Human Rights Pressure on State Behavior," *International Studies Review* 6, no. 2 (June): 213–231.

Chandrasekaran, R. (2006) *Imperial Life in the Emerald City: Inside Iraq's Green Zone*, New York: Alfred A. Knopf.

Cheney, D. (2002) "Vice President Honors Veterans of Korean War," August 29.

Cheney, D. (2003) Interview on *Meet the Press*, www.msnbc.msn.com/id/8987534.

Chicago Council on Foreign Relations and German Marshall Fund (CCFR/GMF) (2002) Poll: "A World Transformed: Foreign Policy Attitudes of the U.S. Public after September 11," June, www.worldviews.org/docs/U.S.9–11v2.pdf.

Cirincione, J., Mathews, J. T., and Perkovich, G. (2004) *WMD in Iraq: Evidence and Implications*, Washington, DC: Carnegie Endowment for International Peace.

Clarke, R. A. (2004) *Against All Enemies: Inside America's War on Terror*, New York: Free Press.

Claude, I. (1962) *Power and International Relations*, New York: Random House.

Daalder, I. H. and Lindsay, J. M. (2003) *America Unbound: The Bush Revolution in Foreign Policy*, Washington, DC: Brookings Institution Press.

Department of Defense (DoD) (2001) "Transcript of Usama Bin Laden Video Tape," www.defenselink.mil/news/Dec2001/d20011213ubl.pdf.

Dorrien, G. (2004) *Imperial Designs: Neoconservatism and the New Pax Americana*, New York: Routledge.

Dueck, C. (2004) "Ideas and Alternatives in American Grand Strategy, 2000–2004," *Review of International Studies* 30, no. 4 (October): 511–535.

Duelfer, C.A. (2004) "Comprehensive Report of the Special Advisor to the DCI on Iraq's WMD," September 30, www.cia.gov/cia/reports/iraqwmd2004.

Duffield, J. S. (2005) "Oil and the Iraq War: How the United States Could Have Expected to Benefit, and Might Still," *Middle East Review of International Affairs* 9, no. 2 (June): 109–141.

Durkheim, E. (1964) *The Rules of Sociological Method* [1895], ed. George Catlin, trans. Sarah A. Solovay and John H. Mueller, New York: Free Press.

Edsall, T. B. and Milbank, D. (2003) "White House's Roving Eye for Politics: President's Most Powerful Adviser May Also Be the Most Connected," *Washington Post*, March 10, A1.

Farrell, T. (2002) "Constructivist Security Studies: Portrait of a Research Program," *International Studies Review* 4, no. 1 (Spring): 49–72.

Feaver, P. D. and Gelpi, C. (2003) *Choosing Your Battles: American Civil–Military Relations and the Use of Force*, Princeton: Princeton University Press.

Feith, D.J. (2008) *War and Decision: Inside the Pentagon at the Dawn of the War on Terrorism*, New York: HarperCollins.

Finnemore, M. (2003) *The Purpose of Intervention: Changing Beliefs about the Use of Force*, Ithaca: Cornell University Press.

Finnemore, M. and Sikkink, K. (2001) "Taking Stock: The Constructivist Research Program in International Relations and Comparative Politics," *Annual Review of Political Science* 4: 391–416.

Friedman, T. L. (1999) *The Lexus and the Olive Tree*, New York: Farrar, Straus and Giroux.

Friedman, T. L. (2003) "The Long Bomb," *New York Times*, March 2.

Frum, D. (2003) *The Right Man: The Surprise Presidency of George W. Bush*, New York: Random House.

Frum D. and Perle, R. (2003) *An End to Evil: How to Win the War on Terror*, New York: Random House.

Gaddis, J. L. (2002) "Bush's Security Strategy," *Foreign Policy* 133 (November–December): 50–57.

Gaddis, J. L. (2004) *Surprise, Security, and the American Experience*, Cambridge, MA: Harvard University Press.

Gallup (2001) November 26–27 November, http://brain.gallup.com.

Gallup (2002a) February 8–10, http://brain.gallup.com.

Gallup (2002b) June 17–19, http://brain.gallup.com.

Gerecht, R. M. (2001) "Crushing al Qaeda is Only a Start," *Wall Street Journal*, December 19.

Gordon, M. R. (2003) "U.S. Air Raids in '02 Prepared for War in Iraq," *New York Times*, July 20, A1.

Gordon, P. (2003) "Bush's Middle East Vision," *Survival* 45, no. 1 (Spring): 155–165.

Haass, R. (2002) "Towards Greater Democracy in the Muslim World," December 4, Council on Foreign Relations.

Hall, P. (1989) *The Political Power of Economic Ideas: Keynesianism across Nations*, Princeton: Princeton University Press.

Halper, S. and Clarke, J. (2004) *America Alone: The Neo-Conservatives and the Global Order*, Cambridge: Cambridge University Press.

Hanson, V. D. (2002) *An Autumn of War: What America Learned from September 11 and the War on Terrorism*, New York: Random House.

Hayworth, J. D. (2003) "Year of the Horse: We Can't Cut and Run from Iraq," National Review Online, November 3.

Hersh, S. M. (2004) *Chain of Command: The Road from 9/11 to Abu Ghraib*, New York: HarperCollins.

Hoffmann, S. (2003) "The High and the Mighty: Bush's National-Security Strategy and the New American Hubris," *American Prospect* 13 (January): 28–31.

Hopf, T. (2002) *Social Construction of International Politics: Identities and Foreign Policies, Moscow, 1955 and 1999*, Ithaca: Cornell University Press.

Hughes, K. (2004) *Ten Minutes to Normal*, New York: Penguin.

Huntington, S. (2002) "American Ideals versus American Institutions," in *American Foreign Policy*, ed. G. J. Ikenberry, New York: Longman, 204–237.

Ikenberry, G. J. (2004) "The End of the Neo-Conservative Moment," *Survival* 46, no. 1 (Spring): 7–22.

International Institute for Strategic Studies (IISS) (2002) *The Military Balance, 2001–2002*, London: Oxford University Press.

Jervis, R. (1976) *Perception and Misperception in International Politics*, Princeton: Princeton University Press.

Jervis, R. (2003a) "The Compulsive Empire," *Foreign Policy* 137 (July/August): 83–87.

Jervis, R. (2003b) "Understanding the Bush Doctrine," *Political Science Quarterly* 118, no. 3 (Fall): 365–388.

Jervis, R. (2008–2009) "War, Intelligence, and Honesty: A Review Essay," *Political Science Quarterly* 123, no. 4 (Winter): 645–675.

Johnston, A. I. (1995) *Cultural Realism: Strategic Culture and Grand Strategy in Chinese History*, Princeton: Princeton University Press.

Kagan, R. (2003) *Of Paradise and Power: America and Europe in the New World Order*, New York: Alfred A. Knopf.

Kagan, R. and Kristol, W. (eds.) (2000) *Present Dangers: Crisis and Opportunity in American Foreign and Defense Policy*, San Francisco: Encounter.

Kakutani, M. (2003) "How Books Have Shaped U.S. Policy," *New York Times*, April 5, D7.

Kang, D. C. and Cha, V. D. (2003) "Think Again: The Korea Crisis," *Foreign Policy* 136 (May–June): 20–28.

Kaplan, L. F. and Kristol, W. (2003) *The War over Iraq: Saddam's Tyranny and America's Mission*, San Francisco: Encounter.

Katzenstein, P. (ed.) (1996) *The Culture of National Security: Norms and Identity in World Politics*, New York: Columbia University Press.

Kay, D. (2003) "Statement by David Kay on the Interim Progress Report on the Activities of the Iraq Survey Group (ISG)," Testimony before the House Permanent Select Committee on Intelligence, the House Committee on Appropriations, Subcommittee on Defense, and the Senate Select Committee on Intelligence, October 2.

Kay, D. (2004) "Iraqi Weapons of Mass Destruction Programs," Testimony before the Senate Armed Services Committee, January 28.

Keck, M. E. and Sikkink, K. (1998) *Activists beyond Borders: Advocacy Networks in International Politics*, Ithaca: Cornell University Press.

Khalilzad, Z. (1995) *From Containment to Global Leadership? America and the World after the Cold War*, Santa Monica: RAND.

Kier, E. (1997) *Imagining War: French and British Military Doctrine between the Wars*, Princeton: Princeton University Press.

Klare, M. T. (2005) "Mapping the Oil Motive," *TomPaine.com*, March 18.

Krebs, R. (2005) "Selling the Market Short? The Marketplace of Ideas and the Iraq War," *International Security* 29, no. 4 (Spring).

Kristol, I. (1995) *Neoconservatism: The Autobiography of an Idea*, New York: Free Press.

Kristol, W. (2002) "Testimony of William Kristol to the Senate Foreign Relations Committee," February 7.

Kristol, W. and Kagan, R. (1996) "Toward a Neo-Reaganite Foreign Policy," *Foreign Affairs* 75, no. 4 (July/August): 18–32.

Kubalkova, V. (ed.) (2001) *Foreign Policy in a Constructed World*, Armonk: M. E. Sharpe.

Kull, S., Ramsay, C. and Lewis, E. (2003–2004) "Misperceptions, the Media, and the Iraq War," *Political Science Quarterly* 118, no. 4 (Winter): 569–598.

Lapid, Y. and Kratochwil, F. (eds.) (1996) *The Return of Culture and Identity in IR Theory*, Boulder: Lynne Rienner.

Ledeen, M. (2002) *The War against the Terror Masters*, New York: St. Martin's.

Leffler, M. P. (2004) "Bush's Foreign Policy," *Foreign Policy* 144 (September/October): 22–28.

Legro, J. W. (2000a) "The Transformation of Policy Ideas," *American Journal of Political Science* 44, no. 3 (July): 419–432.

Legro, J. W. (2000b) "Whence American Internationalism," *International Organization* 54, no. 2 (Spring 2000): 253–289.

Legro, J. W. (2005) *Rethinking the World: Great Power Strategies and International Order*, Ithaca: Cornell University Press.

Lewis, B. (1990) "The Roots of Muslim Rage," *Atlantic Monthly*, September, 47–60.

Lewis, B. (2002a) "What Went Wrong with Muslim Civilization?" *Atlantic Monthly*, January, 43–45.

Lewis, B. (2002b) *What Went Wrong: Western Impact and Middle Eastern Response*, New York: Oxford University Press.

Lieber, R. J. (2003) "The Folly of Containment," *Commentary*, April, 15–21.

Lindsay, J. M. (ed.) (2004) *American Politics After September 11*, 3rd edn, Cincinnati: Atomic Dog Publishing.

Lipset, S. M. (1996) *American Exceptionalism: A Double-Edged Sword*, New York: W. W. Norton.

Mailer, N. (2003) *Why Are We at War?* New York: Random House.

March, J. G. and Olsen, J. P. (1989) *Rediscovering Institutions: The Organizational Basis of Politics*, New York: Free Press.

March, J. G. and Olsen, J. P. (1999) "The Institutional Dynamics of International Political Orders," in *Exploration and Contestation in the Study of World Politics*, ed. Peter J. Katzenstein, Robert O. Keohane, and Stephen D. Krasner, Cambridge, MA: MIT Press.

Mead, W. R. (2001) *Special Providence: American Foreign Policy and How it Changed the World*, New York: Alfred A. Knopf.

Mearsheimer, J. J. and Walt, S. M. (2003) "An Unnecessary War," *Foreign Policy* 134 (January/February): 50–59.

Niebuhr, R. (1944) *The Children of Light and the Children of Darkness: A Vindication of Democracy and a Critique of its Traditional Defence*, New York: Scribner's.

Norton, A. (2004) *Leo Strauss and the Politics of American Empire*, New Haven: Yale University Press.

Okrent, D. (2004) The Public Editor, "Weapons of Mass Destruction? Or Mass Distraction?" *New York Times*, May 30.

Organski, A. F. K. (1968) *World Politics*, 2nd edn, New York: Alfred A. Knopf, 272–299.

Packer, G. (2002) "The Liberal Quandary over Iraq," *New York Times Magazine*, December 8, 104–107, 156.

Packer, G. (2005) *The Assassins' Gate: America in Iraq*, New York: Farrar, Straus, and Giroux.

Pew Research Center for the People and the Press and Council on Foreign Relations (Pew/CFR) (2002) "Americans Favor Force in Iraq, Somalia, Sudan, and…," January 22.

Pew Research Center for the People and the Press (2002a) "Bush Engages and Persuades Public on Iraq," September 19, http://people-press.org/reports/display.php3?ReportID=161.

Pew Research Center for the People and the Press (2002b) "Support for Potential Military Action Slips to 55%," October 30, http://peoplepress.org/reports/display.php3?ReportID=163.

Pew Research Center for the People and the Press (2003) "U.S. Needs More International Backing," February 20, http://people-press.org/reports/display.php3?ReportID=173.

Pipes, D. (2003) "100 Bin Ladens on the Way?" *New York Post*, April 8.

Project for the New American Century (PNAC) (1997), www.newamericancentury.org/aboutpnac.htm.

Project for the New American Century (PNAC) (1998) "An Open Letter to President Clinton: 'Remove Saddam from Power,'" January 26, in *The Iraq War Reader: History, Documents, Opinions*, ed. M. L. Sifry and C. Cerf, New York: Simon & Schuster, 2003, 199–201.

Ratner, M., Green, J., and Olshansky, B. (2003) *Against War in Iraq: An Anti-War Primer*, New York: Seven Stories Press.

Rice, C. (2000) "Promoting the National Interest," *Foreign Affairs* 79, no. 1 (January/February).

Rice, C. (2004) "Dr. Condoleezza Rice's Opening Remarks to Commission on

Terrorist Attacks," National Commission on Terrorist Attacks Upon the United States, Washington, DC, April 8.

Ricks, T. E. (2003) "Centcom's Renaissance Man: New Chief Abizaid Is Departure from Previous Army Leaders," *Washington Post*, August 3, A18.

Ricks, T. E. (2006) *Fiasco: The American Military Adventure in Iraq*, New York: Penguin.

Robin, C. (2004) *Fear: The History of a Political Idea*, New York: Oxford University Press.

Rosen, G. (ed.) (2005) *The Right War? The Conservative Debate on Iraq*, Cambridge: Cambridge University Press.

Ruggie, J. (1982) "International Regimes, Transitions, and Change: Embedded Liberalism in the Postwar Economic Order," *International Organization* 36, no. 2 (Spring): 194–230.

Ruggie, J. (1999) "What Makes the World Hang Together? Neo-Utilitarianism and the Social Constructivist Challenge," in *Exploration and Contestation in the Study of World Politics*, ed. Peter J. Katzenstein, Robert O. Keohane, and Stephen D. Krasner, Cambridge, MA: MIT Press, 215–245.

Rumsfeld, D. (2002) "21st-Century Transformation," remarks delivered at National Defense University, Fort McNair, Washington, January 31.

Rumsfeld, D. (2003a) "Secretary Rumsfeld Contrasts Iraq and North Korea," United States Department of Defense, January 20.

Rumsfeld, D. (2003b) "Testimony before the U.S. Senate Armed Services Committee," July 9.

Satloff, R. B. (ed.) (2002) *War on Terror: The Middle East Dimension*, Washington, DC: Washington Institute for Near East Policy.

Snyder, J. (2003) "Imperial Temptations," *The National Interest* 71 (Spring): 29–40.

Stelzer, I. (ed.) (2004) *The Neocon Reader*, New York: Grove Press.

Stevenson, R. W. and Elder, J. (2004) "Support for War is Down Sharply, Poll Concludes," *New York Times*, April 29, A1.

Suskind, R. (2004) *The Price of Loyalty: George W. Bush, the White House, and the Education of Paul O'Neill*, New York: Simon & Schuster.

Suskind, R. (2007) *The One Percent Doctrine: Deep Inside America's Pursuit of Its Enemies since 9/11*, New York: Simon & Schuster.

Tanenhaus, S. (2003) "Bush's Brain Trust," *Vanity Fair*, no. 515 (July): 114–119, 164, 169.

Tenet, G., with Harlow, B. (2007) *At the Center of the Storm: My Years at the CIA*, New York: HarperCollins.

Vidal, G. (2002) *Dreaming War: Blood for Oil and the Cheney-Bush Junta*, New York: Thunder's Mouth Press.

Waldman, P. (2004) "A Historian's Take on Islam Steers U.S. in Terrorism Fight," *Wall Street Journal*, February 3, 1.

Waltz, K. N. (1979) *Theory of International Politics*, New York: McGraw-Hill.

Washington Post (2004) "Washington Post-ABC News Poll: Politics and Campaign 2004," www.washingtonpost.com/wp-srv/politics/polls/vault/stories/data030804.htm.

Weinstein, K. R. (2004) "Philosophic Roots, the Role of Leo Strauss, and the War in Iraq," in *The Neocon Reader*, ed. I. Steltzer, New York: Grove Press.

Wendt, A. (1999) *Social Theory of International Politics*, New York: Cambridge University Press.

White House (2002) *The National Security Strategy of the United States of America.*

Wolfers, A. (1962) *Discord and Collaboration,* Baltimore: Johns Hopkins University Press.

Wolfowitz, P. (2000a) "Statesmanship in the New Century," in *Present Dangers: Crisis and Opportunity in American Foreign and Defense Policy,* ed. Robert Kagan and William Kristol, San Francisco: Encounter, 307–336.

Wolfowitz, P. (2000b) "Remembering the Future," *The National Interest* 59 (Spring): 35–45.

Wolfowitz, P. (2003a) "Deputy Secretary Wolfowitz Q&A Following IISS Asia Security Conference," May 31.

Wolfowitz, P. (2003b) "Winning the Battle of Ideas: Another Front in the War on Terror," Oscar Iden Lecture, Georgetown University, October 30.

Woodward, B. (2002) *Bush at War,* New York: Simon & Schuster.

Woodward, B. (2004) *Plan of Attack,* New York: Simon & Schuster.

Yetiv, S. A. (2003) "Groupthink and the Gulf Crisis," *British Journal of Political Science* 33, no. 3 (Summer): 419–443.

Yetiv, S. A. (2005) *Explaining Foreign Policy: U.S. Decision-Making and the Persian Gulf War,* Baltimore: Johns Hopkins University Press.

5 Explaining the Iraq War

The Israel lobby theory

Jerome Slater

The Iraq War is often likened by its opponents to the Vietnam War. While there are important differences between the wars, there is at least one striking similarity: not only is there conflict over *whether* the United States should have fought either war, there is conflict over their very *purpose*.

Throughout the Vietnam War the question was repeatedly asked: why are we in Vietnam? Amazingly, even high US policy-makers evidently weren't too sure, for we now know that in their internal studies they repeatedly posed that question to themselves. Over the course of the war a variety of explanations were offered, both to the public and within the government: to prevent the fall of one nation after another if South Vietnam were "lost" (the domino theory); to defend freedom and democracy; to uphold the principle of self-determination; to resist international aggression; or to maintain US international commitments, such as SEATO. More jaundiced explanations by critics of the war included the belief that we had somehow semi-unwittingly blundered into Vietnam and then became trapped there (the quagmire theory); the fear of domestic political consequences if Vietnam should be "lost" to communism; or even psychological explanations focusing on the ego-needs of insecure presidential personalities, who feared the effects on their prestige and their place in history if their policies on Vietnam should fail.

A similar and equally revealing debate has been occurring over the Iraq War since 2003: as Jane Cramer and Trevor Thrall write in the introduction to this volume, "The simple question remains: why *did* the United States invade Iraq?" Once again, a variety of theories or explanations have been offered, as reviewed elsewhere in this book and briefly summarized later in this chapter. As was the case in Vietnam, the very variety of explanations is deeply troubling. That is, rational states should not go to war unless their most vital interests are clearly at stake, and if serious observers disagree over whether they are, it is tempting to conclude that they aren't.

In some wars, vital interests are indeed clearly at stake. For example, during World War II there was not much of a debate about why we were fighting it, and hardly anyone argues today that it was a mistake to do so. While not quite as clear-cut as World War II, some recent wars are widely accepted as having been unavoidable: there is no mystery about why the United States went to war in Afghanistan after 9/11, nor do we really ask if the United States should have gone to war against Saddam's Iraq in the Persian Gulf War of 1990–1991, following the Iraqi invasion of Kuwait and an apparently imminent threat to Saudi Arabia, a close US ally and the largest supplier of our Mideast oil.

The "Israel lobby" theory

In their famous 2007 book, *The Israel Lobby and U.S. Foreign Policy*, John J. Mearsheimer and Stephen M. Walt provide their answer to the question of why we are in Iraq: the "Israel lobby," defined as "a loose coalition of individuals and organizations that actively work to shape U.S. foreign policy in a pro-Israel direction," played the decisive role in convincing the Bush administration to go to war in Iraq (Mearsheimer and Walt 2007: 112). More generally,

> the activities of the groups and individuals who make up the lobby are the main reason why the United States pursues policies in the Middle East that make little sense on either strategic or moral grounds. Were it not for the lobby's efforts.... U.S policy in the Middle East would be significantly different than it is today.
>
> (Mearsheimer and Walt 2007: 111–112)

There is no doubt that the *Israel Lobby* is a major work of foreign policy analysis that has already had a great impact on how scholars, journalists, and perhaps even the general public think about US policy in the Middle East. In a sense (as I have argued elsewhere, see Slater 2009), the book is really two books. The first book focuses on the substance of US policies, and its analysis is broad ranging, extensively documented, and generally compelling: if Mearsheimer and Walt's recommendations for major changes in US policy were adopted by the government, both the national interest and the moral standing of this country would be greatly served.

Unfortunately, it is what I call the second book of Mearsheimer and Walt, focusing on the policy-making process, that has received the overwhelming attention of almost all the critics—unfortunately, because the argument of the second book is not nearly so compelling, is vulnerable to serious criticism, and has all but drowned out the *Israel Lobby*'s policy critique. Even so, some of the criticisms of the book—for example, that it is anti-Semitic—are noxious, and others—for example, that its "methodology" is badly flawed—are unpersuasive. In general, nearly all the most vociferous if not downright nasty attacks on Mearsheimer and Walt clearly stem from outrage over their criticism of the near unconditional US support of Israeli policies as much as from their argument that the power of the Israel lobby largely explains US policies.

In fact, the power or influence of the Israel lobby *is* the best explanation for some aspects of US policies in the Mideast, especially in accounting for the remarkable support of Israel in Congress. As Mearsheimer and Walt discuss in great detail, the Israel lobby is famously well-organized and efficient, is generously financed, has easy access to legislators and their staffs, has close allies in congressional constituencies, and either has or is presumed to have the ability in close elections to help elect friendly Congressmen or defeat allegedly unfriendly ones. Indeed, the evidence of the power of the lobby in Congress—by no means limited to that discussed by Mearsheimer and Walt—is so overwhelming that its denial by the book's "pro-Israel" critics is simply absurd.

What is significantly less persuasive, though, is Mearsheimer and Walt's broader argument that it is the power of the lobby that is the main explanation for the strong support of Israel in the mass media, in the general public, and—above all—among presidents and other key executive-branch officials and institutions.[1] It is the White House and the executive branch that are the main locus of power over most foreign policy decisions, not Congress: thus, the overall persuasiveness of the *Israel Lobby* depends largely on its demonstrating the lobby's power in presidential decisions on national security and high foreign policy issues.

To sustain their overall argument, then, Mearsheimer and Walt need to show much more than that the lobby has great power in Congress; their theory must also show the following:

First, that the domestic politics of Israeli-related issues would be very different if there were no organized Israel lobby. Put differently, while it is clear that political considerations play a major role in the determination of US policies toward Israel, Mearsheimer and Walt must show that it is the Israel lobby that largely creates the pro-Israel electoral attitudes.

Second, that the lobby has power in Congress not only over US policies toward Israel but in overall US policies in the Middle East.

Third, that there is a causal connection not only between pressures by the Israel lobby and congressional actions (which there clearly is) but also between the policies favored—or demanded—by the lobby and its congressional allies and the policies ultimately adopted by the president and the executive branch.

Fourth, that the lobby usually prevails over the president and the executive branch when their policy goals are in conflict.

Fifth, that when US officials say that support of Israel in its policies and actions toward the Palestinians is required by our own national interest, to a significant degree they are concealing their true motivation, which is to avoid clashes with the Israel lobby.

The *Israel Lobby* argument is vulnerable to criticism on all these criteria. First, the argument conflates the power of the organized Israel lobby with broader domestic pro-Israel sentiment in accounting for US policies toward Israel. Though there is, of course, a considerable overlap between these explanatory variables, nonetheless they need to be distinguished. That is, even if there were no organized lobby, pro-Israeli groups in the United States (mostly but by no means exclusively Jewish) would be important in molding public opinion because of their power and influence in the mass media, and they would still play a significant role in the electoral process, both because of their central role in campaign contributions and their potential swing vote in close elections. Obviously, the fact that there really *is* a powerful pro-Israel lobby is significant, but even in its absence the domestic politics of Israeli-related issues would weigh heavily in Congress, and to a lesser but still important extent, in the executive branch.

Second, as I will shortly discuss in connection with the Iraq case, the evidence is strong that the organized lobby has less influence in the US policy-making process over Middle East issues generally than it does over issues directly relating to Israel. It is not difficult to show that the lobby has a major role in determining congressional legislation and other actions concerning US diplomatic, economic and military aid to Israel, but it is considerably more difficult to show the lobby's power over other issues, such as the two wars against Iraq, or the debate over whether the United States should attack Iran's nuclear installations.

Third, even when the lobby seemingly gets its way, as when the government's policies parallel those of the lobby and Congress, Mearsheimer and Walt do not give sufficient attention to the possibility that factors other than the power of the lobby may have been more important, particularly presidential beliefs or ideologies. Put differently, while the *policies* demanded by the lobby and those adopted by the government have sometimes converged—as in the Iraq War, as I shall shortly discuss—the *goals* of the government may have substantially differed, or at least were far broader, than those of the lobby.

Indeed, there have even been some cases in which it appears that presidents chose "pro-Israel" policies not because of the lobby's pressures but despite them. For example, Truman's biographers agree that he decided to recognize the state of Israel and provide important diplomatic support of it, even though he was quite annoyed with Jewish lobbying on behalf of Israel. Another example might be Richard Nixon's support of Israel, despite not only his anger at Jewish lobbying but even his personal anti-Semitic inclinations.

Fourth, while it is certainly true that there have been important cases in which the combined force of Israeli and Israel lobby pressures seem to be the main explanation for US policies—most notably, recently, in the progressive abandonment by the Obama administration of serious pressures on Israel over its ongoing expansion of its "settlements" in the West Bank and East Jerusalem[2]—there have also been important cases in the past in which the Israel lobby was opposed by the president and lost, and more recently the Bush administration did not bow to serious Israeli, congressional, and lobby pressures to adopt a tougher line on Syria.[3]

Similarly, for many years the lobby has pressed for a pre-emptive US attack on the Iranian nuclear facilities, but failed to persuade, let alone "pressure," either the Bush or Obama administrations into authorizing such an attack—or even to cooperate with or accede to an Israeli attack. And even if Obama finally does authorize an attack, almost surely it will be not be because of lobby pressures but because of a wider range of policy considerations as well as Obama's own concerns over the national security stakes for the United States if Iran goes nuclear: general Mideast stability worries, the fear that if Iran gets nuclear weapons it will embolden it to more actively support anti-American terrorist groups, potential threats to Mideast oil producers, considerations of American prestige and credibility, and a fear of the domestic political consequences in the United States if current policies fail to work.

Mearsheimer and Walt downplay these other factors when they write that "If a war [against Iran] does occur, it would be in part on Israel's behalf, and the lobby would bear significant responsibility" (Mearsheimer and Walt 2007: 305). As Mearsheimer and Walt themselves point out, however, Israel and the lobby have been unsuccessfully pressing for an attack since 1993, strongly suggesting that if the United States does finally attack Iran, other factors will be more important. Moreover, the logic of their argument must lead to the conclusion that if the United States continues to refuse to attack Iran, that would demonstrate the failure rather than the power of the lobby. And for some eighteen years, that, in fact, has been the case.

Fifth, Mearsheimer and Walt do not sufficiently distinguish between the true national interest (assuming widespread agreement on what it is) and misperceptions of the national interest, for the underlying premise of the *Israel Lobby* is that policies that are bad for the US national interest are best explained by the power of a group that has a narrow interest in convincing the government to adopt them and succeeds in doing so. That is not necessarily the case, for it excludes the possibility of simple error, or misperceptions—that is, US policy-makers may not be intentionally disregarding the national interest in the Mideast, merely foolishly so. Indeed, this failure to give sufficient weight to the problem of misperceptions is one of the weakest points in the *Israel Lobby* theory.[4]

The Iraq War

I have argued that the Israeli lobby theory constitutes a powerful explanation for congressional actions relating to Israel (legislation, declarations, hearings, etc.), and to a lesser but still significant extent, congressional actions concerning the Middle East as a whole. It is considerably less persuasive in accounting for presidential/executive branch policies toward Israel—although it would be more persuasive if the theory were to be broadened to refer to domestic politics as a whole, not just active lobbying by pro-Israeli groups, organizations, or intellectuals. And, the theory is still less persuasive in explaining presidential policies toward the Mideast in general, and the Iraq War in particular.

Mearsheimer and Walt devote one chapter in *The Israel Lobby* to the Iraq War. They begin by arguing that "the decision to overthrow Saddam Hussein even now seems difficult to fathom," that Iraq was militarily weak and "effectively contained," the UN sanctions had eliminated the WMD problem, and Saddam had nothing to do with 9/11 (Mearsheimer and Walt 2007: 229). In effect, then, they are arguing that since there was no US national interest at stake, we must look elsewhere to understand why the United States attacked Iraq. In part, they suggest, the explanation lies in the combination of great military power and deep but excessive security concerns. However,

> there was another variable in the equation, and the war would almost certainly not have occurred had it not been present. That element was the Israel lobby, and especially a group of neoconservative policy makers and pundits who had been pushing the United States to attack Iraq since well before 9/11.
>
> (Mearsheimer and Walt 2007: 230)

After 9/11, their argument continues,

> the neoconservatives were able to help convince Bush and Dick Cheney that it made sense to oust Saddam.... Thus we concluded that the neoconservatives' efforts were necessary to make the war happen—they dreamed up the idea and were the only important forces promoting it until September 11.
>
> (Mearsheimer and Walt 2009: 71)

How hard did the lobby push for war?

There are a number of problems with this argument. To begin, the evidence is thin that the lobby as a whole, as distinct from some neoconservative intellectuals, pushed hard for the war. The Israel lobby normally takes its position from that of the Israeli government—and invariably so from rightwing governments—and (as Mearsheimer and Walt themselves point out), some Israeli leaders were initially ambivalent about the war, fearing it might divert US attention from Iran, and concerned that "the war look like it was being fought for Israel" (Mearsheimer and Walt 2007: 238). Consequently,

> although there was hardly any opposition to the war among the major Jewish organizations, there was disagreement about how vocal they should be in backing it ... the main concern was the fear that too

open support for an invasion would make it look like the war was being fought for Israel's sake.

(Mearsheimer and Walt 2007: 241)

Still, the argument continues, the Sharon government in Israel "never tried to convince the Bush administration not to go to war against Iraq" (Mearsheimer and Walt 2007: 233–234) and after its initial caution "Israel did join forces with the neoconservatives to help sell the war to the Bush administration and the American people" (Mearsheimer and Walt 2007: 234). Consequently, as Mearsheimer and Walt do show, a number of Israel lobby members did push Congress to support the war. However, in this case the overall argument focuses not on *lobbying* for the war by either Israel or the US groups—perhaps because, as they point out, most American Jews strongly opposed the war—but simply on their *support* of the war or even their unwillingness to actively *oppose* it. "AIPAC is not the only major group in the lobby to stick with Bush on Iraq, or *at least not come out against the war*" (Mearsheimer and Walt 2007: 243, emphasis added), Mearsheimer and Walt write, as if this would constitute powerful evidence to support their argument. However, not joining others in opposing the war was not the same as pushing for it, let alone that the absence of lobby opposition was a major factor in explaining why Bush went to war.

How important was the Israel lobby in the decision to attack Iraq?

Whatever the extent of neoconservative or AIPAC lobbying, the more important question is whether or how much that lobbying mattered. Thus, a second problem in the *Israel Lobby* argument is that the evidence the authors point to, let alone the other evidence that has since emerged, does not demonstrate that the lobby, even in Mearsheimer and Walt's initially relatively cautious assessment, "played an important role in making the case for war with Iraq" (Mearsheimer and Walt 2007: 200). Moreover, their argument becomes increasingly strong: "while pressure from Israel and the lobby was not the only factor behind the Bush administration's decision to attack Iraq," it was a "critical element" (Mearsheimer and Walt 2007: 230) or "a necessary but not sufficient condition for the war" (Mearsheimer and Walt 2007: 253). And their overall assessment is even less qualified: "the war would almost certainly not have occurred ... [in the absence] of the Israel lobby," especially from the "small band of neoconservatives" who were "the driving force behind the Iraq war" (Mearsheimer and Walt 2007: 230, 238).

Much of the *Israel Lobby* argument is based on the fact that until the intensity of neoconservative lobbying increased, following 9/11, the Bush administration had rejected the arguments for going to war against Iraq. However, the inference drawn by Mearsheimer and Walt—that therefore it was the neoconservative lobbying that led the administration to change its mind—does not necessarily follow. In this connection, there is a puzzling passage in the *Israel Lobby*: Robert Kagan, Mearsheimer and Walt write, "put the point well" when he stated that "September 11 is the turning point. *Not anything else*" (Mearsheimer and Walt 2007: 246, quoting Kagan, emphasis added). But that would seem to undercut their argument, not support it, for Kagan was in essence saying that 9/11 was both necessary *and* sufficient to explain the hardened position of the administration.

Put differently, if Kagan was right, the Israel lobby was irrelevant because it was 9/11 that changed the administration's position, not pressure from the lobby. Still, it is worthwhile exploring further whether the lobby influenced the administration's decision to attack Iraq. Mearsheimer and Walt do provide evidence of considerable neoconservative lobbying in favor of an attack, and point out that many public figures, former government officials, and journalists "either said or strongly hinted that pro-Israel hardliners ... were the principal movers behind the Iraq war" (2007: 232).

On the other hand, more recently a number of informed accounts of the decision-making process during the Iraq War by former high officials as well as journalists and scholars downplay or even fail to mention any influence of Israel or the Israel lobby. It is noteworthy that all the other chapters in this book, devoted to explaining why the United States invaded Iraq, either fail to even mention the efforts of the Israel lobby or dismiss its influence out of hand. Further, it is particularly instructive that Flynn Leverett and Hillary Mann Leverett, themselves fierce critics of the Israel lobby, recently wrote that

> As individuals who served at the White House on the National Security Council staff in the run-up to the invasion of Iraq, we saw no evidence that Israeli officials and leaders of the American Jewish community (as opposed to some pro-Israel intellectuals ... and neoconservative policy makers in the Bush Administration) goaded the United States into invading Iraq.
>
> (Leverett and Leverett 2010)

In short, there is not much evidence that pressures from the Israel lobby were a major factor in the policy-making process within the Bush administration, let alone that they were a "necessary condition" for the Iraq War.

The Israel lobby: power or influence?

Still, let us suppose that Mearsheimer and Walt were right that the pro-Israel neoconservatives had a significant role in the decision of the Bush administration to go to war against Iraq; even so, it still would be important to distinguish between the power of the lobby to pressure the administration to do something it did not want to do and the influence or persuasiveness of its arguments. Throughout the *Israel Lobby*, Mearsheimer and Walt's emphasis is on the outright power of the lobby to pressure policy-makers, as in "pressure from Israel and the lobby ... was a critical element" in explaining Bush's policies.

However, Mearsheimer and Walt essentially treat power and influence as if they were synonymous. To be sure, it is not necessarily wrong to define the term "power" to include both the capacity to prevail over opposition and the capacity to persuade, but the differences between them are important. The first form of power—perhaps it would help to call it "raw power"—stems from the ability to reward and punish, whereas the second form, influence, is largely a function of the ability to make arguments that convince those who have the real power in the foreign policy process. Put differently, raw power means the ability to say, "do what I want, or else," and make it stick. There is no "or else," however, in the case of influence, or the power to persuade.

There is no doubt that sometimes the Israel lobby *does* exercise raw power, especially in Congress over issues that directly affect Israel, for it can make or break the electoral futures of many legislators—or, at least, is widely *perceived* to have that power, which is sufficient to have a major impact on how those legislators behave. Consequently, it is well known that many Congressmen dutifully support whatever the Israel lobby wishes, even though they privately admit that it is against their better judgment.

Matters are different with regard to the president and his key advisors, however, for they are much less susceptible to the exercise of raw power. This seems especially to be the case with regard to Iraq policy, even in the Mearsheimer and Walt analysis: their emphasis, essentially, is on the *influence* of the neoconservatives—meaning the success of their arguments in convincing high officials of the Bush administration to attack Iraq. To repeat earlier quotations from *The Israel Lobby*: "the neoconservatives were able to help *convince* Bush and Dick Cheney that it made sense to oust Saddam," or "To repeat, Bush and Cheney opted for war because the neoconservatives helped *convince* them it was a good idea" (Mearsheimer and Walt 2009: 71, 72, emphases added).

At most, then, what Mearsheimer and Walt really show is that the Bush administration, already ideologically sympathetic to the views of the Israel lobby, after 9/11 became persuaded by the neoconservative arguments that an attack on Iraq was a vital US national security interest. Of course, Mearsheimer and Walt argue—and rightly so—that the US government should *not* have been persuaded by such arguments, whether emphasizing Israeli security or the US national interest, but that's a different issue.

What motivated the Bush administration?

As I have suggested, it is important to distinguish between the motives of neoconservatives who argued for attacking Iraq and those of the Bush administration. It is certainly plausible that the neoconservatives were primarily concerned about an Iraqi threat to Israel, but were the motives of the Bush administration the same?[5] Although carefully qualified—"the war was motivated at least in good part by a desire to make Israel more secure" (Mearsheimer and Walt 2007: 231)—the overall weight of the Mearsheimer and Walt argument is to emphasize the Israeli connection.

As is emphasized by a number of contributors to this book, there were a number of other likely factors that accounted for the Bush administration's decision to go to war in Iraq, of which concern over Israeli security may have been one but almost certainly not the most important. The first, of course, is the WMD issue, which by itself may well have been not only a necessary condition for the war but also a sufficient one. A number of scholars, most notably Robert Jervis (Jervis 2009 as well as in his contribution to this book), have persuasively argued that at the time the most reasonable interpretation of the actions of Saddam Hussein was that he had a nuclear weapons program, that "as far as we can tell all intelligence services, even those in countries that opposed the war, came to conclusions similar to those held by American intelligence," and that—most importantly—the WMD issue was not a pretext for war but was genuinely believed by Bush and his top officials.[6]

In addition to the honest (and not stupid) belief that for reasons of regional stability or even of a potential threat to the United States itself, it was intolerable to risk allowing a homicidal psychopath with a proven record of mass murder and reckless expansionism to get nuclear or biological weapons, whether or not he already had them, there were other factors which taken together might be more than sufficient to explain the war: the obvious grip of Wilsonian ideology on George Bush, particularly on the belief that the United States has the moral right and the military power to spread democracy throughout the world, especially (in this case) in the Middle East in general and to Iraq in particular; the intensification of concern over terrorism after 9/11 and the belief that Saddam might come to support Islamic terrorism, whether or not he was already doing so;[7] the longstanding US foreign policy goal of maintaining a pro-Western "stability" in the Middle East, in order to preserve US access to oil; George Bush's desire to "finish the job" left uncompleted by the first Bush administration in the earlier Gulf War, together with his desire for vengeance for Saddam's apparent efforts to assassinate his father; and even, perhaps, genuine humanitarian concerns—the Saddam Hussein regime, after all, was certainly one of the most violent and cruel in the world, and at the time it was reasonable to assume that the overthrow of his regime would greatly improve the human rights of the Iraqi people.

It is not difficult to show that because of some mix of these reasons many Americans—and, for that matter, many Iraqis—either supported the war or were ambivalent about it. Many of those who shared some of these concerns—including the writer of this chapter—were not in the US government, were not connected to the oil industry, were not neoconservatives, were not friendly to the Israeli rightwing, and could not be either persuaded or pressured by the Israel lobby. That being the case, there is no reason to essentially dismiss the possibility that similar concerns were also important factors in the motivations of many officials in the Bush administration.

More generally, as I argued above, the *Israel Lobby* theory does not sufficiently account for the problem of errors and misperceptions, particularly of "the national interest." Though Mearsheimer and Walt do concede that the US officials, in the Iraq case and others, genuinely believed that their policies served the national interest, the overall weight of their argument and rhetoric suggests an implicit premise that US policies in Iraq and throughout the Middle East are so obviously foolish that the only plausible explanation of them is the power of a narrow special interest group whose agenda is not determined by the national interest and is often antithetical to it.

It is perfectly possible to agree with most of Mearsheimer and Walt's criticisms of US policies but to disagree with their explanation of them. With the benefit of hindsight it is easier now than it was in 2003 to conclude that the national interest stakes of the United States in Iraq were not sufficiently critical to have justified the war, but even if that is the case it probably only demonstrates that the national interest was genuinely misperceived by the Bush administration—and many others.

In the final analysis, the *Israel Lobby*'s explanation of the Iraq War is unpersuasive: aside from the absence of concrete evidence, it simply is not very plausible that the highest officials in the government, with all their institutional as well as political power—the President, the Vice President, the Secretary of Defense, the Secretary of State, and the National Security Adviser, none of them either Jewish or neoconservatives—were pressured into going to war because of the position of the Israeli government or the domestic power of the Israel lobby.

As for the real explanation for the Iraq War, there is still no consensus answer. That in itself, however, suggests a useful rule of thumb for possible future wars: if you have to ask why you're in them, you shouldn't be.

Notes

1 There is some recent polling evidence that support of Israel is declining. Even so, it is still relatively high and, more importantly, declining support for Israel has not been accompanied by increased support for the Arab world in general or the Palestinians in particular. As a result, it remains the case that there is no electoral incentive for politicians to take more critical positions on Israel.

2 Even in these cases, Mearsheimer and Walt use excessively strong language regarding the sheer power of Israel and the Israel lobby within the US government, as when they write that during the Bush administration Ariel Sharon's Israeli government "forced the president to retreat" from its earlier opposition to Israeli attacks in the West Bank, indeed that "Sharon had humiliated Bush"

(Mearsheimer and Walt 2009: 69). But it is far from clear that Bush had to be "forced" to change his earlier very mild criticisms of Israeli actions, as opposed to genuinely coming to share Sharon's views of what must be done against "international terrorism," especially, of course, after 9/11.

3 For a summary of these cases, see Slater (2009: 27, 50–52). In responding to my critique of their book, Mearsheimer and Walt wrote that:

> We never said the lobby wins all the time; on the contrary, we wrote that "we do not believe the lobby is all-powerful," and we discussed a number of prominent cases where "the lobby did not get its way." Our argument ... is that cases where the lobby loses "are becoming increasingly rare." Thus it is not surprising that almost all of his [Slater's] examples date from before 1992.
>
> (Mearsheimer and Walt 2009: 70)

That is not really accurate, however, for as I discuss above the limitations on the lobby's power have been also revealed in recent US policies toward Syria and—so far, anyway—Iran. In any case, I agree with the contention of nearly all other serious critics of the *Israel Lobby* that Mearsheimer and Walt's main emphasis is on the power of the lobby, not on the limitations of its power.

4 In their response to my earlier criticisms, in effect Mearsheimer and Walt deny that they give insufficient weight to the problem of misperceptions: for example, they write that the key Bush administration decision-makers "chose war [in Iraq] because they thought it would be in the American national interest" (Mearsheimer and Walt 2009: 72). It is true that the *Israel Lobby* contains some language to that effect, but in my judgment the overwhelming emphasis of the book is on the power of the Israeli government and the US lobby to induce the US government to go to war, even though it was not in the national interest to do so: for one example out of many, Mearsheimer and Walt wrote that the war "would almost certainly not have occurred" if not for the actions of the Israel lobby (Mearsheimer and Walt 2007: 230).

5 Mearsheimer and Walt concede that the neoconservatives also had broader concerns:

> even the neoconservative architects of the war did not advocate it solely to benefit Israel. Rather, they believed that removing Saddam from power would be good for both countries. For them what is good for Israel is good for the United States and vice-versa.
>
> (Mearsheimer and Walt 2009: 72)

6 For example, Colin Powell has said, in effect, that he supported the war only because he believed in the Iraqi WMD threat.

7 Jervis (2008–2009), for example, notes that Saddam did have links with terrorists other than al-Qaeda.

References

Jervis, R. (2008–2009) "War, Intelligence, and Honesty: A Review Essay," *Political Science Quarterly*, 123: 645–675.

Jervis, R. (2010) "The CIA & Iraq: How the White House Got Its Way – An Exchange," July 15. Accessed at www.nybooks.com/articles/archives/2010/jul/15/cia-iraqhow-white-house-got-its-way-exchange on October 15, 2010.

Leverett, F. and Leverett, H. (2010) "Who Will Be Blamed for a U.S. Attack on Iran?" Posted July 11. Accessed at www.raceforiran.com/who-will-be-blamed-for-a-u-s-attack-on-iran on October 15, 2010.

Mearsheimer, J. and Walt, S. (2007) *The Israel Lobby and U.S. Foreign Policy*, New York: Farrar, Straus and Giroux.

Mearsheimer, J. and Walt, S. (2009) "Is It Love or the Lobby? Explaining America's Special Relationship With Israel," *Security Studies*, 18: 58–78.

Slater, J. (2009) "The Two Books of Mearsheimer and Walt," *Security Studies*, 18: 4–57.

6   Neoconservatism and American hegemony

Michael Lind

The role of neoconservative policymakers and opinion leaders in promoting the Iraq War and shaping US foreign policy during the presidency of George W. Bush is a subject that continues to generate more heat than light. Some defenders of Bush administration policies claimed that the influence of neoconservatives was exaggerated—or even that there is no such thing as neoconservatism and never was. Many critics of the war attribute it solely or primarily to a desire to protect Israel on the part of Jewish conservatives or to create profits for the oil industry or the government contractor Halliburton.

As a former neoconservative who worked in the early 1990s as executive editor of *The National Interest,* the foreign policy quarterly edited by Owen Harries and published by Irving Kristol, the "godfather of neoconservatism," I was able to witness the evolution of the strategic thinking that led to the debacle in Iraq. Neoconservatism is a coherent political ideology, like libertarianism or communitarianism. Reductionist explanations of neoconservatism as camouflage for special interests, ranging from those of Americans committed to Israel or to US oil companies, fail to do justice to the movement as a worldview. The debacle in Iraq was the result of the failed global strategy of American hegemony—a strategy supported by neoconservatives as well as other groups in the US foreign policy establishment and electorate. To paraphrase Talleyrand, the Iraq War was worse than a crime—it was a mistake.

What is neoconservatism?

No myth about neoconservatism is more erroneous than the idea that Jewish conservatives like Paul Wolfowitz and Richard Perle are the only true neoconservatives and that their non-Jewish allies like Dick Cheney and Donald Rumsfeld must be assigned to a different category of "nationalists." When combined with the idea that the gentiles were mere figureheads for their Jewish staffers, this line of analysis resembles anti-Semitic conspiracy theorizing. As a non-Jewish former neoconservative, I can state with confidence that neoconservatism is an ideology, not an ethnicity.

In foreign as well as domestic policy, neoconservatism originated as "paleoliberalism"—an attempt to defend and maintain the tradition of Franklin Roosevelt, Harry Truman, John F. Kennedy and Lyndon Johnson at a time when the Democratic Party, the original home of most neoconservatives, was being reshaped by opponents of the Vietnam War and the Cold War of which it was part. The term "neoconservative," an insult applied by the social democrat Michael Harrington, was less apt than "paleoliberal."

Many first wave neocons were allied with the traditionally anticommunist AFL-CIO. The American labor movement had long campaigned against the repression of free trade unions like Lech Walesa's Solidarity by Marxist-Leninist dictatorships. Furthermore, many American trade unionists in the 1930s and 1940s had resisted efforts by American communists working for Moscow to infiltrate and take over American unions (one such anticommunist trade unionist was Ronald Reagan, who had headed the Screen Actors Guild and voted for Franklin Roosevelt four times). A number of early neoconservatives had been democratic socialist followers of Trotsky, Max Schachtmann and Norman Thomas. The disproportionate Jewish membership of the neoconservative movement reflected the historic affinity between American Jews and liberalism and leftism.

The origins of neoconservative ideology on the left are apparent. The fact that most of the younger neocons were never on the left is irrelevant; they are the intellectual (and, in the case of William Kristol and John Podhoretz, the literal) heirs of older ex-leftists. The idea that the United States and similar societies are dominated by a decadent, post-bourgeois "new class" was developed by thinkers in the Trotskyist tradition like James Burnham and Max Schachtmann who influenced an older generation of neocons. The concept of the "global democratic revolution" has its origins in the social-democratic Fourth International. The economic determinist idea that liberal democracy is an epiphenomenon of capitalism, promoted by neocons like Michael Novak, is simply Marxism with entrepreneurs substituted for proletarians.

The organization as well as the ideology of the neoconservative movement has Marxist origins. PNAC is modeled on the Committee on the Present Danger, which in turn was modeled on the Congress for Cultural Freedom (CCF), a CIA-funded network of the anticommunist center-left which sought to counter Stalin's international cultural front groups between the 1940s and the 1960s. Many of the older neocons are veterans of the CCF, including Irving Kristol, who with Stephen Spender co-edited *Encounter*, the CIA-bankrolled magazine of the movement. European social democratic models inspired the quintessential neocon institution, the National Endowment for Democracy (NED).

Along with other traditions that have emerged from the socialist left, neoconservatism has appealed to many Jewish intellectuals and activists, but it is not, for that reason, a Jewish, much less a Zionist, movement. Like other schools on the left, neoconservatism recruited from diverse "farm teams," including liberal Catholics (William Bennett and Michael Novak began on the Catholic left) and populists, socialists and New Deal liberals in the South and Southwest (the pool from which Jeane Kirkpatrick and I were drawn). There were, and are, very few Northeastern WASP mandarins in the neoconservative movement for the same reason that there were few on the older American left, which tended to mirror the New Deal coalition of ethnic and regional outsiders.

In the 1970s, these Truman-Kennedy-Johnson liberals, many of whom worked for Hubert Humphrey or Washington Senator Henry "Scoop" Jackson, found themselves under attack from the left and the right. To the left was the New Left or "McGovernite" wing of the Democratic Party, dominated by veterans of the anti-Vietnam War movement. Its activists wanted to unilaterally end the confrontation with the Soviet bloc, replace New Deal welfare capitalism with democratic socialism or social democracy, and replace the liberal ideal of racial integration with the radical approach of militant multiculturalism. To the right were the traditional economic conservatives who opposed the New Deal and the white working-class populists led by George Wallace who opposed the Civil Rights Revolution. These centrists, finding themselves a minority in the Democratic Party, worked for both Democratic and Republican presidents. Brzezinski and Huntington joined the Carter administration, while Daniel Patrick Moynihan worked for Nixon and his successor Gerald Ford.

During the 1980s, the early neoconservative movement splintered. One faction, including Jeane Kirkpatrick, Irving Kristol, William Bennett and others, joined the Reagan administration. Reagan himself was a sort of neocon—a former trade union leader who had voted four times for FDR, the president he most admired—and his movement rested on a broad coalition of Main Street Republicans, Wall Street libertarians, Moral Majority Protestants, working-class Catholic Reagan Democrats, New Right populists, and Cold War liberals. Over time, as the price of their acceptance by the Republican Party, most of these Reagan officials repudiated their earlier liberal positions on trade unions and the New Deal welfare state, although not on racial integration (they continued to defend the liberal integrationist position of the 1960s in civil rights, opposing both white racism and racial preferences for blacks and Latinos).

Neoconservative editors like Irving Kristol (*The Public Interest*) and Norman Podhoretz (*Commentary*) turned their formerly-centrist publications into mouthpieces for their new-found allies on the Religious Right, publishing writers who denounced Darwin's theory of evolution and global warming as liberal hoaxes. In response to this rightward shift, the sociologist Daniel Bell resigned his position as one of the editors of *The Public Interest*. Other neoconservatives remained in the Democratic Party. The most prominent of these was Daniel Patrick Moynihan. As a US Senator from New York in the Reagan years, he objected to the contempt for international law and the growing unilateralism of the Reagan administration.

As the original neoconservative movement dispersed during the Reagan years, one faction grew in importance. In 1974, Albert Wohlstetter, a theoretician of the arms race at the University of Chicago, accused the CIA of underestimating the Soviet threat. George Herbert Walker Bush, then Director of Central Intelligence, organized a group of outside experts called "Team B" to second-guess the CIA's conclusions. The roster of Team B overlapped considerably with the Committee on the Present Danger, a public pressure group organized by Paul Nitze to agitate for tougher policies in the Cold War.

The secret Team B report, issued in 1976 and declassified in 1992, claimed that the CIA had grossly underestimated Soviet military power. In fact, it became clear after the fall of the Soviet Union that the CIA in the 1970s had *overestimated* Soviet military power. The neocon estimates of Soviet strength, we now know, were ridiculous exaggerations. The leading neocons got it wrong. One exception was Moynihan, who in 1979 claimed that the USSR was weak and in danger of disintegrating.

In the 1990s, many Team B veterans organized the Project for the New American Century (PNAC) headed by Irving Kristol's son William, the editor of *The Weekly Standard*. The leading theorist of PNAC during the Clinton years and the major organizer of George W. Bush's bungled Iraq war, Deputy Secretary of Defense Paul Wolfowitz, was a student of Wohlstetter who had served on the original Team B commission. As Team B had exaggerated the threat from the Soviet Union in the late 1970s arguing it was on the verge of world conquest, PNAC likewise manipulated intelligence data to support preconceived conclusions—that the Soviet Union was on the verge of world conquest in the late 1970s, that China in the 1990s was a Nazi or Soviet-style "peer competitor," and that Iraq in the spring of 2003 threatened the United States and the West with a vast arsenal of weapons of mass destruction. Threat inflation by neoconservative defense experts, from the late Carter years to the present, has served conservative Republican politicians well, by allowing them falsely to portray not only Democrats but moderate Republicans as "appeasers" who are "weak on national defense."

Neocons, nationalists and realists

Many critics of neoconservatism during the 2000s distinguished neoconservatives in the Bush administration from a group called nationalist conservatives or sometimes Western conservatives, to which non-Jewish policymakers like Dick Cheney and Donald Rumsfeld were assigned. The assumption seems to have been that only Jews can be neoconservatives. An entertaining but flawed documentary entitled *Arguing the World* about Irving Kristol, Daniel Bell and Nathan Glazer spread the misleading impression that the typical neoconservative was a former Jewish leftist who had attended City University of New York (Dorman 1998).

In reality the neoconservative movement had always included non-Jewish thinkers and policymakers like Daniel Patrick Moynihan, James Q. Wilson and Jeane Kirkpatrick who helped to define it. In foreign policy, non-Jews like Donald Rumsfeld, James Woolsey, John R. Bolton and Dick Cheney were among the leading neoconservatives. James Woolsey, like Jeane Kirkpatrick a Protestant native of Oklahoma, worked for both Democratic and Republican administrations and started out in politics as a supporter of Eugene McCarthy. Today he is an outspoken supporter of efforts to address climate change. Dick and Lynne Cheney in particular had always been allied in Republican Party politics with Bill Bennett, another non-Jewish neoconservative, against the paleoconservatives associated with Patrick Buchanan. Like many neoconservatives, the Cheneys were hawkish on foreign policy but moderate or liberal on social issues like gay rights, even if they downplayed their views in order not to alienate Republican social conservatives. It is mistaken to create a fictitious category of "nationalist" conservatives to which non-Jewish neoconservatives are assigned.

The genuine ideological divisions over foreign policy on the Republican right during the Bush years were among three groups: neoconservatives (non-Jewish and Jewish), realists and isolationists. During the Bush years, Dick Cheney as Vice President was the most prominent neoconservative and Colin Powell as Secretary of State was the most important realist. Isolationists on the right, a group that includes both paleoconservatives and libertarians, had no influence.

Neoconservatives and realists drew different lessons from the debacle of Vietnam and the US experience in the 1970s and 1980s. Powell concluded that the lesson of Vietnam was that the United States should use military force only as a last resort and then with overwhelming firepower—the "Powell Doctrine." Powell and other realists, like Nixon and Kissinger, saw the United States as a status quo power that should engage in traditional great power strategies like concerts and balancing.

The same traumatic experiences of the 1970s led many eminent neoconservatives, some of them veterans of Team B, to completely different conclusions. They claimed that Nixon's and Kissinger's *Realpolitik* and détente policy had encouraged Soviet aggression. They believed that the Cold War was an ideological struggle rather than a pure Bismarckian power struggle and attributed the defeat of the Soviet Union in part to the appeal of liberal democratic ideals. They believed that post-Watergate restrictions of presidential power, and the Church Committee's exposure of CIA methods, had crippled the ability of the United States to respond to foreign threats.

It was this shared worldview, and not a desire to guarantee profits for Halliburton nor to make Israel secure as isolated motives, that shaped the neoconservative strategy of the Bush administration between 2001 and 2006, when the replacement of Donald Rumsfeld by Robert Gates marked a shift toward a realist policy. The fact that the mindset of the leading neoconservatives had been shaped during the Cold War between the Vietnam-Watergate period and the fall of the Berlin Wall cannot be over-emphasized. It explains their radical claims for presidential prerogatives and their rejection of realism. It explains their eagerness to adopt the claim of Eliot Cohen (2001) that the campaign against Islamist terrorism was "World War IV" (World War III having been the Cold War).

Most important, a naïve equation between communism and jihadism (and secular Ba'athism as well) explains many otherwise puzzling aspects of the invasion and occupation of Iraq. Many neoconservatives knew far more about the Soviet bloc and European totalitarianism than about the Middle East. Abram Shulsky of the Defense Department's Office of Special Plans, for example, had been editor of *Problems of Communism* during the Cold War. It is not clear whether the neoconservatives truly expected the downfall of Saddam to produce a toppling of authoritarian regimes throughout the Middle East, similar to the domino effect that led to the end of communism in Eastern Europe and Russia. However, it is clear that the disastrous policy of "de-Baathification" that turned low-level soldiers in Iraq into unemployed, desperate enemies of the new regime and the American occupiers was based on post-1945 "de-Nazification" in Germany and its equivalent in Japan. In this and other cases, errors driven by ideology, like misleading equations between Nazism, communism and Ba'athism, explain more than conspiracy theories that treat the neoconservatives as cunning puppet masters rather than incompetent bunglers.

Ideology, Israel and neoconservative grand strategy

The origins of neoconservatism in the anti-totalitarian liberalism and leftism of the mid-twentieth century remained clear from the frequent resort by the second wave neocons to the imagery of World War II and the early Cold War. American foreign policy was portrayed by neoconservatives as a crusade by "the democracies" against totalitarianism, identified with radical Islam or sometimes China. The neoconservative manifesto by Richard Perle and David Frum, *An End To Evil* (2003), refers to a possible threat from China in terms evoking World War II and the Cold War: "Eventual Korean unification will reinforce the power of the world's democracies against an aggressive and undemocratic China, should China so evolve." The UN "has traduced and betrayed" the dream of world peace. There are the Neville Chamberlain appeasers and the Decadent Europe theme: "To Americans, this looked like appeasement. But it would be a great mistake to attribute European appeasement to cowardice—or cowardice alone" (Perle and Frum 2003).

In the neocon ideology that guided the Bush administration, the United States was reliving the experience of Britain three-quarters of a century before. Osama bin Laden (or Saddam or Yasser Arafat, whom William Bennett called "the godfather of world terrorism," or the Chinese leadership) was the new Hitler. Bush was the new Churchill, as Reagan had been earlier. Moderate Republicans and conservative realists, as well as liberal Democrats, were the new Neville Chamberlains. The lower-class Protestant fundamentalists of the rural and suburban American South were equated with the bourgeois dissenting Protestants of Victorian England. The American university was the new Bloomsbury, full of decadent liberals and leftists sapping the morale of young Americans, who could need to be drafted to fight a series of wars abroad to promote democracy. Kagan and Kagan (2000) published a book called *While America Sleeps: Self Delusion, Military Weakness and the Threat to Peace Today*, which compared the United States to Britain in the late 1930s. For the neocons, the United States was the Britain of Churchill and Chamberlain, and it was always 1939.

The global strategy of the second wave neocons, then, was essentially non-ethnic and ideological, a crusade in the name of democracy inspired by mid-twentieth century anti-totalitarian liberalism and leftism. But their Middle East strategy of alignment with Israel's Likud Party, a party inspired by the Jewish fascism of Lev Jabotinsky, who admired (and was admired by) Mussolini, was incompatible with their stated liberal Enlightenment principles. So was their alliance with Likud's major constituency in the American electorate, the Protestant fundamentalist religious right, an alliance which has inspired neoconservative editors to open their pages to articles expressing the views on abortion, gay rights and "Darwinism" of the Southern Baptists and Assemblies of God.

In theory at least, neoconservative ideology, with its emphasis on the non-ethnic state based on universal Enlightenment principles, was more compatible with Israeli post-Zionism than with either the Labor Zionist or Revisionist Zionist forms of Jewish ethnic nationalism. The neoconservatives were always denouncing American "paleoconservatives" for claiming that American nationality must be founded on race (Caucasian) or religion (Christianity)—and yet they defended Israeli politicians and thinkers whose blood-soil-and-religion nationalism is even less liberal than the "Buchananism" the neocons denounce in the US context. In the pages of *The Weekly Standard*, David Brooks made the astonishing argument that the United States, a Lockean liberal democracy, must defend Israel, another Lockean liberal democracy, against "Palestinian organic nationalism" (Brooks 2001). The idea that Israeli identity has nothing to do with blood-and-soil nationalism might hearten post-Zionist proponents of Israel as "a state of all its citizens," but will come as a surprise to Labor Zionists as well as to the Likud and Shas parties.

Unlike David Brooks, Douglas Feith was honest about the ethnic nature of Israeli nationalism. In an essay entitled "Reflections on Liberalism,

Democracy and Zionism," Feith, who went on to become the third most powerful official in Bush's Pentagon, denounced "those Israelis" who "contend that Israel like America should not be an ethnic state—a Jewish state—but rather a 'state of its citizens.'" Feith argued "that there is a place in the world for non-ethnic nations and there is a place for ethnic nations" (quoted in Sniegoski 2008). Feith's theory, unlike that of Brooks, permits pro-Likud neocons to preach post-ethnic universalism for the United States and blood-and-soil nationalism for Israel. While solving one rhetorical problem, Feith creates others. He legitimates multiculturalism, which the neocons despise—how can one justify Israel-centered Jewish nationalism while denouncing Afrocentrism? Even worse, Feith's theory seems to endorse the false claim of anti-Semites that Jews are essentially foreigners in the nations in which they are born or reside. Indeed, according to the Jabotinskyite ideology shared by Sharon, Netanyahu and many (not all) of their neocon allies, there are only two kinds of Jews in the world: Israelis and potential Israelis. For generations many if not most Jewish Americans have rejected this illiberal conception.

There are Jewish as well as non-Jewish neoconservatives who are indifferent to Israel, and not all Jewish neoconservatives are Likud apologists. Indeed, it is possible to imagine a version of neoconservatism that would have been less partial to Israel and more supportive of Arab rights, including the right of self-determination. Their ethnic commitments, not their universalist neoconservative philosophy, explain the alliance between some Jewish neoconservatives and the far right in Israel and its American Protestant fundamentalist supporters. But it does not explain the Iraq War, which was part of the larger overall project of establishing US global hegemony after the Cold War—a project that was and still is supported by the mainstream US foreign policy establishment.

Why the US foreign policy establishment sided with the neocons

The question remains of why the idiosyncratic neoconservative faction in US foreign policy was more successful in shaping US foreign policy than other factions, like liberal internationalism, realism or neo-isolationism. The panic inspired by the 9/11 attacks was not, in itself, sufficient to justify the adoption of neoconservative strategy by the Bush administration, nor the widespread support of that strategy on the part of many Democrats and opinion leaders in the media. Realists in the tradition of Colin Powell would have retaliated against al-Qaeda, but they would not necessarily have invaded Iraq or declared that the United States was engaged in "World War IV."

The answer is that neoconservative strategy, for all its idiosyncrasies, fit into the post-Cold War US foreign policy consensus in favor of a US grand strategy of hegemony. While practically all neoconservatives of the 2000s supported American global hegemony, not all supporters of a hegemonic strategy were neoconservatives.

Neoconservative publicists sometimes blurred the distinction between hegemony and empire (Odom and Dujarric 2004; Bacevich 2004; Johnson 2004; Ferguson 2004). The neoconservative Robert Kagan (1998) described the United States as a "Benevolent Empire." "The United States needs an imperial strategy," Elliot Cohen, a leading neoconservative defense analyst, wrote in 1998. "Defense planners could never admit it openly, of course, and most would feel uncomfortable with the idea, but that is, in fact, what the United States at the end of the twentieth century is—a global empire" (Cohen 1998). Stephen Peter Rosen, another neoconservative thinker, wrote that the United States, "if it is to wield imperial power, must create and enforce the rules of a hierarchical inter-state empire" (Rosen 2002). Neoconservative civilian appointees in George W. Bush's Defense Department invited historians to private discussions of alleged lessons that the United States could learn from empires of the past (Thomas 2000; Kakutani 2003).

In 2001 in the neoconservative journal *The Weekly Standard*, the journalist Max Boot published an essay entitled "The Case for American Empire" in which he argued: "Afghanistan and other troubled lands today cry out for the sort of enlightened foreign administration once provided by self-confident Englishmen in jodhpurs and pith helmets" (Boot 2001). Boot also published a manifesto calling on the United States to engage in colonial wars around the world, borrowing his title *The Savage Wars of Peace* from Rudyard Kipling's poem "The White Man's Burden" praising US imperialism in the Philippines in 1898. Kipling called on Americans to join the British empire in conquering and ruling nonwhite peoples like the Filipinos against their will: "Take up the White Man's Burden—The savage wars of peace" in order to govern "your new-caught, sullen peoples,/Half-devil and half-child" (Boot 2002).

This kind of romanticism, however, was not typical of supporters of American hegemony. A more influential justification for converting America's temporary hegemony within its Cold War alliance system into indefinite US global hegemony after the Cold War was provided by the theory of the "security dilemma." The idea is simple. All sovereign states are naturally suspicious of each other. If any country builds up its military forces for defense, other countries will assume that it will use those forces for aggression, and feel compelled to build up their own militaries in response. The result inevitably will be a cycle of arms races that can spin out of control into all-out war.

The only possible way to prevent the security dilemma from producing arms races and wars, according to the hegemony school, is "hegemonic stability." One powerful state, the hegemon, should more or less monopolize military force and provide free security to other countries. In effect, the hegemonic power acts as a de facto government for a regional or global system of sovereign states. In civilized countries individuals do not feel the need to amass weapons in their homes out of fear of their neighbors, because they trust the government to protect them from crime. In the same way, states that trust a benevolent hegemon to protect their existence and interests can relax, reduce their armaments to a minimum and focus on civilian pursuits like trade.

In *The Case for Goliath: How America Acts as the World's Government in the 21st Century,* the political scientist Michael Mandelbaum invokes American hegemony as the solution to the security dilemma in Asia, Europe and the Middle East:

> Reassurance ensures against what *might* happen, and the need for it arises from the structure of the system of sovereign states. Because no superior power controls relations among them, an attack by one against another is always possible. Governments therefore tend to take steps to prepare to defend themselves. ... But military preparations that one country undertakes for purely defensive reasons can appear threatening to others, which may then take military measures of their own and so set in motion a spiral of mistrust and military buildups.
>
> (Mandelbaum 2005)

Fortunately, according to Mandelbaum, US hegemony eliminates this dilemma:

> The American military presence in Europe acts as a barrier against such an undesirable chain of events. It reassures the Western Europeans that they do not have to increase their armed forces to protect themselves against the possibility of a resurgent Russia. ... At the same time, the American presence reassures Russia that its great adversary of the first half of the twentieth century, Germany, will not adopt policies of the kind that led to two destructive German invasions in 1914 and 1941.
>
> (Mandelbaum 2005: 34–35; see also Jervis 1997; Mandelbaum 1995; Friedberg 1993–1994)

The alternative to US hegemony would be a far more dangerous world:

> At best, an American withdrawal would bring with it some of the political anxiety typical during the Cold War and a measure of the economic uncertainty that characterized the years before World War II. At worst, the retreat of American power could lead to a repetition of the great global economic failure and the bloody international conflicts the world experienced in the 1930s and 1940s.
>
> (Mandelbaum 2005: 224)

William Kristol and Robert Kagan made the same argument based on the security dilemma, advocating perpetual US global hegemony:

> The more Washington is able to make clear that it is futile to compete with American power, either in size of forces or in technological capabilities, the less chance there is that countries like China or Iran will entertain ambitions of upsetting the present world order. And that means the United States will be able to save money in the long run, for it is much cheaper to deter a war than to fight one.
>
> (Kristol and Kagan 1996)

Mackubin Thomas Owens of the Naval War College agrees: "The basis of [U.S.] primacy is hegemonic stability theory. According to the theory of hegemonic stability, a decline in relative US power could create a more disorderly, less peaceful world" (Owens 2006: 2).

The hegemony strategy requires that the United States engage in three policies: dissuasion, reassurance and coercive nonproliferation.

First, the United States will outspend all other great military powers combined, with the goal, in the words of the Pentagon's 1992 Defense Planning Guidance draft, of dissuading or "deterring potential competitors from even aspiring to a larger regional or global role" (*New York Times*, March 8, 1992). "Americans should be glad that their defense capabilities are as great as the next six powers combined," the neoconservative journalists William Kristol and Robert Kagan wrote in 1996.

> Indeed, they may even want to enshrine this disparity in U.S. defense strategy. Great Britain in the late 19th century maintained a "two-power" standard, insisting that at all times the British navy should be as large as the next two naval powers combined, whoever they might be. Perhaps the United States should inaugurate such a two- (or three-, or four-) power standard of its own, which would preserve its military supremacy regardless of the near-term global threats.

Kristol and Kagan argued that the United States should perpetually spend as much on defense (roughly 23 percent of GNP) as it did during the Cold War (Kristol and Kagan 1996).

Second, the United States must be willing to go to war, if necessary, to "reassure" its dependent allies in Asia, Europe and the Middle East by protecting them against purely local threats, whether or not the United States itself is threatened. To quote the 1992 Defense Planning Guidance again, "Second, in the non-defense areas, we must account sufficiently for the interests of the advanced industrial nations to discourage them from challenging our leadership or seeking to overturn the established political and economic order." The United States indefinitely should provide security for other great powers like Japan, China, Russia and Germany both in their own regions and in areas of concern to all of the great powers like the Persian Gulf: "[W]e must account sufficiently for the interests of the advanced industrial nations to discourage them from challenging our leadership" (*New York Times* article on Pentagon's Plan).

Finally, in order to achieve the first two goals, the United States must discourage the proliferation of advanced weapons to hostile countries, in order to maintain maximum freedom of action for the US military to coerce countries in American spheres of influence by threatening them or attacking them at minimal cost to the United States (for a more detailed discussion see Lind 2006).

The hegemony strategy and Iraq

Given the premises of the hegemony strategy, deposing Saddam Hussein in order to install a friendly government in Iraq served two of the purposes of the strategy—protecting the interests of other industrial nations as well as the United States in the security of oil supplies, and preventing the possible proliferation of weapons of mass destruction that could be used to deter US power projection. This explains why so many members of the American foreign policy establishment supported the Iraq War when the neoconservatives pushed for this war in the wake of 9/11. The establishment supported the logic of US hegemony, even though they did not share other elements of neoconservative ideology.

The hegemonic logic underlying the Iraq War should not be confused with the pretexts used by the Bush administration to rally public support, like false claims about Iraq's alleged weapons of mass destruction or alleged ties to al-Qaeda. On July 23, 2002, Richard Dearlove, the chief of British intelligence, briefed British Prime Minister Tony Blair after returning from a trip to Washington to meet with Bush administration officials. According to the minutes of that briefing, Dearlove told Blair: "Military action was now seen as inevitable. Bush wanted to remove Saddam, through military action, justified by the conjunction of terrorism and WMD. But the intelligence and the facts were being fixed around the policy" (Risen 2006). In May 2003, after US inspectors failed to find any weapons of mass destruction in Iraq, Deputy Secretary of Defense Paul Wolfowitz, one of the chief architects of the Iraq War as well as of the strategy of US global hegemony, admitted in an interview: "The truth is that for reasons that have a lot to do with the U.S. government bureaucracy we settled on the one issue that everyone could agree on which was weapons of mass destruction as the core reason" for the war. After it was proven that Saddam had no ties with al-Qaeda as well as no weapons of mass destruction, the Bush administration hastily changed its justification for the war, alleging that its main purpose all along had been to bring democracy to Iraq and the Arab world in general. Wolfowitz, however, admitted that bringing democracy to Iraq "is a reason to help the Iraqis but it's not a reason to put American kids' lives at risk, certainly not on the scale we did it" (Tanenhaus 2003).

Instead of weapons of mass destruction or spreading democracy, as we have seen, the most important strategic rationale for the US invasion of Iraq was the hegemonic strategy divulged in a document drawn up for Wolfowitz called "Rebuilding America's Defences: Strategies, Forces and Resources for a New Century." This policy document, published in September 2000 by the Project for the New American Century, the neoconservative think tank affiliated with Wolfowitz, Rumsfeld, Cheney and other high-ranking members of the Bush administration, reads:

> The United States has for decades sought to play a more permanent role in Gulf regional security. While the unresolved conflict with Iraq provides the immediate justification, the need for a substantial American force presence in the Gulf transcends the issue of the regime of Saddam Hussein.
>
> (Mackay 2002)

The Iraq War is now widely considered to have been a mistake, but the hegemony strategy continues to form the bipartisan basis for US foreign policy. Because neoconservative grand strategy is only one version of the hegemony strategy, the discrediting of neoconservatism does not discredit other variants of the strategy.

The hegemony strategy needs to be criticized on its merits. The security dilemma theory that justifies US hegemony strategy assumes that the nature of a country's government is irrelevant to its foreign policy—in apparent contradiction to the neoconservative belief in an "alliance of democracies." It is not necessary to endorse the theory that democracies will never go to war with each other in order to reject the idea that Britain, France, Germany and Russia, in the absence of US hegemony in Europe, would inevitably become enemies. Germany is not ruled by Junkers or Nazis craving *Lebensraum* (living space) in the East, Russia is not ruled by communists trying to overthrow capitalism, and British policies toward Europe are no longer driven by fears of a continental threat to British colonies overseas.

If the theory of an inevitable security dilemma among great powers is mistaken, then the major argument for US hegemony in terms of American national security collapses. This is because the cost-benefit analysis of US hegemony depends on whether the security dilemma exists or not. If the alternative to perpetual US military hegemony in Europe or Asia is a local arms race that might spiral out of control into World War III, then the costs of US hegemony in those regions, including the costs of occasional small reassurance wars by the United States as local policeman, are relatively minor by comparison to the benefits. But if the alternative to perpetual US hegemony in Europe and Asia is likely to be peace among the local great powers, if only a tense and armed peace, rather than new rounds of Sino-Japanese or Russo-German war, then American taxpayers need to ask their elected leaders why it is necessary to continue to encircle China and Russia, to continue to treat Japan and Germany as US protectorates, and to continue unilaterally to threaten or wage war against lesser states hostile to US hegemony in Asia, Europe and the Middle East like North Korea, Saddam's Iraq and Iran.

While neoconservatism as Cold War liberalism ended with the Cold War, the second wave of neoconservatism enjoyed suprising influence in the 1990s and 2000s. But neoconservatism in the United States is unlikely to enjoy a third act. A public that has turned against the wars in Iraq and Afghanistan is unlikely to support further adventures, and in the new politics of budgetary austerity promoted by the right as a result of the Great Recession, defense spending is certain to be reduced. But while the neoconservatives are in decline, a strategy of US global hegemony remains the consensus among American foreign policy elites of both parties. Neoconservatism may be discredited, but the case against American hegemony has yet to succeed.

Note

This chapter draws on material I have previously published (Lind 2003, 2004, 2006).

References

Bacevich, A. (2004) *American Empire: The Realities and Consequences of U.S. Diplomacy,* Cambridge, MA: Harvard University Press.

Boot, M. (2001) "The Case for American Empire," *The Weekly Standard,* October 15.

Boot, M. (2002) *The Savage Wars of Peace: Small Wars and the Rise of American Power,* New York: Basic Books.

Brooks, D. (2001) "The Death of Compromise: There's No More Middle in the Middle East," *The Weekly Standard,* July 2–9, p. 18.

Cohen, E. (1998) "Calling Mr. X," *New Republic,* January 19, pp. 17–19.

Cohen, E. (2001) "World War IV," *Wall Street Journal,* March 20.

Dorman, R. (1998) *Arguing the World,* First Run Features.

Ferguson, N. (2004) *Colossus: The Price of America's Empire,* New York: Penguin.

Friedberg, A. L. (1993–1994) "Ripe for Rivalry: Prospects for Peace in a Multipolar Asia," *International Security,* 18.

Jervis, R. (1997) *System Effects: Complexity in Political and Social Life,* Princeton: Princeton University Press.

Johnson, C. (2004) *The Sorrows of Empire: Militarism, Secrecy, and the End of the Republic,* New York: Metropolitan Books.

Kagan, D. and Kagan, F. W. (2000) *While America Sleeps: Self-Delusion, Military Weakness, and the Threat to Peace,* New York: St. Martin's Press.

Kagan, R. (1998) "The Benevolent Empire," *Foreign Policy,* 111.

Kakutani, M. (2003) "How Books Have Shaped U.S. Policy," *New York Times*, April 5, p. D7.

Kristol, W. and Kagan, R. (1996) "Towards a Neo-Reaganite Foreign Policy," *Foreign Affairs*, 75.

Lind, M. (2003) "The Weird Men Behind George W. Bush's War," *The New Statesmen*, April 7.

Lind, M. (2004) "A Tragedy of Errors," *The Nation*, February 23.

Lind, M. (2006) *The American Way of Strategy*, London: Oxford University Press.

Mackay, N. (2002) "Bush Planned Iraq 'Regime Change" Before Becoming President," *Sunday Herald*, September 15.

Mandelbaum, M. (1995) "Preserving the New Peace," *Foreign Affairs*, 74.

Mandelbaum, M. (2005) *The Case for Goliath: How America Acts as the World's Government in the 21st Century*, New York: PublicAffairs.

Odom, W. E. and Dujarric, R. (2004) *America's Inadvertent Empire*, New Haven: Yale University Press.

Owens, M. T. (2006) "A Balanced Force Structure to Achieve a Liberal World Order," January 20. Foreign Policy Research Institute, www.fpri.org/enotes/20060120.military.owens.balancedforcestructure.html.

Perle, R. and Frum, D. (2003) *An End to Evil*, New York: Random House.

Risen, J. (2006) *State of War: The Secret History of the CIA and the Bush Administration*, New York: The Free Press.

Rosen, S. P. (2002) "An Empire If You Can Keep It," *The National Interest*, Spring.

Sniegoski, S. J. (2008) *The Transparent Cabal: The Neoconservative Agenda, War in the Middle East, and the National Interest of Israel*, Norfolk, VA: Ihs Press.

Tanenhaus, S. (2003) "Interview with Paul Wolfowitz," *Vanity Fair*.

Thomas, E. (2000) "The 12 Year Itch," *Newsweek*, March 31, p. 54.

7 Blood for oil, in Iraq and elsewhere

Michael T. Klare

In the months leading up to the invasion of Iraq, Bush administration officials were adamant in their insistence that oil played no role in the US planning for a possible military assault. "The only interest the United States has in the [Persian Gulf] region is furthering the cause of peace and stability, not [Iraq's] ability to generate oil," presidential spokesperson Ari Fleischer famously declared on October 30, 2002 (Fleischer 2002). When Fleischer first uttered these words, the "cause of peace and stability" was said to reside in the elimination of Saddam Hussein's weapons of mass destruction (WMD). But when no WMD were found in Iraq, it was said to lie in the elimination of Hussein himself and the establishment of a democratic regime. Later, when democracy failed to flourish, it was said to entail the stabilization of Iraq and the defeat of "Islamo-fascism." As all of these endeavors have come up empty-handed, suspicion as to the Bush administration's actual motive for invading Iraq has inevitably circled back to what was widely assumed to be the original impulse: oil.

Certainly anyone who was paying attention to the administration's planning for the invasion would have seen ample evidence of Washington's interest in securing control over Iraq's prolific oil reservoirs (for a summary see Klare 2004: 98–101). There was, for example, the Working Group on Oil and Energy, a cadre of pro-American expatriate Iraqi oil managers assembled by the US Department of State in late 2002 to establish the guidelines for the privatization of the Iraqi oil industry once Hussein was removed and a new regime put in place in Baghdad (Cummins 2003; Veith 2003). Equally revealing was the creation of a special military task force whose primary mission was to seize control of Iraqi oil fields at the very onset of the invasion. "Without going into great detail," a senior Pentagon official explained on January 24, 2003, "it's fair to say that our land component commander and his planning staff have crafted strategies that will allow us to secure and protect these fields as rapidly as possible" (DoD 2003). And if that wasn't enough, the very first military action of the invasion itself was an armed raid on Iraq's offshore oil facilities. "Swooping silently out of the Persian Gulf night," an overly excited reporter for the *New York Times* wrote on March 22, 2003, "Navy

Seals seized two Iraqi oil terminals in bold raids that ended early this morning, overwhelming lightly armed Iraqi guards and claiming a bloodless victory in the battle for Iraq's vast oil empire" (Dao 2003).

In considering these phenomena, it is easy to reach the conclusion that the Bush administration's primary motive was to gain control over the Iraqi oil industry and to parcel it out to American energy firms. Lending credibility to this view is the fact that Iraq possesses the world's second-largest reserves of conventional petroleum – an estimated 115 billion barrels, or 9.5 percent of the known global supply – and is believed to sit atop large reservoirs of as-yet unexplored oil, possibly boosting its net holdings by as much as 100 percent (BP 2007; US Department of Energy, Energy Information Administration 2006). There is also ample evidence that officials of top US oil companies met with Ahmed Chalabi and other US-backed Iraqi expatriates in the months leading up to the American invasion to discuss their participation in Iraq's oil sector once Saddam Hussein was removed and the industry had been privatized in accordance with Washington's wishes (Morgan and Ottaway 2002). But while there is no question that American oil giants like Exxon Mobil and Chevron would like to operate in Iraq if given the chance, gaining access to Iraqi reserves was only a part of Washington's motive for invading Iraq; far more significant is the *geopolitical* objective of maintaining control over the entire Persian Gulf region – the source of three-fifths of the world's oil supply (Klare 2004: Ch. 4 introduces this argument).

Bordering the Persian Gulf are a handful of oil producers that together possess an estimated 749 billion barrels of oil, or 56 percent of the world's proven reserves as of the end of 2009 (BP 2010). These include Saudi Arabia, the world's number one producer, along with Iran, Iraq, Kuwait, Oman, Qatar, and the United Arab Emirates (UAE). These suppliers are important not only because they house such a large percentage of the world's known reserves, but also because they possess a greater capacity than most other producers to boost production in the years ahead to meet rising world supply. Because oil fields in the global North – the United States, Canada, Europe, the former Soviet Union – were developed earlier in the Petroleum Age, they have largely reached their peak levels of production and are now in decline; the fields of the global South, however, were largely developed later and so are still capable of producing more oil before they, too, will peak and decline. And of all the fields in the world, none are more likely to produce more in the years ahead than those in Saudi Arabia and neighboring Gulf states – making them even more important to the world economy in the future than they have been in the past (US Department of Energy, Energy Information Administration 2007; Deffeyes 2001).

No top American official understood all this better than Vice President Dick Cheney – arguably the principal architect of the 2003 US invasion of Iraq. Cheney first revealed his grasp of Persian Gulf geopolitics on September

11, 1990, when, as Secretary of Defense in the first Bush administration, he testified before the Senate Armed Services Committee on the justification for US intervention in the first Gulf War:

> We obviously have a significant interest because of the energy that is at stake in the Gulf. Iraq controlled 10 percent of the world's reserves prior to the invasion of Kuwait. Once Saddam Hussein took Kuwait, he doubled that to approximately 20 percent of the world's known oil reserves. Of course, within a couple of hundred miles of the border of Kuwait, in the Eastern Province of Saudi Arabia, reside another 24 or 25 percent of the world's known reserves. So, we found ourselves in a situation where suddenly, as a result of his invasion of Kuwait on August 2, he was indeed in control of the Persian Gulf's key reserves without ever having actually taken any more territory than Kuwait itself. Once he acquired Kuwait and deployed an army as large as the one he possesses, he was clearly in a position to be able to dictate the future of worldwide energy policy, and that gave him a stranglehold on our economy.
>
> (US Congress, Senate, Committee on Armed Services 1990: 10–11)

Under these circumstances, he explained, the President saw no option but to deploy US troops in the area to deter an Iraqi invasion of Saudi Arabia and thereby prevent Hussein from gaining such a "stranglehold." Revealingly, Cheney used very similar language to justify the US invasion of Iraq twelve years later. In his most important speech on the war, delivered to the Veterans of Foreign Wars on August 25, 2002, he returned to the themes he first aired in 1990:

> Armed with an arsenal of [WMD] and a seat atop 10 percent of the world's oil reserves, Saddam Hussein could then be expected to seek domination of the entire Middle East, take control of a great portion of the world's energy supplies [and] directly threaten America's friends throughout the region.
>
> (Cheney 2002; see also Harding 2003)

Again, claimed Cheney, the logic was inescapable: the United States must take military action to prevent such a catastrophe.

Seen from this perspective, the 2003 American invasion of Iraq was fully consistent with long-term US policy. Ever since the Carter administration of 1977–1981, it has been explicit US policy to employ military force as needed to prevent any hostile power from achieving a position from which it could threaten the safe flow of Persian Gulf oil to the United States and its allies. As explained by Cheney, the United States will never allow another power – other than itself – to "dominate" the Gulf or to gain a "stranglehold" over its economy. This dictum – widely known as the

"Carter Doctrine" – was first applied to the Soviet Union (following the 1979 Soviet invasion of Afghanistan) and has since been applied to any nation that appeared to pose a threat to the flow of Persian Gulf oil. Both the Gulf War of 1990–1991 and the 2003 invasion of Iraq must be seen in this context.

The origins of the Carter Doctrine

The origins of the Carter Doctrine can be traced back to February 1945, when the United States first established a protectorate over Saudi Arabia and committed itself to the use of military force to protect Persian Gulf oil. This move was triggered by Washington's concern over the nation's declining oil output and a desire to ensure the safety of its overseas supplies. Until that point, the United States had been largely self-sufficient in petroleum production and, in most years, produced a surplus allowing exports to foreign consumers as well. But the requirements of wartime consumption plus intimations of an eventual decline in US output led President Franklin D. Roosevelt to seek control over foreign sources of petroleum. By 1943, he had concluded that Saudi Arabia was likely to assume the role of principal foreign supplier to the United States after World War II, and, by 1945, had determined that the United States must extend some sort of protective umbrella over Saudi Arabia's prolific oil fields. With this in mind, he arranged to meet with King Abdul Aziz ibn Saud, the founder of the modern Saudi dynasty, aboard the USS *Quincy* following the February 1945 Allied leadership conference in Yalta (Painter 1986; Stoff 1980).

President Roosevelt met with King Abdul Aziz for five and a half hours on February 14, 1945, discussing a wide range of issues of concern to both leaders. No record was kept of this meeting, but most scholars have concluded that Roosevelt and Abdul Aziz agreed to establish a tacit alliance, whereby the United States would assume permanent responsibility for protecting the House of Saud against its foreign and domestic enemies in return for exclusive US access to Saudi oil. In line with this arrangement, the United States undertook a variety of measures aimed at providing a defensive shield around Saudi Arabia and its oil fields. These included the establishment of a permanent US military base at Dhahran (beginning in 1946), the supply of advanced US arms to Saudi forces, and the deployment of hundreds (later thousands) of American military instructors and advisers in the kingdom (Miller 1980: 128–131; Long *et al.* 1985).

Despite this buildup, the United States initially relied on Great Britain – for many decades the dominant power in the region – to maintain security in the region. However, when London announced that it could no longer perform this role and that it would remove its forces from the Gulf by the end of 1971, Washington chose to confer responsibility for regional stability on the Shah of Iran, then its principal ally in the area. This approach – known in Washington as the "surrogate strategy" – prevailed until January 1979, when the Shah was overthrown and replaced by radical Islamic clerics loyal to the Ayatollah Khomeini. This traumatic event coincided with the Soviet invasion of Afghanistan, placing Soviet troops a mere 300 miles from the vital Strait of Hormuz – the narrow waterway connecting the Persian Gulf to the Indian Ocean and oil ports around the world. The Carter Doctrine, entailing direct US responsibility for Persian Gulf security, was largely adopted in response to these unexpected developments.

When first enunciated in President Carter's State of the Union address of January 23, 1980, the doctrine was aimed specifically at the oil resources of the greater Gulf region. This area, Carter declared, "contains more than two-thirds of the world's exportable oil," and so must not be allowed to fall under the dominion of a hostile power.

> Let our position be absolutely clear: an attempt by any outside force to gain control of the Persian Gulf region will be regarded as an assault on the vital interests of the United States of America, and such an assault will be repelled by any means necessary, including military force.
>
> (Carter 1980; see also Palmer 1992: 103–111)

Because the United States did not at that time possess any forces specifically earmarked for operations in the Gulf area, Carter also announced the establishment of a new combat contingent for this purpose, the Rapid Deployment Joint Task Force (RDJTF).

The Carter Doctrine after Carter

Although critical of President Carter on many issues, President Ronald Reagan wholeheartedly endorsed the Carter Doctrine and lent it fresh impetus. On January 1, 1983, he elevated the RDJTF to a full-scale regional headquarters, the US Central Command (CENTCOM), and charged it with the task of protecting the flow of oil from the Persian Gulf to markets in the West – a task which it retains today (Priest 2003). Reagan also demonstrated his adherence to the Carter Doctrine by actually putting it into practice. When, at the height of the Iran–Iraq War of 1980–1988, Iranian forces began to attack Kuwaiti oil tankers traveling through the Persian Gulf (presumably to discourage Kuwait from providing loans to Iraq for arms procurement), Reagan authorized the "reflagging" of Kuwaiti tankers with the American ensign and their protection by US naval forces. Such action was essential, Reagan declared, to demonstrate the "U.S. commitment to the flow of oil through the Gulf" (Palmer 1992: 123, 128–149).

The Iran–Iraq War drew to a close in August 1988, with the exhausted and impoverished belligerents agreeing to a ceasefire and peace talks. But peace in the Gulf reigned only briefly. Disappointed with the outcome of the war and facing a mountain of accumulated wartime debt, Saddam Hussein viewed Kuwait – which was refusing to forgive the debt Baghdad had built up during the war to pay for arms – as the major source of his problems and a potential source of income. After issuing a series of increasingly threatening (and unheeded) ultimatums to Kuwait, Hussein ordered Iraqi forces to invade and occupy the country on August 2, 1990. Although American officials had viewed Saddam Hussein in a generally friendly light up until this point, the White House instantly concluded that the Iraqi invasion of Kuwait posed an indisputable threat to US strategic interests in the Gulf, as encapsulated in the Carter Doctrine. At a meeting at Camp David on August 3, President George H. W. Bush ordered the Department of Defense to begin making plans for military action to defend the Saudi fields, and three days later authorized Defense Secretary Cheney to begin deploying American troops in the kingdom (Woodward 1991: 224–273). It was this move that Cheney was called on to justify in his September 11, 1990 testimony before the Senate Armed Services Committee.

Oil, and the fate of Saudi Arabia, stood at the center of White House deliberations in the early days of the crisis. In a nationally televised address on August 8, 1990, announcing his decision to use military force in the Gulf, Bush Senior cited US energy needs as his primary impetus. "Our country now imports nearly half the oil it consumes and could face a major threat to its economic independence," and so "the sovereign independence of Saudi Arabia is of vital interest to the United States" (Bush 1990). Only later, when American troops were girding for combat with the Iraqis, did administration officials articulate other justifications for war – the need to liberate Kuwait, to destroy Iraqi WMD, and so forth. As Cheney's testimony before the Armed Services Committee makes clear, however, the President and his senior associates initially viewed the invasion of Kuwait through the lens of the Carter Doctrine: as a threat to Saudi Arabia and the free flow of oil from the Gulf (Woodward 1991: 225–226, 230, 236–237).

Despite the terrible drubbing Iraqi forces received during the 1991 Gulf War, Hussein's armies were still seen afterwards as posing a significant threat to US strategic interests in the Persian Gulf. President Bush Senior and his successor, Bill Clinton, sought to mitigate this threat through a draconian system of economic sanctions, but these efforts were widely seen as having failed in their intended purpose. The fact that Saddam Hussein was also thought by many in Washington to be persisting in his efforts to acquire WMD only added to the impression of a substantial Iraqi threat. Ultimately, President George W. Bush concluded that the only way to eliminate this threat and thereby protect vital US interests in accordance with the precepts of the Carter Doctrine was to invade Iraq and destroy the Hussein regime once and for all (Hersh 2001: 58–63; Woodward 2004).

This history provides critical context for the debate over whether the 2003 Iraq War was prompted by the pursuit of oil. While the administration can claim that it was primarily motivated by concern over the military threat posed by Iraq and not by a desire to seize Iraq's oil, the threat that Hussein was said to pose was, in fact, directed at the United States' continued control of the Persian Gulf area – control which, since Carter's time, has been viewed as essential to the uninterrupted flow of Persian Gulf oil. From a geopolitical perspective, then, oil was at the heart of the administration's outlook, as acknowledged by Vice President Cheney in his address to Veterans of Foreign Wars on August 25, 2002.

The globalization of the Carter Doctrine

Despite all the anguish over the war in Iraq, despite all the blood that has been spilt in that devastated country, the Carter Doctrine remains alive and well – and has now been successfully extended to other areas of the world. Indeed, even though US combat troops have officially been withdrawn from Iraq, CENTCOM continues to maintain a significant military presence in the greater Gulf area and stands ready, when called upon to do so, to employ military force to overcome threats to the free flow of Persian Gulf oil.

With Iraq currently subdued by US military occupation, the next most potent threat to American domination is said to emanate from Tehran. At present, the greatest danger posed by Iran is said to be its pursuit of nuclear weapons, but US strategists are also concerned over the conventional Iranian military threat to the Strait of Hormuz – the narrow passageway connecting the Persian Gulf with the Indian Ocean and the world at large (Katzman 2006). To ensure that Iran will not try to close the strait by firing on tankers crossing through it, CENTCOM ships and planes patrol the waterway daily and remain poised for an immediate clash with Iranian forces. Late in the Bush administration, the country's chief geopolitician, Dick Cheney, took the lead in signaling continued US resolve: in a speech delivered aboard the aircraft carrier USS *John C. Stennis* while deployed in the Persian Gulf (along with another US carrier, the *Nimitz*) just 150 miles off the coast of Iran, Cheney warned that the United States was fully prepared to use force to protect the flow of oil. "With two carrier strike groups in the Gulf, we're sending clear messages to friends and adversaries alike," he declared. "We'll keep the sea lanes open. We'll stand by our friends in opposing extremism and strategic threats" (Sanger 2007). The Obama administration may have changed the tone slightly, but the policy of protecting the Persian Gulf oil flow remains the same.

But this ongoing Gulf policy is only part of the story. First during the Clinton administration and with greater alacrity during the Bush Junior administration, the policy of using military force to protect vital sources of petroleum was steadily extended to other oil-producing regions of the world, and now covers much of the planet. This effort – best described as the globalization of the Carter Doctrine – reflected both a growing US concern over the safety of oil supplies from the Gulf and a desire to "diversify" US sources of crude petroleum (Klare 2004: 132–145 advances this argument).

The globalization of the Carter Doctrine began in earnest in the late 1990s, when President Clinton determined that the Caspian Sea basin – until 1992 largely under the control of the Soviet Union – should become a major source of oil for the United States and its allies, thereby helping to lessen US dependence on the ever-turbulent Gulf area. The newly-independent states of Azerbaijan and Kazakhstan were eager to sell their petroleum wealth to the West, but they lacked an autonomous conduit for exports (at that time, all existing pipelines from the land-locked Caspian passed through Russia) and also faced serious challenges from ethnic minorities and internal opposition movements. To safeguard the future flow of Caspian Sea oil to the West, Clinton agreed to assist in the construction of a new oil pipeline from Azerbaijan to Turkey via Georgia (thus bypassing Russia) and to help these states enhance their military capacity (the Clinton-backed oil conduit, known as the Baku-Tbilisi-Ceyhan or BTC pipeline, went on line in 2006).

While modest in comparison to the military aid provided to Saudi Arabia and other Gulf producers, American assistance to the Caspian Sea states has resulted in the establishment of close ties with military forces in the region. Typically, US aid to these states has been justified in terms of sustaining the fight against terrorism. A close reading of State and Defense Department documents suggests, however, that the protection of oil remains a paramount concern. In requesting $51.2 million in assistance to Azerbaijan for fiscal year 2005, for example, the State Department affirmed that "U.S. national interests in Azerbaijan center on the strong bilateral security and counter-terrorism cooperation [and] the advancement of U.S. energy security" (DoS 2005). At the same time, in Kazakhstan, the United States was helping to refurbish the old Soviet air base at Atyrau, near the giant offshore Kashagan oil field (which is partly owned by ExxonMobil, ConocoPhillips, and Royal Dutch/Shell). This base was to be used to house a Kazakh "rapid reaction brigade" whose task, according to the Department of State, was to "enhance Kazakhstan's capability to respond to major terrorist threats to oil platforms or borders" (Nichol 2002: 3).

To help protect the BTC pipeline, a significant source of oil for the West which passes near several areas of instability (including Chechnya, South Ossetia, and Abkhazia), the United States provided the Republic of Georgia with substantial military aid and deployed a contingent of combat instructors in the country to help train the Georgian troops responsible for pipeline security. Such assistance is intended "to underscore America's very strong support for stability and security and the territorial integrity here in Georgia," then Secretary of Defense Donald Rumsfeld declared during a December 2003 visit to the country (DoD 2003a). This relationship is "strategically important" to the United States, a high Pentagon official accompanying Rumsfeld told reporters, both in terms of the war on terror and "in terms of energy," because of the presence of the BTC pipeline (DoD 2003b).

A similar pattern of ever-expanding US military involvement was also evident at the time of the Iraq invasion and occupation in the Andean region of South America, another key oil-producing region that has been plagued by internal disorder and conflict. The violent situation in Colombia was a source of particular concern for American officials. Colombia was once a leading oil supplier to the United States and has the potential to provide larger volumes in the future; however, the civil war that had gripped the country over the past few decades had discouraged exploration in new areas and lowered its oil output. Contending that the violence in Colombia had produced an atmosphere of lawlessness in which the illegal drug trade could flourish, the United States had long provided arms and assistance to that country's army and police forces. In 2002, however, the Bush administration announced another key objective for US military assistance: to help the Colombian government protect its vulnerable oil pipelines.

Colombia's extensive pipeline network had often been attacked by anti-government guerrillas, reducing Colombia's net petroleum exports and depriving the government of a critical source of income. To counter this danger, the White House requested $98 million in fiscal year 2003 to bolster security along the Caño Limón-Coveñas pipeline, a 480-mile conduit carrying oil from Occidental Petroleum's fields in the northeast to Coveñas on the Caribbean coast. These funds – plus another $147 million requested in fiscal year 2004 – were used to train and equip elite battalions of the Colombian army to guard the Caño Limón-Coveñas pipeline and to fight rebel forces operating in the vicinity (DoS 2004; Forero 2002). By intervening in this manner, Washington hoped to make the region safer for oil exploration and thus increase Colombia's future exports to this country.

American military involvement in sub-Saharan Africa was at a less advanced stage at this time, but here, too, concern over oil supplies spurred a major increase in US assistance. The growing importance of Africa in satisfying America's energy needs was first highlighted in the Bush administration's National Energy Policy of May 2001:

> Sub-Saharan Africa holds 7 percent of world oil reserves and comprises 11 percent of world oil production. Along with Latin America, West Africa is expected to be one of the fastest growing sources of oil and gas for the American market.
>
> (National Energy Policy Development Group 2001: Ch. 8)

This gave Africa a strategic dimension it did not possess before. "African oil is of national strategic interest to us," Assistant Secretary of State Walter Kansteiner observed in 2002, "and it will increase and become more important as we go forward" (Crawley 2002).

Having been designated as a "national strategic interest" of the United States, African oil was then exposed to the same sort of military initiatives that had been pursued in other oil-producing regions in accordance with the Carter Doctrine. As in the other oil areas, the opening wedge of US involvement in Africa was military assistance and training – an approach that facilitates the establishment of close ties with the region's (often dominant) military elites. Military aid to the African oil producers was supplied both in the form of bilateral assistance to individual nations as well as through multilateral security initiatives. Angola and Nigeria were the principal recipients of bilateral aid at this time, jointly receiving approximately $180 million in Fiscal Years 2004–2006. This included transfers of arms and military equipment via the Foreign Military Sales (FMS) and Foreign Military Sales Financing (FMF) programs, along with specialized training given to Angolan and Nigerian military personnel under the International Military Education and Training (IMET) program. Other West African recipients of IMET assistance have included Chad, Congo-Brazzaville, Equatorial Guinea, and Gabon (US DoS 2006: 191–198, 287–289, 443, 587–590; Klare and Volman 2006).

But just as US aid to the Caspian states was followed by the insertion of a permanent American military presence in the region, the Department of Defense expanded its footprint in Africa as it searched for permanent bases there, ultimately creating a new Pentagon command there, AFRICOM, in February 2007. Another highly visible expression of growing US military involvement at the time was an increased Navy presence along Africa's west coast, the location of its most promising offshore oil fields (Cobb 2003). Recognizing, moreover, that American combat troops might at some point be deployed on the ground in West Africa, the Department of Defense was recorded as looking for potential basing locations in and around the major oil zones. According to media reports, the Pentagon was seeking "bare-bones facilities" – essentially, airstrips with modest logistical capabilities – in Ghana, Kenya, Mali, Senegal, and Uganda (Jaffe 2003; Schmitt 2003). While military officials tend to emphasize the threat of failed states, humanitarian disaster, and terrorism when discussing the need for such facilities, they have told reporters from the *Wall Street Journal* that "a key mission for U.S. forces [in Africa] would be to ensure that Nigeria's oil fields, which in the future could account for as much as 25 percent of U.S. oil imports, are secure" (Jaffe 2003).

In Africa, then, as in the Gulf area, the Caspian basin, and Latin America, the US Department of Defense was systematically enhancing its capacity to engage in direct military operations to protect the flow of oil at the same time as the Iraq invasion and occupation, and since. Typically, these developments have been reported piecemeal, as a series of unconnected events, or, at best, as part of a generalized expansion of American military capabilities. But the information provided above suggests something far more intentional and specific – a determined US effort to insert military power into the world's major oil-producing areas and to prepare for future conflict and wars over energy. It would appear, moreover, that the best way to characterize this process is as the steady expansion of the Carter Doctrine's purview from the Persian Gulf to the rest of the oil-producing world.

From this perspective, the 2003 invasion of Iraq should be viewed as not the first – and certainly not the last – of a long series of wars and military interventions over the control of foreign oil. These wars, if allowed to happen, are certain to claim an increasing toll in human life and will definitely impose a severe and growing strain on the US treasury. For members of the American Armed Forces, moreover, these commitments will demand years of dangerous and ignoble work as protectors of pipelines and refineries. From a moral perspective, then, it is time to say: "no more blood for oil!" Surely, there is no justification for sacrificing the life of a single human being – whether American, Iraqi, Colombian, or of some other nationality – so that we might fill the tanks of obscenely fuel-inefficient vehicles with another tank of imported petroleum.

The futility of using military force to protect the flow of oil

But some might still inquire: moral scruples aside, can military force play a useful role in protecting the global flow of oil? The answer, revealed across time, and most recently and painfully learned in Iraq, is no. In attempting to demonstrate this, I advance three main lines of argument: first, that the conspicuous deployment of American forces to protect overseas oil installations arouses more animosity than it quells; second, that military force is a costly and largely ineffective tool for protecting oil installations; and third, that the very reliance placed on military action to protect oil distracts us from the necessary task of undertaking the necessary transition to a post-petroleum energy system (Klare 2007 first outlined this argument).

The US experience in Saudi Arabia offers perhaps the best cautionary tale about the dangers arising from the conspicuous deployment of US military forces in oil-producing regions abroad. When the United States first sought to station troops in that country at the end of World War II, King Abdul Aziz opposed the plan because, as the US ambassador told his superiors at the time, he thought it would provoke "violent criticism from reactionaries and fanatics" (Foreign Relations of the United States 1945). Forty-five years later, when then Secretary of Defense Cheney asked Ibn Saud's successor, King Fahd, for permission to station hundreds of thousands of US troops on Saudi territory to conduct the Gulf War of 1990–1991, he was greeted with similar concerns. Eventually, Fahd agreed to the plan – but only after Cheney promised that the troops would be withdrawn just as soon as Iraqi forces were driven out of Kuwait. As things turned out, however, Bush Senior decided to retain many of the troops in Saudi Arabia in order to enforce the containment of Iraq, and this continued presence of American "infidels" in the Islamic "Holy Land" later became the rallying cry for Osama bin Laden in his efforts to recruit young Saudis for his terrorist campaign against the United States (Klare 2004: 50–55; Woodward 1991: 253–256, 258–261).

More recently, the war in Iraq appears to confirm the view that the deployment of US troops to protect oil installations often arouses more hostility than it affords protection. The United States made its priorities clear when, following the initial US entry into Baghdad in April 2003, US troops guarded the Oil Ministry building while allowing the rest of the city to be sacked by mobs and looters. This confirmed many Iraqis' suspicions that the United States' sole interest in Iraq was to seize its oil. This suspicion was given further credence by reports that funds intended for municipal reconstruction were instead used to protect oil pipelines, refineries, and loading facilities (Cloud and Jaffe 2004). No matter how hard US officials have since sought to affirm Washington's commitment to Iraq's well-being, nothing they have done has entirely erased the perception among a large share of the Iraqi population that the United States' principal interest in Iraq is its oil.

Much doubt can also be raised about the actual *effectiveness* of using military force to protect the flow of energy. Despite the many billions of dollars that have been spent to increase the security of pipelines and other oil infrastructure in Iraq, insurgents have continued to damage these facilities on a regular basis, severely undercutting the government's capacity to finance itself through the export of oil. Many reasons have been given for this, including the obvious difficulty of protecting exposed and inherently vulnerable installations, the need to rely on incompetent and corrupt security forces, and the insurgents' obvious daring and determination; nevertheless, the bottom line is that every effort by the Iraqi government and its US backers to enhance the security of Iraq's oil infrastructure has met with extensive failure (Watkins 2005; Miller 2004; Worth and Glanz 2006). A very similar picture could be seen in southern Nigeria, where government efforts to protect oil installations from attack by the Movement for the Emancipation of the Niger Delta (MEND) and other rebel groups proved equally ineffective (Polgreen 2006).

It should be noted, moreover, that such operations are inherently expensive, thus not cost-effective. Although it is impossible to put an exact price tag on the cost of global enforcement of the Carter Doctrine, a reasonable estimate would run to over $100 billion per year, or approximately one-sixth of the US defense budget. This would exclude the direct costs of the war in Iraq but encompass the day-to-day operations of other forces assigned to the Central Command plus some share of forces in the

European, Pacific, and Southern Commands that are engaged in oil-protection services of one sort or another. Also included would be the billions of dollars in military aid to such oil-producing or oil-transporting states as Angola, Azerbaijan, Colombia, Georgia, Kazakhstan, and Nigeria. If any portion of the war in Iraq is added to this tally, the net cost of protecting oil would, of course, rise much higher.

Finally, and perhaps most significantly, all of these costly and dangerous efforts represent a distraction from the main task facing US leaders in the energy field: to prepare for the day when petroleum must be replaced with other, more environmentally friendly sources of energy. Although it is likely that oil will remain plentiful for another five to ten years (or perhaps even a bit longer), a growing chorus of experts believe that we are fast approaching the moment when global oil output will reach its peak level and begin an irreversible decline – at which point alternatives must be available to take up the slack or the United States will face an energy shortfall and a severe economic meltdown. Equally urgent, the United States must begin to shift from its reliance on fossil fuels like oil and natural gas to other sources of energy in order to substantially reduce its emissions of carbon dioxide – the principal source of the "greenhouse gases" that are heating up the atmosphere and causing catastrophic climate change. President Obama has made statements acknowledging these severe problems, and he has taken some steps to address these issues, but he has not significantly changed US policies.

Overall, while this is not the place to weigh in on the specific comparative advantages and disadvantages of the various alternatives to oil, one thing can be said of them all in common: developing them on a large enough scale to replace petroleum in time to avert economic and environmental disaster will require investment on a massive scale, comparable to that devoted to the Manhattan Project of World War II or the Apollo Moon Project. It is not an impossible task, but it is likely that the United States cannot spend $100 billion or more per year on enforcement of the Carter Doctrine *and* devote a similar amount – as surely will be required – in order to develop petroleum alternatives on the scale needed. This is the task required of President Obama and future administrations. Hence, rejection of the globalized Carter Doctrine, which policy President Obama has inherited, is a prerequisite of sorts for making the transition from a petroleum-based to a post-petroleum energy system.

In conclusion, the use of military force to protect the flow of imported oil has been a clear pattern of American policy, however quietly pursued, and certainly explains US continued interests in Iraq. Using military force to protect oil flows is neither justifiable in moral terms nor effective in ensuring the actual delivery of energy. Instead of squandering our national wealth and the blood of men and women in uniform in the futile pursuit of "energy security" through military means, we should repudiate the globalized Carter Doctrine and embrace a new definition of energy security that relies first and foremost on the development of petroleum alternatives that do not entail reliance on the use of force to ensure their availability and that do not contribute to global environmental degradation.

Note

The original version of this chapter appeared in *Lessons from Iraq: Avoiding the Next War*, edited by Miriam Pemberton and William D. Hartung, Boulder: Paradigm Publishers, 2008, pp. 32–39.

References

British Petroleum (2007) *Statistical Review of World Energy June 2007*, London: BP.

British Petroleum (2010) *Statistical Review of World Energy June 2010*, London: BP.

Bush, G. H. W. (1990) Address on Iraq's Invasion of Kuwait, August 8. Accessed at http://millercenter.org/scripps/archive/speeches/detail/5529 on June 6, 2011.

Carter, J. (1980) *State of the Union Address 1980*. Accessed at www.jimmycarterlibrary.gov/documents/speeches/su80jec.phtml on June 6, 2011.

Cheney, R. (2002) From the transcript of Cheney's address in "Eyes on Iraq: In Cheney's Words: The Administration's Case for Removing Saddam Hussein," *New York Times*, August 27.

Cloud, David S. and Jaffe, G. (2004) "U.S. Diplomat Wants More Funds for Iraqi Security," *The Wall Street Journal*, August 30.

Cobb, C. (2003) "Larger US Troops Presence May be Needed in Africa, says NATO Commander," *AllAfrica* news, May 2. Accessed at http://allafrica.com/stories/printable/200305020307.html on June 6, 2011.

Crawley, M. (2002) "With Mideast Uncertainty, US Turns to Africa for Oil," *Christian Science Monitor*, May 23.

Cummins, C. (2003) "Expatriate Iraqis Say Oil Fields Should be Opened," *Wall Street Journal*, March 3.

Dao, J. (2003) "Navy Seals Easily Seize 2 Oil Sites," *New York Times*, March 22.

Deffeyes, K. S. (2001) *Hubert's Peak. The Impending World Oil Shortage*, Princeton: Princeton University Press.

Department of State (DoS) (2004) FY 2004 International Affairs Budget, Congressional Budget Justification for Foreign Operations. Accessed at http://2001-2009.state.gov/s/d/rm/c11411.htm on June 6, 2011.

Department of State (DoS) (2005) FY 2005 International Affairs Budget, Congressional Budget Justification for Foreign Operations. Accessed at http://2001-2009.state.gov/s/d/rm/c11411.htm on June 6, 2011.

Department of State (DoS) (2006) FY 2006 International Affairs Budget, Congressional Budget Justification for Foreign Operations. Accessed at http://2001-2009.state.gov/s/d/rm/c11411.htm on June 6, 2011.

Fleischer, A. (2002) "Press Briefing by Ari Fleischer," The White House, October 30. Accessed at www.whitehouse.gov on August 13, 2007.

Forero, J. (2002) "New Role for U.S. in Columbia: Protecting a Vital Oil Pipeline," *New York Times*, October 4.

Harding, J. (2003) "The Figure in the White House Shadows Who Urged the President to War in Iraq," *Financial Times*, March 22–23.

Hersh, S. (2001) "The Iraq Hawks," *The New Yorker*, December 24, pp. 58–63.

Jaffe, G. (2003) "In Massive Shift, U.S. is Planning to Cut Size of Military in Germany," *Wall Street Journal*, June 10.

Katzman, K. (2006) *The Persian Gulf States: Issues for U.S. Policy, 2006*, Washington, DC: Congressional Research Service, August 21.

Klare, M. T. (2004) *Blood and Oil: The Dangers and Consequences of America's Growing Dependency on Imported Petroleum*, New York: Metropolitan Books.

Klare, M. (2007) "The Futile Pursuit of 'Energy Security' by Military Means," *Brown Journal of World Affairs*, 13: 139–153.

Klare, M. and Volman, D. (2006) "America, China, and the Scramble for Africa's Oil," *Review of African Political Economy*, 33: 297–309.

Long, D. E., Reich, B., and Gasiorowski, M. (1980) *The Government and Politics of the Middle East and North Africa*, New York: Westview Press.

Miller, A. D. (1980) *Search for Security: Saudi Arabian Oil and American Foreign Policy, 1939–1949*, Chapel Hill: University of North Carolina Press.

Miller, T. C. (2004) "Oil Sabotage Threatens Iraq Economy, Rebuilding," *Los Angeles Times*, September 18.

Morgan, D. and Ottaway, D. B. (2002) "In Iraq War Scenario, Oil is Key," *Washington Post*, September 15.

Nichol, J. (2002) *Central Asia's New States: Political Developments and Implications for U.S. Interests*, Washington, DC: Congressional Research Service.

Painter, D. S. (1986) *Oil and the American Century: The Political Economy of U.S. Foreign Oil Policy, 1941–1954*, Baltimore: Johns Hopkins University Press.

Palmer, M. A. (1992) *Guardians of the Gulf: A History of America's Expanding Role in the Persian Gulf, 1833–1992*, New York: Free Press.

Polgreen, L. (2006) "Armed Group Shuts Down Part of Nigeria's Oil Output," *New York Times*, February 25.

Priest, D. (2003) *The Mission: Waging War and Keeping Peace with America's Military*, New York: W. W. Norton & Company.

Sanger, D. E. (2007) "Cheney, on Carrier, Warns Iran to Keep Sea Lanes Open," *New York Times*, May 12.

Schmitt, E. (2003) "Threats and Responses: Expanding U.S. Presence; Pentagon Seeking New Access Pacts for Africa Bases," *New York Times*, July 5.

Stoff, M. B. (1980) *Oil, War, and American Security: The Search for a National Policy on Foreign Oil, 1941–1947*, New Haven: Yale University Press.

US Congress, Senate, Committee on Armed Services (1990) *Crisis in the Persian Gulf Region: U.S. Policy Options and Implications*, Hearings, 101st Congress, 2nd Session, Washington, DC: Government Printing Office.

US Department of Defense (DoD) (2003a) Transcript: Secretary Rumsfeld Press Conference with Acting Georgian President Burdzhanadze, December 5. Accessed at www.defense.gov/Transcripts/Transcript.aspx?TranscriptID=2774.

US Department of Defense (DoD) (2003b) Transcript: Background Briefing En Route to Georgia, December 5. Accessed at www.defense.gov/Transcripts/Transcript.aspx?TranscriptID=2773.

US Department of Energy, Energy Information Administration (2006) *International Energy Outlook 2006*. Washington, DC.

US Department of Energy, Energy Information Administration (2007) *International Energy Outlook 2007.* Washington, DC.

Veith, W. (2003) "Privatization of Oil Suggested for Iraq," *Los Angeles Times,* February 21.

Watkins, E. (2005) "Corruption, Sabotage Hinder Iraq's Postwar Efforts," *Oil and Gas Journal,* May 2, pp. 36–37.

Woodward, B. (1991) *The Commanders,* New York: Simon & Schuster.

Woodward, B. (2004) *Plan of Attack,* New York: Simon & Schuster.

Worth, R. F. and Glanz, J. (2006) "Oil Graft Fuels the Insurgency, Iraq, and the U.S. Say," *New York Times,* February 5.

8 Oil and the decision to invade Iraq

John S. Duffield

Introduction

What role did oil play in the decision to invade Iraq in 2003? We still do not know exactly why the Bush administration went to war against Iraq, and we may never know. Certainly, no compelling evidence, either in the form of declassified documents or participants' memoirs, has yet emerged indicating that oil was a prominent factor or constant consideration in the thinking of decision-makers within the Bush administration. But oil is nevertheless critical to understanding the decision to invade Iraq and remove Saddam Hussein from power. Oil did not make a US war against Iraq inevitable. But it did much to set the stage for war, greatly increasing the incentives to topple Saddam, by any means possible. Indeed, it is hard to imagine the invasion of Iraq ever having occurred but for oil. Only by understanding the ways in which oil has infused the US strategic calculus in the Persian Gulf can we fully make sense of the war.

Why is this the case? The United States has had a number of interests in the Persian Gulf, but it has been the region's oil, more than any other factor, that has caused the United States to regard the Gulf as strategically important. In particular, the United States has long had a substantial interest in seeing that Persian Gulf oil flowed steadily, and in large quantities, on to world markets. For many years, this interest has motivated – and been used to justify – an ever deeper degree of US involvement and intervention in the region.

In the early 2000s, moreover, it was the regime of Saddam Hussein that represented the principal threat to the stability of the Gulf and its ability to supply the world with oil. Saddam had long harbored ambitions to dominate the region, and he had twice invaded neighboring countries in an effort to realize those ambitions. In addition, despite the constraints placed on Iraq's military capabilities by the Gulf War of 1991 and the subsequent UN sanctions, many observers both inside and outside the Bush administration believed that Iraq possessed at least some chemical and biological weapons and might one day acquire nuclear weapons. And armed with a combination WMD and conventional military capabilities,

Saddam might once again conclude that he could move against his oil-rich neighbors.

This is not to say that the United States could not have sought to address the regional threat posed by Saddam in other ways. Indeed, it had tried to do so, with considerable success, through a policy of containing and deterring Iraq for a dozen years after the end of the Gulf War. But both the UN sanctions regime and the substantial US military presence in the Gulf on which this policy depended were becoming increasingly difficult to maintain.

Forceful regime change also offered a number of other potential benefits in comparison with the alternatives. In particular, it could remove the constraints that had prevented Iraq from realizing its own substantial potential as an oil producer at a time when long-term trends pointed toward a tighter world oil market. Thus going to war was an increasingly attractive option.

What others have said about the role of oil

Much of what has been said and written about the role of oil in the Bush administration's decision to invade Iraq falls into two categories. On the one hand, there are some, often members of the Bush administration, who hardly mention oil in their accounts or who deny, usually strenuously, that the war had anything to do with oil. On the other hand, there are those who argue that the war was all about oil.

The Bush administration offered a variety of justifications for its decision to go to war against Iraq. During the run up to the invasion, President George W. Bush and other high-level officials emphasized the threat to US national security posed by Iraq's alleged possession of weapons of mass destruction and its ties to international terrorists. Later, they stressed the need to promote democracy in the Middle East. And along the way, they highlighted Saddam Hussein's despotic rule and human rights abuses.

Conspicuously absent from these justifications were the possible oil-related benefits of going to war. With one noteworthy exception, which is cited below, the major public statements made by President Bush, Vice President Dick Cheney, Secretary of State Colin Powell, and Secretary of Defense Donald Rumsfeld contained hardly any references to oil as a reason for war. And when oil was mentioned, it was usually in the context of denying that it was a motivation. Thus Rumsfeld famously insisted that the conflict had "nothing to do with oil, literally nothing to do with oil" (Everest 2004: 248), and Bush speech writer David Frum argued that "The United States is not fighting for oil in Iraq" (cited in Rutledge 2005: 179). Likewise, defenders of the administration's policy outside the government flatly denied that the war had anything to do with oil (e.g. Boot 2003).

This absence of oil-related motives has been a theme of many subsequent accounts of the Bush administration's decision-making. Third-party descriptions based on access to decision-makers, such as those by Bob Woodward (2002, 2004), Ron Suskind (2004), and Thomas Ricks (2006), make little or no mention of oil. Nor do those few biographies and memoirs by former Bush administration officials that have appeared so far (e.g. Feith 2008; McClellan 2008). The principal exception is Alan Greenspan's *Age of Turbulence*, in which the former head of the US Federal Reserve writes that "The Iraq war is largely about oil" (Greenspan 2007: 463). But even Greenspan's claim is too general to be of much use in parsing the role that oil might have played in the administration's decision-making.

In contrast, critics of the war, both at the time and in subsequent years, have often argued that the war was all about oil (e.g., Almond 2003; Diebel 2003; Klare 2003; Lindorff 2003). This argument has taken several different forms, but in each case, oil-related benefits were presumably a central part of the Bush administration's decision calculus.

One popular version is that the Bush administration sought to gain direct control over Iraq's sizeable oil supplies. Indeed, according to a Pew Research Center poll conducted shortly before the war began, a majority of respondents in France (75 percent), Germany (54 percent), and Russia (76 percent) agreed with the statement that "the United States wanted to control Iraqi oil" (Boot 2003). One purpose would have been to make Iraq's oil available for American consumers. Another would have been to restore access to Iraq's lucrative oil fields to American oil companies (Paul 2003; Israeli 2004: 141–177; Rutledge 2005: 176–186; Leach 2006; Maass 2009: 136–150). Iraq had nationalized its oil industry in the 1970s, kicking out the mostly US-based international oil companies. In the years prior to the invasion, however, Saddam Hussein had selectively signed contracts for the development of new oil fields with companies from China, Russia, and other more sympathetic countries. Not only were American oil companies frozen out of the deals, but a significant uptick in Iraqi oil production potentially threatened to drive down the price of oil, thereby hurting US companies (Ferraro 2003).

Others have argued that the control of Iraq's oil was meant to be a means to a larger end: US control over the world's oil supplies more generally. It would have given the United States a tool for pressuring Saudi Arabia and other oil-producing states. It would have enabled the United States "to undercut any Saudi moves to slash production and hike oil prices. No longer would the oil weapon hang over America like the sword of Damocles" (Rutledge 2005: 177; see also Standlea 2006: 39–40; Callincos 2005: 597–602; Israeli 2004). To the contrary, by controlling the amount of oil on the market, the United States would now be able to exert financial pressure on oil-producing states as a means of promoting political and economic reforms. Thus Iraqi oil would be "a weapon for undermining Arab regimes and Iran, bringing 'democracy' to the Middle East and making the region safer for the US and Israel" (Alkadiri and Mohamedi 2003: 20) Finally, controlling Iraq's oil would also eliminate the threat that OPEC would begin to denominate oil sales in euros, thereby reducing the influence of the dollar in world markets (Clark 2005).

A final variant of this argument is that the ultimate goal of the war was to shore up the global US-led liberal economic order. In the words of Stokes and Raphael:

> Saddam was removed not only because he posed a continuing threat to US control of the region's oil reserves but because the act of removal provided an opportunity to replace him with a ruling strata more compliant to the interests of global capital.
>
> (Stokes and Raphael 2010: 96)

Thus war would benefit not just US companies but the entire capitalist system and make Iraq a showcase of neoliberal doctrine (see also Everest 2004: 248–276).

This chapter takes an intermediate position. In a sense, it argues that both those who deny that oil played a role in the Bush administration's decision-making and those who insist that the war was all about oil may be at least partially right. Control of Iraq's oil may not have been the immediate or a conscious reason for going to war, but the purposes of the war were deeply rooted in the region's oil. Just as the existence of the USSR did so much to shape US foreign and security policy during the Cold War, the presence of so much valuable oil in the Persian Gulf has done much to condition US policy toward that region, resulting in a greater degree of involvement and, ultimately, a greater inclination toward war than would otherwise have been the case. The remainder of the chapter elaborates on these connections.

US interests in the Persian Gulf

It goes without saying that the Persian Gulf has mattered a great deal to the United States. But the most important US interest in the region has been and remains its copious supplies of fossil fuels, especially oil. As Richard Haass, the first Director of Policy Planning in the State Department during the Bush administration, has written,

> the principal reason the [Persian Gulf] region matters as much as it does stems from its [oil and gas] resources and their relevance to the world economy ... absent oil and oil's importance the region would count for much less.
>
> (Haass 2009: 76)

This interest does not derive particularly from the United States' own dependence on Persian Gulf oil, however. Although the United States has imported a more or less steadily increasing percentage of the oil it consumes, only a small fraction of that oil has come from the Persian Gulf. In 2002, just prior to the Iraq War, the United States consumed approximately 19.8 million barrels per day (MBD) of oil. Of this, 10.5 MBD (53 percent) represented net imports, but only 2.3 MBD of the imported oil – about 12 percent of US consumption and 22 percent of US net imports – came from the Middle East (USEIA 2010: 129, 135).

Rather, the US interest in the region has been due primarily to the dependence of the world economy as a whole on Persian Gulf oil. Since the mid-1960s, oil has been the single most important global energy source, and in 2002, it accounted for 38 percent of total world energy consumption (BP 2010). And for the last four decades, except for a few years in the mid-1980s, the Persian Gulf has been the largest oil-producing region. In 2002, it accounted for nearly 30 percent of global oil production and nearly 40 percent of all oil exports (BP 2010).

Consequently, although the United States has never depended on the Persian Gulf for more than a small percentage of the oil it consumes, the health of the US economy has been highly sensitive to developments in the region, in two ways. First, a disruption of Persian Gulf oil supplies would cause oil prices to rise in the United States, even if it imported not a single barrel of oil. This is because "the United States and the other major oil importers are all part of a single, seamless oil market driven by supply and demand" (Telhami *et al.* 2002). Second, an oil shock originating in the region would harm the economies of major US economic partners in Europe and Asia, which have been more heavily dependent on imported oil in general and Persian Gulf oil in particular, with deleterious consequences for production and employment in the United States (see also Klare 2004a: 78; 2008: 186).

And during the first years of the Bush administration, it appeared that the importance of Persian Gulf oil would only increase in the coming decades. In early 2003, the US Energy Information Administration (USEIA) projected that global oil demand would grow from 77.1 MBD in 2001 to 118.8 MBD by 2025, an increase of 54 percent (USEIA 2003b: Table C4). An increasing percentage of that oil, moreover, was expected to come from the Persian Gulf. The USEIA projected that the Middle East's share of global oil production might increase to more than 34 percent in 2025 (USEIA 2003a: Table C21) and that the Gulf's share of all oil exports would reach almost 60 percent by 2020 (USEIA 2001: 59).[1]

The main reason for the centrality of the Persian Gulf in these projections was the fact that nearly two-thirds of the world's proven oil reserves were estimated to lie in the region. In 2002, Saudi Arabia alone was attributed with a quarter of all proven oil reserves (262 billion barrels), with most of the balance being provided by Iraq itself (112.5 billion barrels), the United Arab Emirates (98 billion barrels), Kuwait (96.5 billion barrels), and Iran (90 billion barrels) (BP 2003).

In sum, during the decades leading up to the Iraq War, US interests in the Persian Gulf derived primarily from the region's oil. As veteran Persian Gulf expert Gary Sick has written,

> the interests of the United States in the Persian Gulf region have been very simple and consistent: first, to ensure access by the industrialized world to the vast oil resources of the region; and second, to prevent any hostile power from acquiring political or military control over these resources. ... Other objectives, such as preserving the stability and independence of the Gulf states or containing the threat of Islamic fundamentalism, were derivative concerns and were implicit in the two grand themes of oil and containment.
>
> (Sick 2003: 291)

Put more simply, in the words of noted Middle East analyst Kenneth Pollack, a former Central Intelligence Agency and National Security Council official, "America's primary interest in the Persian Gulf lies in ensuring the free and stable flow of oil from the region to the world at large" (Pollack 2003: 3). As further evidence of the strategic US interest in Persian Gulf oil supplies, one can point to the repeated US interventions and deepening American involvement in the region, especially since the 1970s. The principal reason for this involvement is that oil production and exports there have been subject to periodic, and occasionally severe, disruptions. Consequently, the United States has been highly motivated to take measures designed to prevent such disruptions and, beyond that, to encourage regional producers to supply the world market with adequate quantities of oil at reasonable prices.

During the first phase of US involvement, in the mid- and late 1970s, American policy-makers tried to avoid a repeat of the first oil embargo and to obtain the help of regional producers in stabilizing the price of oil as well as to exclude Soviet influence from the region. Under the Nixon Doctrine, however, the United States sought to rely primarily on regional powers to maintain order and promote US interests in the Persian Gulf. To that end, successive administrations sold massive amounts of often advanced arms to Iran and Saudi Arabia under the so-called "twin pillars" strategy.

That limited initial approach was undermined by the Iranian Revolution and then the Soviet invasion of Afghanistan, both in 1979. In response, under the Carter Doctrine and the subsequent Reagan Corollary, the United States indicated a new willingness to intervene militarily to prevent any outside power – but especially the Soviet Union – from gaining control of the region's oil resources. It also began to create a dedicated capability to facilitate military intervention, if deemed necessary, including a larger military presence in the region, bases, and new strategic mobility forces. That capability was first put to use in the late 1980s, when the United States agreed to escort Kuwaiti tankers threatened by Iranian attacks (Operation Earnest Will). During the 1980s, the Reagan administration also provided covert assistance to Iraq in order to prevent Iran from dominating the region.

US involvement in the Persian Gulf reached a whole new level during the 1990–1991 Gulf War (Operations Desert Shield and Desert Storm). Several motives lay behind the US intervention, including the imperative to stand up to naked aggression and to uphold international law. But as one of the best histories of the episode notes, "while it was never the case that the Gulf crisis was solely about oil, oil infused every aspect" (Freedman and Karsh 1995: 180). It was bad enough that, with the occupation of Kuwait, Saddam Hussein controlled some 20 percent of the world's oil reserves. But if unchecked, the Iraqi leader was poised to dominate Saudi Arabia and the other oil-producing countries of the region through the threat or actual use of force. "He was clearly in a position to be able to dictate the future of worldwide energy policy," warned Secretary of Defense Dick Cheney, "and that gave him a stranglehold on our economy and on that of most of the other nations of the world as well" (quoted in Klare 2004b: 6. See also Freedman and Karsh 1995: 180; Little 2002: 255 and 259). The stakes for the United States could hardly have been higher. As President Bush himself cautioned: "Our jobs, our way of life, our own freedom and the freedom of friendly countries around the world would all suffer if control of the world's great oil reserves fell into the hands of Saddam Hussein" (Yergin 1991: 773). Thus, he concluded, "We cannot permit a resource so vital to be dominated by one so ruthless. And we won't" (Little 2002: 73).

Following the Gulf War, a small but significant US combat force remained in the theater. It served both to deter possible further aggressive moves by Iraq against its oil-rich neighbors and to enforce the UN sanctions that had been imposed on the country after the war. US naval forces made up much of the multinational Maritime Interception Force operating in the Gulf that enforced the embargo on Iraqi imports and oil exports. Army units repeatedly exercised the prepositioned equipment in Kuwait as a show of force under operations Vigilant Warrior and Desert Spring, and both Army and Marine Corps forces conducted frequent exercises. Most extensive of all, however, were the air operations intended to enforce the no-fly zones imposed over northern and southern Iraq. When the Iraq War began in 2003, US pilots had flown over 286,000 missions (Duffield 2008: 178)

Further evidence of the importance the United States has attached to ensuring the integrity of Persian Gulf oil supplies is suggested by the efforts made by US forces to secure Iraq's oil fields, pipelines, and other oil-related infrastructure, including the Ministry of Oil, during the first days of the Iraq War. Some have argued that this was part of a plan to exert direct control over Iraqi oil or to turn it over to US companies. A more benign interpretation is that the Bush administration wanted to ensure that a future government of Iraq would have the resources needed to pay for the country's reconstruction. Clearly, however, these early actions served the strategic US interest in minimizing the disruption to global oil supplies, even if that goal was later foiled by insurgent attacks on the oil infrastructure.

The threat posed by Iraq under Saddam Hussein

The principal threats to Persian Gulf oil supplies have varied over the years. But in the early 2000s, the greatest threat of all was arguably that posed by Iraq under Saddam Hussein. In the words of General Anthony Zinni, who served as commander in chief of the US Central Command until 2000, Iraq remains the most significant near-term threat to US interests in the Gulf region (quoted in Klare 2004a: 81).

The Iraqi leader continued to harbor a desire to dominate the region, and he might again have the ability to do so, especially if he were able to acquire significant numbers of weapons of mass destruction (WMD).

When the Bush administration took office, Saddam Hussein was widely believed to have expansive regional ambitions. According to a 1998 intelligence community brief, "Saddam is committed to seeing Iraq reemerge as the dominant power in the region" (US Senate 2008: 75). Likewise, a 2001 CIA memorandum asserted that "his strategic aim is to establish Iraq as the preeminent power in the Persian Gulf" (US Senate 2008: 75). Or in the words of Pollack, who made what was arguably the most compelling public case for going to war against Iraq, "Saddam Hussein [was] determined to overturn the status quo to make himself the hegemon of the Persian Gulf region and the leader of the Arab world" (Pollack 2002: 153).

As evidence of these ambitions, one needed only to look at Saddam Hussein's recent behavior toward Iraq's neighbors.[2] In 1980, he had attacked Iran, seeking to exploit the internal turmoil roiling the country to make a variety of political and territorial gains. Then in 1990, just two years after the conclusion of the Iran–Iraq War, Iraq had invaded and quickly occupied Kuwait, and it seemed poised to threaten Saudi Arabia as well. Thus it seemed logical to conclude that, given the opportunity, Saddam would once again make some kind of aggressive move – intimidation, coercion, or even invasion – against one or more of his oil-rich neighbors. But would he get the chance?

Much of Iraq's military capability had been destroyed during the Gulf War, and following the war, the threat posed by Iraq to its neighbors continued to be neutralized by a combination of UN sanctions and a greatly increased US military presence in the region. The former made it difficult for the country to reconstitute its military power, while the latter was intended to deter any future Iraqi attempts at aggression. Nevertheless, many observers believed that Saddam Hussein had abandoned neither his ambitions to dominate the Gulf nor his efforts to develop an arsenal of weapons of mass destruction that would help him to realize that goal. Indeed, the US intelligence community viewed "Baghdad's goal of becoming the predominant regional power" as a key driver behind its WMD program (cited in US Senate 2006: 113). Consequently, as the Bush administration settled into office in 2001, it was possible to imagine that Saddam Hussein might once again make a bid for regional hegemony and control over the Gulf's oil resources if he were allowed to remain in power.

Members of the Bush administration described Iraq in no uncertain terms as possessing a substantial arsenal of weapons of mass destruction that might soon include nuclear weapons. As Cheney told an audience in Nashville in August 2002:

> Simply stated, there is no doubt Saddam Hussein has weapons of mass destruction. There is no doubt that he is amassing them to use against our friends, against our allies, and against us. And there is no doubt that his aggressive regional ambitions will lead him into future confrontations with his neighbors.
>
> (US Senate 2008:79)

As a result, much has been made of the fact that no WMD were found in Iraq. Nevertheless, prior to the war, US and some other Western intelligence agencies believed that Iraq probably possessed significant quantities of chemical and biological weapons (or the ability to produce them) and that it probably maintained a nuclear weapons program (e.g. CIA 2002). Most importantly, many reasonable people feared that Saddam Hussein would be able to acquire a formidable arsenal of nuclear weapons in as little as a few years, if left unchecked.

Pollack presented one of the most compelling cases for military action. In his view, Iraq had essentially figured out how to build nuclear weapons, had been able to hang on to most of the knowledge and equipment that it needed to do so, and was probably working to enrich uranium. Consequently, according to German and US intelligence estimates he cited, Iraq might have been able to make a nuclear weapon in as few as three to five years. And, Pollack concluded, if Iraq was able to buy enriched uranium, as it appeared to be attempting to do, "it could probably build a workable device in a year or two" (Pollack 2002: 168, 173–175).[3]

Largely overlooked in the debates over Iraq's WMD, moreover, were the country's conventional military capabilities. Yet these, too, posed a significant potential threat to its neighbors, just as they had in the past (Klare 2004a: 81). As Pollack observed,

> despite the devastation of the Gulf War and sanctions, Iraqi forces remain large enough to give them an edge over any single Persian Gulf state or any combination of them. ... Moreover, Iraqi forces possess a qualitative edge over the Persian Gulf states that magnifies their quantitative advantage.
>
> (Pollack 2002: 160)

To be sure, the Gulf War and subsequent UN sanctions had exacted a considerable toll, especially in the area of logistics. As a result, "Iraq almost certainly ha[d] lost the ability to mount sustained ground offensives that could threaten GCC [Gulf Cooperation Council] oil production beyond Kuwait and, perhaps, northernmost Saudi Arabia" (Pollack 2002: 165). Nevertheless, he continued,

> in the absence of U.S. forces, the Republican Guards could probably overrun Kuwait again as they did in 1990, albeit with greater difficulty because of the state of Iraqi logistics. Iraqi forces might be able to undertake similarly limited operations versus Saudi Arabia, Jordan, and Iran, although they probably could not replicate the multicorps offensives they staged against Iran in 1988.

Thus, Pollack concluded, "even in their current weakened state, Iraq's [conventional] capabilities would pose a significant threat to regional stability if the United States were ever to pull its forces out of the region" (Pollack 2002: 149, 160).

What might Saddam Hussein have been expected to do with such an arsenal? Even with nuclear weapons, it is almost inconceivable that he would have tried to attack directly the United States or any of its traditional allies, including Israel. Such an attack would certainly have been met by a devastating response. Although he had used WMD (in this case chemical weapons) against Iran and Kurds in Iraq, his victims had lacked the ability to respond in kind. Thus, Iraq would be unable to use or even threaten to use nuclear weapons so long as the United States was able to retaliate (Mearsheimer and Walt 2003).

Hardly more likely was the possibility that Saddam Hussein might clandestinely transfer nuclear weapons to a terrorist group hostile to the United States. The probability of such a nuclear handoff was extremely small, for at least four reasons. First, there was no evidence of any genuine connection between Saddam Hussein and such groups, especially al Qaeda; to the contrary, a history of enmity existed between them. Second, if Saddam Hussein did give nuclear weapons to a terrorist group, he would lose control over how they would be used. Third, if he nevertheless went ahead, he could not be sure that the transfer would go undetected, especially given the US imperatives to monitor the situation carefully. And even if a transfer went undetected, Saddam Hussein could not assume that the United States would not retaliate against him anyway if a terrorist nuclear attack were to occur (Mearsheimer and Walt 2003). Thus, even Pollack flatly admitted, "terrorism is the least of the threats posed by Iraq to the interests of the United States" and "Saddam Hussein is not likely to give weapons of mass destruction to terrorists" (Pollack 2002: 153, 180).

Rather, it was the possible combination of WMD and conventional capabilities that posed the greatest threat. With nuclear weapons in particular, Saddam Hussein might conclude that he could safely use his conventional forces against his neighbors, since an Iraqi nuclear arsenal might deter other states from engaging in a rerun of Operation Desert Storm. Indeed, Saddam might believe that even the United States "would be deterred from taking any steps to reverse effects of Iraqi conventional aggression" (n.a. 2002: 7; see also Pollack 2002: 272).

Thus the principal danger to US interests was that Iraq would have sought to use its military capabilities to realize its regional ambitions. As Vice President Cheney warned in his August 2002 Nashville speech,

> [a]rmed with an arsenal of these weapons of terror, and seated atop ten percent of the world's oil reserves, Saddam Hussein could then be expected to seek domination of the entire Middle East, take control of a great portion of the world's energy supplies, directly threaten America's friends throughout the region, and subject the United States or any other nation to nuclear blackmail.[4]

President Bush echoed this view in his January 2003 State of the Union Address, when he stated that "With nuclear arms or a full arsenal of chemical and biological weapons, Saddam Hussein could resume his ambitions of conquest in the Middle East."[5]

If Saddam Hussein were ever to achieve this objective, the consequences would be dire. In Pollack's words,

> he [would] use this power to advance Iraq's political interests, even to the detriment of its economic interests and the world's. ... If Saddam Hussein were ever to control the Persian Gulf oil resources, his past record suggests that he would be willing to cut or even halt oil exports altogether whenever it suited him to force concessions from his fellow Arabs, Europe, the United States, or the world as a whole. And even if he failed, he could still wreak considerable havoc on the region and world oil supplies.
>
> (Pollack 2002: 152, 272)

Thus, Cheney concluded in a retrospective defense of the decision to go to war, "had we followed the counsel of inaction, the Iraqi regime would still be a menace to its neighbors and a destabilizing force in the Middle East" (Schmitt 2003).

The lack of good alternatives: growing difficulties with containing and deterring Iraq

To be sure, regime change via war was not the only option available to the Bush administration, but it was an increasingly attractive one, relative to the others. One alternative was to pursue regime change by other means. Indeed, this had been a part of official US policy since at least the passage and signing of the "Iraqi Liberation Act of 1998." The problem was that the United States had few other means to achieve this goal. It provided assistance to elements of the democratic opposition in exile, but there was little it could do inside Iraq to set the stage for a transition of power.

More promising was a continuation of the policy of containing and deterring Iraq, which had been in place since the Gulf War. At the end of the war, the UN had mandated the destruction of Iraq's WMD, imposed inspections to verify Iraqi compliance, and erected a tough sanctions regime to prevent Iraq from reconstituting its conventional and unconventional military capabilities. In addition, the United States had established a significant military presence in the Gulf designed to deter any future Iraqi acts of aggression.

For the better part of a decade, these measures had been largely successful at neutralizing the Iraqi threat. In the late 1990s, however, UN inspections were ended, and as time wore on, the sanctions regime and important components of the US military presence had become increasingly difficult to maintain. As a result, one could again imagine a time when Saddam Hussein would once more be free to pursue his goal of dominating the Gulf.

A number of countries, including some permanent members of the UN Security Council, had never been enthusiastic about the sanctions in view of the costs they imposed and the lost economic opportunities they represented. And over the years, the sanctions had come under increasing international criticism because of the humanitarian crisis that they were allegedly causing in Iraq. In the mid-1990s, the Security Council had made a serious attempt to address the latter problem by allowing Iraq to export a considerable amount of oil in order to earn the foreign exchange required to purchase foodstuffs, medicines, and other humanitarian supplies abroad, the so-called "oil for food" program. But the crisis did not seem to abate, in no small part because of Saddam's deft manipulation of the sanctions, and pressure continued to grow to eliminate or at least dilute the sanctions substantially. Thus in December 1999, the Security Council lifted the cap on the amount of oil Iraq could sell and greatly expanded the types of goods it could import.

At the same time, Saddam Hussein was proving increasingly adept at evading the sanctions. Iraq was able to divert a growing amount of oil from legitimate sales via the oil-for-food program to smuggling by truck, pipeline, and boat. In 1999, according to Pollack, the United States estimated that only about 5 percent of Iraq's oil revenues were skirting the UN system, whereas just two years later, that share had grown to roughly 20 percent (Pollack 2002: 101). Simultaneously, Iraq had also managed since 2000 to skim money from the legitimate oil sales by demanding surcharges on each barrel of oil sold. All told, Pollack estimated that Saddam's regime would "rake in $2.5–3 billion, representing 15–22 percent of all Iraqi revenue" in 2002 (Pollack 2002: 214–225). This was a vast sum that Saddam could spend however he liked, and Iraq was "using the money to import prohibited items for its conventional military and WMD programs" (Pollack 2002: 216).

In the face of these mounting challenges to the sanctions regime, the Bush administration initially pursued a two-prong strategy. On the one hand, it agreed to loosen further restrictions on the import of civilian goods, while attempting to ensure that items with overt military applications remained blocked, in order to blunt the political pressure to end sanctions altogether. On the other hand, it sought to deal with the problem of smuggling by bringing illegal oil shipments within the UN program. By mid-2002, however, both efforts had floundered in the face of determined opposition to any toughening of the sanctions from Russia, France, and China, which favored even looser restrictions, and the Security Council could agree on no more than narrowing the list of prohibited dual-use items (Pollack 2002: 218–225; Sengupta 2002).

As a result, US officials could not count on the sanctions regime to remain effective at containing Saddam's military power indefinitely. To the contrary, according to Pollack,

> the changes the U.N. agreed to in the spring of 2002 ... [would] probably allow Iraq to make a partial recovery of its Gulf War military strength. ... Within a period of as little as three to five years, Iraqi may be able to recover its former logistical prowess.
>
> (Pollack 2002: 167)

Of course, a robust US military presence in the Gulf region might have been sufficient to keep even a strengthening Iraq in check, although there was some question as to whether it could deter a nuclear-armed Saddam Hussein. In any case, however, the difficulties of maintaining the critical American military presence were growing. The problem was most acute in Saudi Arabia, where US military facilities had already been subjected to attacks. In fact, the US presence in the land of Islam's two holiest shrines was stoking anti-American sentiment throughout the Muslim world as well as criticism of the Saudi ruling family. Indeed, Osama bin Laden had cited it as a major reason for his war against the United States.

One immediate consequence of this growing antipathy was the imposition of restrictions on how US forces in the region could be employed. Most prominently, Saudi Arabia insisted in 2001 that American bases on its soil not be used to carry out air strikes against the Taliban in Afghanistan, although it did allow the United States to use the command and control center at Prince Sultan airbase to coordinate the air campaign (Gause 2003: 2). More fundamentally, it raised questions about the long-term viability of the American military presence. Indeed, regional expert Gregory Gause concluded, "after the attacks of September 11, 2002, an American military presence in the kingdom [was] no longer sustainable in the political system of either the United States or Saudi Arabia" (Gause 2003: 2). Consequently, as Pollack wrote in mid-2003,

> the best way for the United States to address the rise of terrorism and the threat of internal instability in Saudi Arabia and the other GCC states would be to reduce its military presence in the region to the absolute minimum, or even to withdraw entirely.
>
> (Pollack 2003)

Instead, the United States would have to rely increasingly "on the smaller gulf monarchies to provide the infrastructure for its military presence in the region" (Gause 2003: 2). It had already made use of these countries, especially Kuwait and Bahrain, which had hosted US forces, and there were several reasons to expect greater acceptance of the American military in those states than in Saudi Arabia. Nevertheless, an American presence there was not unproblematic, and Gause concluded, "a close military association with the United States might become more difficult to sustain domestically in the future." Public opinion, where it could be measured, held unfavorable views of US policies in the region, and elections were expected to result in parliaments that were less supportive of US policy objectives than were the ruling regimes (Gause 2003: 23–25).

In view of these developments, it became reasonable to fear that the political-military edifice erected to contain and deter Iraq following the Gulf War might not last. Instead, it would become increasingly difficult to prevent Iraq from acquiring weapons of mass destruction and from embarking once again upon the path of regional domination, with tumultuous consequences for world oil markets. Indeed, this danger was recognized by Rumsfeld and a number of other future high-level Bush administration officials as early as January 1998, in a letter to President Clinton:

> if Saddam does acquire the capability to deliver weapons of mass destruction, as he is almost certain to do if we continue along the present course, the safety of American troops in the region, of our friends and allies like Israel and the moderate Arab states, and a significant portion of the world's supply of oil will all be put at hazard.[6]

The only sure way to avoid this highly undesirable outcome would be to make certain that Saddam did not outlast the UN sanctions regime and the US military presence.

Other benefits of forceful regime change: liberating Iraqi oil

In addition to putting a quick end to the threat that Saddam Hussein posed to the stability of Persian Gulf oil supplies, forceful regime change offered a number of other potential benefits, especially in comparison with a continuation of the status quo (see also, for example, Kubursi 2006). A successful war would send a signal to other potential proliferators that they could not act with impunity. In fact, the initial success of the US invasion may have prompted Iran to offer a dramatic set of concessions regarding its hitherto secret nuclear program in late 2003, and it coincided with Libya's agreement to disclose and dismantle all of its WMD programs, although the war, in combination with a refusal by the Bush administration to negotiate, may also have galvanized North Korea to complete and test a nuclear weapon (Cirincione 2009). Similarly, the overthrow of Saddam would put on notice other state sponsors of terrorism, even if Iraq itself had no meaningful ties to al Qaeda.

In addition, a successful war might have been expected to have several regional benefits beyond ending the threat to Persian Gulf oil. By removing a sworn enemy of Israel, it would have enhanced the security of the principal US ally in the Middle East, even if Saddam had been deterred from launching a direct attack on Israel (Mearsheimer and Walt 2007: 231). Indeed, it might result in the establishment of a new ally that could serve as an alternative host for US military forces in the region. And it might help to open a democratic beachhead in the Persian Gulf that could eventually usher in a broader political and social transformation in the region (Mearsheimer and Walt 2007: 255–257).

Not least important among these other potential benefits, however, was the effect a war might have on Iraq's own contribution to global energy security. By all accounts, Iraq has the potential to be one of the world's largest oil producers and exporters. In 2002, it possessed the second largest proven oil reserves, approximately 112 billion barrels, and its probable and possible reserves had been estimated as high as 220 billion barrels. Ninety percent of the country, including most of its Western desert, had not been explored. Of the seventy-four oil fields that had been discovered and evaluated as of 2002, moreover, only fifteen, containing less than forty billion barrels, had actually been developed (USEIA 2003c).[7]

Based on such considerations, a number of experts estimated that Iraq could, with sufficient investment, produce 4.5 to 6 MBD, which would make it the fourth largest producer and third largest exporter of oil in the world (USEIA 2003c; Yergin 2002). And a few, such as Fadhil Chalabi, a former Iraqi Undersecretary of Oil, and Tariq Shafiz, former Vice President and Executive Director of the Iraq National Oil Company (INOC), estimated that Iraq's reserves could ultimately support a production rate of 10–12 MBD, allowing it to rival Saudi Arabia as the world's largest producer and exporter (Kawach 2002).

Actual Iraqi oil production, however, peaked at 3.7 MBD in 1979 and thereafter remained far below its tremendous potential. One reason was the damage inflicted to Iraq's oil infrastructure during the wars initiated by Saddam Hussein. During the early weeks of the Iran–Iraq War, Iraq's deepwater oil terminal at Al-Bakr in the Persian Gulf was seriously damaged (Chalabi 2000). As a result, Iraqi oil exports plummeted from over 3 MBD to less than 1 MBD in 1981, and Iraq was unable to make oil shipments from its Gulf terminals for eight years (Yergin 1991: 767).

Following the conclusion of the Iran–Iraq War, production grew rapidly, reaching 3.5 MBD in 1990. But hardly had the Iraqi oil industry recovered from that war when it received an even more devastating blow during the 1991 Gulf War. According to the USEIA, an estimated 60 percent of the Northern Oil Company's facilities were damaged in the conflict, and the southern oil industry was decimated (USEIA 2003c). Overall, by one estimate, US-led bombing during the Gulf War cut Iraq's production capacity to 1.1 MBD.[8]

In theory, much of the damage incurred during the Gulf War could have been quickly repaired just at it had been during and immediately after the Iran–Iraq War. This time, however, repairs and reconstruction were obstructed by the comprehensive UN sanctions that were imposed on Iraq in 1990 and left in place after the war. The sanctions prevented Iraq from obtaining the latest technology, spare parts, and foreign investment for its oil fields (Gongloff 2003). Even after Iraq was authorized to spend up to $600 million per year on spare parts and equipment under the oil-for-food program, the actual delivery was largely delayed on account of restrictions imposed by the UN Sanctions Committee (Chalabi 2000).

As a result of these constraints, Iraq's oil production capacity actually declined in the late 1990s and early 2000s. Nor was the situation helped by Saddam Hussein's attempts to manipulate Iraqi oil for political advantage. As recently as early 2002, he had temporarily suspended oil exports in an unsuccessful attempt to exert pressure on the United States and Israel (MacFarquhar 2002). In the process, "Iraq [had] severely tested the resilience of its oil fields by sporadically shutting down oil exports for political reasons over the past two years."[9] Thus just months before the 2003 war, a Council on Foreign Relations/Baker Institute report estimated Iraq's sustainable oil production capacity at no higher than 2.6 to 2.8 MBD, with production levels declining by 100,000 barrels per day each year.[10] And a secret government task force established in fall 2002 offered an even bleaker assessment, pegging Iraq's production capacity at only 2.1 to 2.4 MBD (Gerth 2002).

Thus by 2002, if not much earlier, it had become clear that the quickest way to remove the constraints that had hobbled Iraqi oil production was to remove Saddam Hussein from power. Regime change could occasion the lifting of the UN sanctions and, perhaps even more importantly, facilitate a resumption of investment in exploration and development. It would also mean the end of Saddam's manipulation of Iraqi oil production and exports for political purposes.

Freeing up Iraq's tremendous oil production potential could in turn have been expected to result in several significant benefits. First, it could help to meet anticipated growth in the world demand for oil. In addition, it could contribute to a more stable world oil market through the creation of greater redundancy in oil supplies and, ideally, additional excess production capacity. Since the late 1970s, the world had counted primarily on Saudi Arabia to prevent dramatic price increases by raising production whenever supplies were disrupted elsewhere. Beginning in the early 1990s, however, the kingdom had been producing at levels that limited its ability to respond to unexpected supply disruptions, and growing tensions within Saudi Arabia itself had begun to call into question its very ability to maintain output at existing, not to mention higher, levels. Meanwhile, the potential for supply disruptions – and concomitant sharp price increases – seemed as great as ever. In this context, a significant increase in Iraqi oil production capacity would have been very useful for averting a possible future oil crisis.

Conversely, if worries about Saudi Arabia's production potential were exaggerated, freeing up Iraq's oil production might have been expected to benefit the United States by reducing Saudi influence over world oil markets. US reliance on Saudi Arabia to stabilize world oil markets limited the ability of the United States to criticize Saudi policies and to promote desired domestic political, economic, and social reforms. In addition, Saudi Arabia's spare capacity had given it a degree of influence over the oil market and other oil producers that did not always conform to US interests. The wisdom of relying on Saudi Arabia was further called into question by revelations about the roles played by Saudis in the terrorist attacks of 9/11. Thus, as a controversial July 2002 briefing by a Rand analyst for the US Defense Advisory Board concluded, a pro-Western Iraq could reduce US dependence on Saudi energy exports and enable the United States to force the monarchy to crack down on financing and support for terrorism within its boundaries (Morgan and Ottaway 2002). In this context, the possibility of building up Iraq as an oil-producing counterweight to Saudi Arabia could have appeared very attractive.

Concluding thoughts

This chapter has argued that Persian Gulf oil greatly increased the likelihood of a US invasion of Iraq in the early 2000s. The United States has had a long-standing interest in seeing that the Persian Gulf be able to supply the world reliably with substantial amounts of oil, and in the early

2000s, Saddam Hussein's regime presented the principal threat to that interest. In addition, the alternatives to war – regime change by other means and especially a continuation of the previous policy of containment and deterrence – appeared either unpromising or less and less attractive. Oil is largely the reason why the Persian Gulf and Saddam Hussein mattered.

But neither should the role of oil in the decision to invade Iraq be overstated. The US interest in Persian Gulf oil and the threat posed by Iraq did not make war inevitable. War was not the only plausible option. In particular, the possibilities for containing and deterring Iraq had not been exhausted. Indeed, as the events of late 2002 demonstrated, it was not impossible to re-establish a tough UN inspections regime that, if given more time, might have greatly clarified just how substantial a threat Iraq posed to its neighbors. To explain why the United States chose war in 2003, one must consider other factors, and three in particular stand out.

One obvious factor that often goes unmentioned was that the United States had the ability to go to war. Simply put, the Bush administration invaded Iraq because it could. Even here, however, perceptions played a role. Experts disagreed on how many forces would be necessary and how much opposition they would face. But the potentially controversial belief that the United States could win a rapid and decisive victory at little cost had been reinforced by the swift defeat of the Taliban in late 2001.

A second important factor was the presidential election of 2000. George Bush's narrow victory resulted in a vast attitudinal shift within the corridors of power. The highest levels of the Bush administration were staffed by a number of people who wanted to adopt a more aggressive policy toward Iraq than had members of the Clinton administration. Indeed, some, such as Paul Wolfowitz, the Undersecretary of Defense, made regime change a top priority. It is much harder, if not impossible, to imagine a war being undertaken by a hypothetical Gore administration.

But even the handover of power, alone, might not have been enough. Many in the Bush administration did not assign top priority to Iraq or regard forceful regime change as the best option. Rather, we must also consider the impact of the terrorist attacks of 9/11. They provided both a further reason, however specious, for getting rid of Saddam and, when harnessed to an effective public relations campaign, a compelling justification for war that resonated deeply with the American public. It is possible to imagine a war without the shock of 9/11, but still difficult. 9/11 created a large window of opportunity for those in the administration who preferred war.

Nevertheless, oil did much to set the stage. Indeed, it was a necessary condition for war. One way to appreciate this is by comparing US policy toward other "rogue" states that the Bush administration did not invade, such as Iran, North Korea, Syria, and Libya. Several other states were seeking to acquire nuclear weapons in the first years of the Bush administration, and at least one – North Korea – was closer to having them. Several states had more extensive ties to anti-American terrorists. And a number of other states around the world had fallen equally short of adhering to democratic principles or had engaged in widespread human rights abuses. What made Iraq different? Arguably, it was the threat that it posed to Persian Gulf oil supplies that set Iraq under Saddam Hussein apart from most of the other rogue states against which the United States might have directed its ire. The principal exception to this claim is Iran, but invading that country would have posed a much greater military challenge at the time.

Another way to appreciate the role of oil is to consider the counterfactual, complicated and problematic though it may be. What if the Persian Gulf had never possessed significant amounts of oil? In that case, it is difficult to imagine something like the Iraq War ever having occurred. Even if oil-related considerations played no role in the decision to invade, one can regard the war as a logical – if not the only possible – culmination of a series of prior steps that were taken largely, if not exclusively, because of the region's strategic importance to the United States. Some of these steps, such as the Carter Doctrine, Operation Earnest Will, and Operations Desert Storm and Desert Shield, were explicitly justified in terms of threats to the region's oil supplies. Other measures, such as US arms sales in the 1970s and the enforcement of UN sanctions in the 1990s, were justified on other grounds. But those grounds could be easily understood in terms of threats to the region's oil. In short, no oil, no war.

Notes

This chapter is a substantially revised version of John S. Duffield, "Oil and the Iraq War: How the United States Could Have Expected to Benefit, and Might Still," *Middle East Review of International Affairs* 9, no. 2 (June 2005): 109–141. It also draws upon material in John S. Duffield, *Over a Barrel: The Costs of U.S. Foreign Oil Dependence* (Stanford: Stanford University Press, 2008), and Peter J. Dombrowski and John S. Duffield, "Are We Safer Now?" in John S. Duffield and Peter J. Dombrowski, eds., *Balance Sheet: The Iraq War and U.S. National Security* (Stanford: Stanford University Press, 2009): 158–202. I wish to thank Matthew Schipani, Raluca Viman Miller, and Kristopher Sauriol for research assistance and Gregory Gause and Ed Morse for comments on an earlier version.

1 Likewise, the Report of the National Energy Policy Development Group in 2001 noted that "By 2020, Persian Gulf oil producers are projected to supply between 54 and 67 percent of the world's oil" (p. 8-4). Available at www.ne.doe. gov/pdfFiles/nationalEnergyPolicy.pdf (accessed November 3, 2010).
2 "Presentation – The Case for Action," September 12, 2002. Available at www. waranddecision.com/docLib/20080403_TheCaseforAction.pdf (accessed September 29, 2010).
3 The October 2002 National Intelligence Estimate concluded that "If Baghdad acquires sufficient fissile material from abroad it could make a nuclear weapon within several months to a year." Available at www.fas.org/irp/cia/product/iraq-wmd-nie.pdf (accessed November 1, 2010).
4 Available at http://georgewbush-whitehouse.archives.gov/news/releases/2002/08/20020826.html (accessed November 3, 2010).

5 Available at http://georgewbush-whitehouse.archives.gov/news/releases/2003/01/20030128–19.html (accessed November 3, 2010).
6 Available on the website of the Project for the New American Century at www.newamericancentury.org/iraqclintonletter.htm (accessed November 1, 2010).
7 See also "Guiding Principles for U.S. Post-Conflict Policy in Iraq," Report of an Independent Working Group Cosponsored by the Council on Foreign Relations and the James A. Baker III Institute for Public Policy of Rice University, December 2002, 18. Available at www.cfr.org/content/publications/attachments/Iraq_TF.pdf (accessed November 1, 2010).
8 "Post-sanction Plan," *Oil & Gas*, July 17, 1995.
9 "Guiding Principles," 16.
10 "Guiding Principles," 16.

References

Alkadiri, Raad, and Fareed Mohamedi. 2003. *World Oil Markets and the Invasion of Iraq.* Middle East Report, no. 227 (Summer). Available at www.merip.org/mer/mer227/227_alkadiri_mohamedi.html (accessed November 2, 2010).
Almond, Mark. 2003. "It's All About Control, Not the Price of Petrol." *New Statesman* (April 7).
Boot, Max. 2003. "A War for Oil? Not This Time." *New York Times* (February 13).
BP. 2003. *BP Statistical Review of World Energy 2003* (June).
BP. 2010. *BP Statistical Review of World Energy 2010* (June). Available at www.bp.com/productlanding.do?categoryId=6929&contentId=7044622.
Callinicos, Alex. 2005. "Iraq: Fulcrum of World Politics." *Third World Quarterly* 26, no. 4/5.
Central Intelligence Agency (CIA). 2002. "Iraq's Weapons of Mass Destruction" (October). Available at www.cia.gov/library/reports/general-reports-1/iraq_wmd/Iraq_Oct_2002.pdf (accessed November 1, 2010).
Chalabi, Fadhil. 2000. "Iraq and the Future of World Oil." *Middle East Policy* 7, no. 4 (October). Available at www.mepc.org/public_asp/journal_vol. 7/chalabi.html.
Cirincione, Joseph. 2009. "The Iraq War and the Failure of U.S. Counterproliferation Strategy." In John S. Duffield and Peter J. Dombrowski, eds., *Balance Sheet: The Iraq War and U.S. National Security*, pp. 39–67. Stanford: Stanford University Press.
Clark, R. William. 2005. *Petrodollar Warfare: Oil, Iraq and the Future of the Dollar.* Gabriola Island, Canada: New Society Publishers.
Diebel, Linda. 2003. "Oil War: 23 Years in the Making." *Toronto Star* (March 9).
Duffield, John S. 2008. *Over a Barrel: The Costs of U.S. Foreign Oil Dependence.* Stanford: Stanford University Press.
Everest, Larry. 2004. *Oil, Power, and Empire: Iraq and the U.S. Global Agenda.* Monroe: Common Courage Press.
Feith, Douglas J. 2008. *War and Decision: Inside the Pentagon at the Dawn of the War on Terrorism.* New York: Harper.
Ferraro, Vincent. 2003. "Another Motive for Iraq War: Stabilizing Oil Market." *Hartford Courant* (August 12).
Freedman, Lawrence, and Efraim Karsh. 1995. *The Gulf Conflict, 1990–1991.* Princeton: Princeton University Press.
Gause, F. Gregory. 2003. "The Approaching Turning Point: The Future of U.S.

Relations with the Gulf States." *Brookings Project on U.S. Policy Towards the Islamic World.* Analysis Paper Number Two (May).

Gerth, Jeff. 2002. "Report Offered Bleak Outlook About Iraq Oil." *New York Times* (October 5).

Gongloff, Mark. 2003. "Playing for Iraq's Jackpot." *CNNMoney* (April 16). Available at http://money.cnn.com/2003/04/16/news/economy/war_oil_primer (accessed November 1, 2010).

Greenspan, Alan. 2007. *The Age of Turbulence: Adventures in a New World.* New York: Penguin.

Haass, Richard N. 2009. *War of Necessity, War of Choice: A Memoir of Two Iraq Wars.* New York: Simon & Schuster.

Israeli, Raphael. 2004. *The Iraq War: Hidden Agendas and Babylonian Intrigue.* Eastbourne: Sussex Academic Press.

Kawach, Nadim. 2002. "GCC vs Iraq: Who Benefits after the War?" *Gulf News* (online edition) (December 6).

Klare, Michael T. 2003. "For Oil and Empire? Rethinking the War with Iraq," *Current History* 102, no. 662 (March), 129–135.

Klare, Michael T. 2004a. *Blood and Oil: The Dangers and Consequences of America's Growing Petroleum Dependency.* New York: Henry Holt.

Klare, Michael T. 2004b. "Bush-Cheney Energy Strategy: Procuring the Rest of the World's Oil." *Foreign Policy in Focus.* Washington, DC, and Silver City, NM: Interhemispheric Resource Center/Institute for Policy Studies/SEEN. Available at www.fpif.org/papers/03petropol/politics.html (accessed April 23, 2004).

Klare, Michael T. 2008. *Rising Powers, Shrinking Planet: The New Geopolitics of Energy.* New York: Metropolitan Books.

Kubursi, Atif. 2006. "Oil and the Global Economy." In Rick Fawn and Raymond Hinnebusch, eds., *The Iraq War: Causes and Consequences,* pp. 247–255. Boulder: Lynne Rienner.

Leach, Gary. 2006. *Crude Interventions: The United States, Oil and the New World (Dis) Order.* London: Zed.

Lindorff, Dave. 2003. "Crude History Lesson: Is the War All About Oil after All?" *In These Times* (March 27). Available at www.inthesetimes.com/site/main/article/ crude_history_lesson (accessed May 11, 2004).

Little, Douglas. 2002. *American Orientalism: The United States and the Middle East Since 1945.* Chapel Hill: University of North Carolina Press.

Maass, Peter. 2009. *Crude World: The Violent Twilight of Oil.* New York: Knopf.

MacFarquhar, Neil. 2002. "Iraq Halts Petroleum Exports to Put Pressure on Americans." *New York Times* (April 9).

McClellan, Scott. 2008. *What Happened: Inside the Bush White House and Washington's Culture of Deception.* New York: PublicAffairs.

Mearsheimer, John J., and Stephen M. Walt. 2003. "An Unnecessary War." *Foreign Policy* 134 (January–February), 50–59.

Mearsheimer, John J., and Stephen M. Walt. 2007. *The Israel Lobby and U.S. Foreign Policy.* New York: Farrar, Straus and Giroux.

Morgan, Dan, and David B. Ottaway. 2002. "War-Wary Saudis Move to Increase Oil Market Clout." *Washington Post* (November 30).

Paul, James. 2003. "Oil Companies in Iraq." *Global Policy Forum* (November). Available at www.globalpolicy.org/component/content/article/185/40586.html (accessed October 6, 2010).

Pollack, Kenneth M. 2002. *The Threatening Storm: The Case for Invading Iraq.* New York: Random House.

Pollack, Kenneth M. 2003. "Securing the Gulf." *Foreign Affairs* 82, no. 4 (July/August), 2–16.

Ricks, Thomas E. 2006. *Fiasco: The American Military Adventure in Iraq.* New York: Penguin.

Rutledge, Ian. 2005. *Addicted to Oil: America's Relentless Drive for Energy Security.* London: I. B. Tauris.

Schmitt, Eric. 2003. "Cheney Lashes Out." *New York Times* (October 11).

Sengupta, Somini. 2002. "U.N. Broadens List of Products Iraq Can Import." *New York Times* (May 15).

Sick, Gary. 2003. "The United States in the Persian Gulf: From Twin Pillars to Dual Containment." In David W. Lesch, ed., *The Middle East and the United States*, pp. 291–307. Boulder: Westview Press.

Standlea, David. 2006. *Oil, Globalization, and the War for the Arctic Refuge.* Albany: State University of New York Press.

Stokes, Doug, and Sam Raphael. 2010. *Global Energy Security and American Hegemony.* Baltimore: Johns Hopkins University Press.

Suskind, Ron. 2004. *The Price of Loyalty: George W. Bush, the White House, and the Education of Paul O'Neill.* New York: Simon & Schuster.

Telhami, Shibley, Fiona Hill, Abdullatif A. Al-Othman, and Cyrus H. Tahmassebi. 2002. "Does Saudi Arabia Still Matter? Differing Perspectives on the Kingdom and Its Oil." *Foreign Affairs* 81, no. 6 (November/December).

US Energy Information Administration (USEIA). 2001. *Annual Energy Outlook 2002.* Washington, DC: US Department of Energy, December.

US Energy Information Administration (USEIA). 2003a. *Annual Energy Outlook 2003.* Washington, DC: US Department of Energy, January.

US Energy Information Administration (USEIA). 2003b. *International Energy Outlook 2003.* Washington, DC: US Department of Energy, May.

US Energy Information Administration (USEIA). 2003c. Iraq Country Analysis Brief (August). Available at www.eie.doe.gov/emeu/cabs/iraqfull.html.

US Energy Information Administration (USEIA). 2010. *Annual Energy Review 2009.* DOE/EIA-0384(2009) (August). Washington, DC: US Department of Energy.

US Senate. Select Committee on Intelligence. 2006. "Report on Postwar Findings About Iraq's WMD Programs and Links to Terrorism and How They Compare With Prewar Assessments." 19th Cong., 2nd Sess. (September 8). Available at http://intelligence.senate.gov/phaseiiaccuracy.pdf (accessed November 2, 2010).

US Senate. Select Committee on Intelligence. 2008. "Report on Whether Public Statements Regarding Iraq By U.S. Government Officials Were Substantiated By Intelligence Information." 110th Cong., 2nd Sess. (June). Available at http://intelligence.senate.gov/080605/phase2a.pdf (accessed November 2, 2010).

Woodward, Bob. 2002. *Bush at War.* New York: Simon & Schuster.

Woodward, Bob. 2004. *Plan of Attack.* New York: Simon & Schuster.

Yergin, Daniel. 1991. *The Prize: The Epic Quest for Oil, Money, and Power.* New York: Simon & Schuster.

Yergin, Daniel. 2002. "A Crude View of the Crisis in Iraq." *The Washington Post* (December 8).

9 Tony Blair nurtures the special relationship

Jane M. O. Sharp

Introduction

Tony Blair's decision to embrace George Bush's war against Iraq has four root causes. First, a perception of the dangers of weapons of mass destruction (WMD) and, after 9/11, the possibility that biological, chemical and nuclear agents might fall into the hands of terrorists. Second, a Manichean sense of good and evil and a religiosity which did not sit well in secular Britain, but which facilitated his relationship with the born-again George W. Bush. Third, his perception that British military operations, especially when justified as humanitarian intervention, were usually successful, short-lived and relatively free of risk, based on recent "successes" in Kosovo in 1999, Sierra Leone and East Timor in 2000, and Afghanistan in 2001. Fourth, and most influential, his judgment (fortified by the myth of the Special Relationship and his friendship with Bill Clinton in 1997–2000) that Britain must always try to stay close to the United States.

In April 1999, one month into NATO's bombing of Serbia, and impatient with Bill Clinton's resistance to the deployment of American troops in Kosovo, Blair delivered his Doctrine of the International Community speech to the Economic Club of Chicago, which explored the legal and moral basis for military intervention "in other peoples' conflicts." Blair noted that many recent problems had been caused by two ruthless and dangerous men: Slobodan Milosevic and Saddam Hussein. He admitted that the international community could not step in to stop all barbarous acts by undemocratic regimes, so suggested five criteria that must be met before taking military action, basically a re-hash of the Just War theory espoused by Aquinas:

1 Are we sure of our case? War is an imperfect instrument for resolving conflict so we cannot rush into a situation on the basis of media reports of terrible events.
2 Have we exhausted all diplomatic means?
3 Are there military operations we can practically take?
4 Are we prepared for the long term because we cannot simply walk away once the fighting is over?
5 Do we have a national interest involved?

In Blair's view British involvement in Kosovo met all these criteria, and probably encouraged his belief that ousting Saddam would be relatively uncomplicated. Blair showed little interest in foreign or defense policy before he became prime minister, but once in office he quickly came to see the use of military force as the answer to most foreign policy problems. Nevertheless, it remains a puzzle to many in Britain that an otherwise successful center-left government could lock itself into a subservient military relationship with the most right-wing unilateralist US administration in any of their lifetimes (Kettle 2010). This chapter is an effort to understand how Blair could *risk* his reputation on such a deeply misguided adventure.

The focus is on British policy toward Iraq between Operation Desert Storm in 1991 and the launch of Operation Iraqi Freedom in March 2003. It shows how the lessons which Blair took from 9/11 were much closer to those of George Bush than to those of his own senior advisers in the Ministry of Defence (MOD) Foreign and Commonwealth Office (FCO), the intelligence agencies – MI6 (foreign), MI5 (domestic), and Defence Intelligence Staff (DIS) – as well as most parliamentarians. Britons had suffered from Irish terrorism for decades and had disrupted several Al Qaeda attacks during the 1990s, so the public were not as traumatized by 9/11 as their American cousins. Most already knew Al Qaeda was a serious threat. By contrast, as revealed at the Iraq Inquiry, Tony Blair did not have Osama Bin Laden on his radar before 9/11, not having read his intelligence briefings on Al Qaeda. He was thus better able to understand the traumatic impact of 9/11 in the United States, and more receptive, than most in Britain, to Bush's argument that the prospect of Saddam acquiring weapons of mass destruction, and perhaps passing them on to terrorists, was sufficient reason to launch a full scale war against Iraq.

This chapter begins by examining UK policy toward the containment of Iraq between 1991 and 2003. It traces the growing tensions over policy towards Iraq in the UN Security Council, between the United States and the UK on the one hand, and Russia, China, and France on the other. From George Bush senior through two Clinton administrations into the presidency of George Bush junior, the United States, with the UK in its wake, imposed increasingly punitive sanctions, more intrusive weapons inspections, and what was virtually a continuous air war against Iraq through the inter-war period. Blair endorsed the notion of regime change in partnership with Clinton in the latter's second term, and with Clinton first authorized the use of British forces against Iraq in December 1998. Thus, far from being bullied or pressured into war by Bush, Blair was an enthusiast for regime change even before 9/11.

The second section explores how Blair was able to obtain parliamentary consent for his Iraq war despite the absence of a convincing threat. As Blair's advisers pointed out, the Bush claims about Iraq were wholly unconvincing. Britain had a long and troubled history of colonial relations with Iraq. Policy-makers knew about Saddam's WMD programs in the

1980s because Britain had provided much of the equipment and expertise in support of Iraq's war against Iran (Cook 2003: 363). But British intelligence in 2001 saw no link between secular Saddam and Al Qaeda, and knew that UN inspectors had overseen the destruction of Saddam's WMD stockpiles between 1991 and 1998, with no sign that the programs had been revived since then. With no inspectors in Iraq since 1998, Blair and his team thus had to *present* the limited intelligence available to suggest the existence of active WMD programs.

Inflating the threat did not initially cut much ice with UK government lawyers, who were increasingly unhappy in 2002 with claims by Blair and his ministers about the legality of war against Iraq. The final section details the striving for a legal rationale which occupied the Blair team for the twelve months between March 2002 and March 2003. Bush's advisers, notably Vice President Cheney and Secretary of Defense Donald Rumsfeld, were not enthusiastic about involving the United Nations, but Blair persuaded Bush that if he wanted British support there would have to be Security Council authorization. Moreover, regime change was not an acceptable *casus belli*. The issue would have to be Saddam's refusal to disarm as required by Resolution 687, the cease-fire agreement that ended the Gulf War in 1991. To this end the Blair team (together with Bush administration lawyers) designed a new set of demands that they believed Saddam could not possibly meet. His failure to do so would then provide a legal rationale for war. The Security Council was not so malleable, however, and in the absence of UN authority the UK Attorney General had to be leaned upon by Bush administration lawyers, as well as Blair's kitchen cabinet, before he came up with the "correct" advice.

Containment: UN sanctions and unauthorized no-fly zones

Two main sets of instruments served to contain Iraq after the Gulf War. The first were sanctions authorized by the UN and monitored by a special UN Commission (UNSCOM). The second were (unauthorized) US-led air strikes conducted over Iraq between April 1991 and March 2003, ostensibly to patrol no-fly zones over northern and southern Iraq, but which grew increasingly proactive and punitive.

Saddam invaded Kuwait on August 2, 1990. As Iraqi troops approached the border with Saudi Arabia, King Fahd asked the United States, Britain, and France for military assistance. With smaller contingents from other UN member states a multinational force of 680,000 troops assembled on January 17, 1991 to launch Operation Desert Storm (Operation Granby in the UK). These operations were fully authorized by the UN, and the subsequent debates about the legality of Operation Iraqi Freedom (Operation Telic in the UK) in 2002–2003 stem from UN resolutions adopted during and after the first Gulf War. The most important of these were:

- Resolution 678 on November 29, 1990, demanded Iraq withdraw from Kuwait by January 15, 1991, after which UN member states were authorized "to use all necessary means to restore international peace and security in the area."
- Resolution 687, adopted on April 3, 1991, required Iraq to disarm and destroy all chemical and biological weapons and not to acquire nuclear weapons (Article 8); established UNSCOM (Article 9); stated that sanctions would be lifted once Iraq *had* met its disarmament obligations (Article 22), and agreed to formalize the ceasefire agreement of February 27 only if and when Iraq agreed to all previous UN demands (Article 33).

In the aftermath of Iraq's defeat, uprisings broke out among the Shia in the south and the Kurds in the north, which Saddam ruthlessly suppressed. In response, on April 5, 1991 the UNSC adopted Resolution 688 which condemned the treatment of civilians by the regime and demanded that Saddam respect human rights for all Iraqi citizens. Resolution 688 was not a Chapter VII resolution, so not a call to arms. It did not authorize any member state to conduct air strikes over Iraq to force Saddam to stop repressing the Kurds in the north or the Shia in the south of Iraq. Nevertheless in April 1991 the United States and France invoked 688 to establish a no-fly zone (NFZ) over northern Iraq, and in August 1992 another one over southern Iraq. The UK joined the United States and France in patrolling the NFZs, but did not invoke 688 as its legal authority. The UK claimed instead that customary international law allowed the use of force to avert a humanitarian catastrophe.

During President Bill Clinton's first term (1993–1996) US and UK air strikes in the NFZs tended to be reactive, discrete, and proportional, prompting the neoconservatives in Washington to accuse the president of being soft on Iraq, by responding to Saddam's provocations with pinpricks instead of forceful and punitive strikes. Clinton's Iraq policy came under even greater strain during his second term (1997–2000) when Republicans controlled both the House and the Senate, and the Project for the New American Century was calling for the removal of Saddam. In 1997 Clinton made some cabinet changes that toughened up his Iraq policy. Sandy Berger replaced the more dovish Anthony Lake at the National Security Council, while Madeleine Albright replaced Warren Christopher at State. This matched the replacement of Rolf Ekeus by Richard Butler as head of UNSCOM. Ekeus thought UNSCOM worked well to contain Saddam, whereas Butler took a much harder line and wanted more intrusive inspections.

UNSCOM successes

Despite the harsher Clinton policy toward Iraq, by the mid 1990s there was a growing consensus in the wider UN community that UNSCOM had discovered and destroyed Saddam's active nuclear, biological, and chemical weapons programs. With respect to nuclear assets, although Iraq had produced missiles that could reach Israel before the Gulf War it had not been able to produce either a fissile core or an implosive device (Ritter 1999: 102–103). Between 1991 and 1994 UNSCOM and IAEA stripped the nuclear weapons development program down to its roots, and removed all known plutonium and highly enriched uranium. With respect to biological weapons, on September 8, 1994, the UK Joint Intelligence Committee (JIC) reported that Iraq had no stocks of biological agents suitable for weaponization. With respect to chemical weapons, by 1994 UNSCOM had destroyed or verified destruction of 28,000 chemical-weapons munitions, almost 500,000 liters of chemical weapons agents and two million liters of chemical weapons precursors (Knights 2005: 172).

There was a spike of alarm in August 1995 when Saddam's son-in-law Hussein Kamil defected to the West with good news and bad news (Powell IIT 2010: 52) The good news was that Saddam had destroyed all his biological weapons in 1991; the bad news was that the Iraqi records were poor and did not show when and where previous stockpiles had been stored or destroyed. Nevertheless, as Tony Blair became prime minister in 1997, Iraq was seen as an aspiring rather than an actual WMD proliferator (Knights 2005: 171). This was confirmed (unwittingly perhaps) by Tony Blair in a hawkish speech about Saddam in January 1998 to the Labour Party policy forum in London, when Blair said: "He (Saddam) must be either persuaded by diplomacy or made by force to yield up his long cherished ambition to develop nuclear, chemical and biological weapons" (Seldon *et al.* 2008: 85).

Operation Desert Fox December 1998

If Saddam no longer had active WMD programs in the late 1990s, he was not always cooperative, especially after Richard Butler replaced Rolf Ekeus as head of UNSCOM. Saddam accused Butler of exploiting the inspection regime to gather military intelligence for the United States and the UK; a charge that was well founded. With respect to the UK, in 1997 Butler and ex-marine Scott Ritter initiated a new "Shake the Tree" operation which involved close cooperation between UNSCOM and British intelligence. Rachel Davis, formerly with the UK Defence Intelligence Staff (DIS), headed up UNSCOM's Information Assessment Unit in Bahrain, from where she developed close working relationships with Britain's GCHQ in Cheltenham, the CIA, SIS, Israeli intelligence (Aman), and the German national intelligence service (BND). Under Operation Rockingham, UNSCOM inspectors were briefed and debriefed before and after each mission to Iraq (Knights 2005: 174–175; Jones 2010: 29–30).

In 1998 Saddam declared eight presidential sites off-limits to UNSCOM inspectors at which stage Blair was more eager for military action than

Clinton. He was worried about Labour Party opposition, however, so Alastair Campbell, Blair's communications director, produced the first of his dossiers on Iraqi WMD on November 12, 1998. It was a rough-and-ready document, but it defused some of Blair's backbench opposition. Foreign Secretary Robin Cook reminded Blair that he would still need specific UN authority for military action. Blair then consulted UK Attorney General John Morris, who argued that 1205 (adopted on November 12, 1998) as a Chapter VII Resolution would serve to revive Resolutions 687 and 678 which was sufficient cover for Blair to proceed. No other Security Council member approved the Operation, however, and at least one FCO lawyer thought the 1205 justification "a bit of a stretch" (Wilmshurst IIT 2010). Clinton and Blair nevertheless scheduled four days of intense air and cruise missile strikes to begin on November 14. UNSCOM inspectors left Iraq on November 11 only to return on November 17 when the mission was aborted after a diplomatic intervention by Kofi Annan. Eventually the strikes were launched in mid December, but not before Clinton again warned UNSCOM inspectors to leave the country. This time they would not return until November 2002.

Although Blair claimed Desert Fox successfully degraded Saddam's WMD assets, the record suggests otherwise. Former UNSCOM inspector Scott Ritter noted that the strikes were mostly against empty buildings. The DIS in London concurred. They refused to endorse MOD claims that the operation had been a success, because they had no evidence of any active biological or chemical warfare related facilities left in late 1998 (Jones 2010: 38–39). Analysts who studied the target list questioned the stated purpose of the operation (degrading WMD) because they included all aspects of Iraq's military infrastructure: intelligence HQ, military barracks, airfields, Ba'ath Party buildings, with a great deal of collateral damage to schools and hospitals. Coming so soon after the passage of the Iraq Liberation Act in October, Desert Fox looked more like the beginning of a US effort to oust Saddam. Russia, China, and France, as well and Turkey and several of the Gulf States, condemned the United States and UK for taking matters into their own hands (Ross ITT 2010).

Desert Fox was hugely controversial not only at the UN, but also in Washington and London. Russia, France, and China called for lifting the eight-year oil embargo on Iraq and for the firing of Richard Butler. France had ceased to patrol the northern NFZ in 1996, and now pulled out of the southern zone as well. Critics in the United States accused Clinton of merely trying to divert attention from threats of impeachment at home. In Britain, slavishly following the US lead was never popular because it alienated British allies in Europe and in the Middle East. Europhile Brits were also upset that precisely when Britain was holding the six-month EU Presidency in the second half of 1998, Blair chose to act bilaterally with Clinton instead of trying to develop an EU consensus on how to deal with Saddam. Lord Healey, a former Labour Defence Minister, warned Blair that his actions had done him no good and had enormously weakened Britain's influence with Russia, China, the Middle East, and the EU. Nor was the operation popular with the British military establishment. General Sir Peter de la Billiere, who commanded British troops in the Gulf War in 1991, told David Frost on BBC TV that "You can't bomb people into submission; it tends to make them defiant. I think there is a considerable risk this will happen not just in Iraq, but across the Islamic world" (Grice 1998).

Seeking smarter UN sanctions after Operation Desert Fox

The Iraq issue was quieter at the UN during 1999 and 2000, but Desert Fox destroyed Security Council unity and put the UK under pressure. Russia and China now opposed all Anglo-American proposals on Iraq, as did France. Arab countries claimed that the United States and UK had double standards with respect to UN resolutions, for example, ignoring Israel's responsibility to withdraw from the occupied territories, as mandated by UNSC Resolution 242 in 1967, but expecting 100 percent compliance from Iraq. To counter the ill will, the UK mission in New York tried to regenerate a comprehensive P-5 effort to design smarter, fairer sanctions that would ease the hardship suffered by most Iraqis while still containing Saddam's aspirations to acquire WMD. Resolution 1284, adopted on December 17, 1999, established the UN Monitoring, Verification and Inspection Commission for Iraq (UNMOVIC) as a successor inspection team to UNSCOM, which was designed to meet concerns the other UN members had about the previous inspectors being too close to Western intelligence agencies. From the perspective of the UK, Resolution 1284 aimed to get Iraq to the point where sanctions might be suspended, but it did not convince Russia, China, or France who all abstained, claiming it did not offer Iraq a clear path to sanction relief (Ross IIT 2010: 48).

As UNSCOM departed Iraq, the consensus in London – including the FCO, MOD, and the JIC – was that the inspections had worked reasonably well. UK intelligence was satisfied that Iraq was not importing weapons systems and was not able to rearm, so was not a threat to other states. William Patey (head of the Middle East department at the FCO) told the Iraq Inquiry that: "had we not had sanctions Saddam would have been able to develop missiles over 150km range and he would have been able to make further progress with his WMD program. So we did constrain him in that respect" (Ricketts, Patey and Webb IIT 2009). This view was backed up by Simon Webb (the Political Director at the MOD in 2001) who told the Iraq Inquiry that: "Our military capacity and broad international consensus to maintain the arms embargo severely limited Iraq's ability to rearm and rebuild." In February 2001 the FCO Policy Advisory Board (PAB) stated that: "inspectors were the best way to limit Iraq's WMD programme," in other words containment was working and the UN was the place to pursue it, diplomatically not militarily. The Attorney General's office had also warned the FCO and the MOD, in February 2001, that the legality of patrolling the NFZs was very dubious (Brummell Doc. 2001).

Blair and Bush: the impact of 9/11

Before 9/11 the new Bush administration seemed to prefer a more aggressive containment regime rather than a full-scale war against Iraq. Blair claimed that Iraq was not high on the agenda at his first get-together with the newly elected President George W. Bush at Camp David in February 2001, though his adviser John Sawers remembered it was definitely the first topic Bush, Blair and Colin Powell discussed on that occasion (Sawers ITT 2009: 13). The new US CENTAF Commander Lt General Charles Wald, definitely had Iraq high on his agenda: "With the new (Bush) administration it would be the perfect time to change how we were doing things. You can't do this tit for tat thing. ... Our recommendation was that we do something more aggressive" (Knights 2005: 235). The first example of this more aggressive policy, and the new President's first military action, took place on February 16 when the United States and UK conducted raids within five miles of central Baghdad, well beyond either the northern or southern NFZs as defined in 1991 and 1992. So just as Tony Blair began his first term as prime minister by bombing Iraq in partnership with Bill Clinton, so too did Blair and Bush begin the latter's first term. At the FCO the Middle East Department found this disturbing. Patey told the Iraq Inquiry that the FCO feared others would associate Blair with the new American president's policy of regime change in Iraq, as trailed by Condi Rice in her 2000 *Foreign Affairs* article (Rice 2000).

Blair was in Brighton, about to deliver a speech to the annual trade union congress when Al Qaeda hit the twin towers in New York on September 11, 2001. He dashed back to London and called in his intelligence chiefs to ask, "who did this?" The answer was "most likely Osama bin Laden's organization." Blair's response was extraordinary: "Did I know about this?" Stephen Lander (head of MI5) reminded Blair that he had been receiving regular Joint Intelligence Committee (JIC) bulletins about Al Qaeda, the most recent being on July 16 warning that Al Qaeda was in the final stages of planning an attack on the West (Seldon *et al.* 2008: 12). In his first public remarks on 9/11 Blair spoke of standing shoulder to shoulder with the United States and he worked hard to forge as large a coalition as possible to deal with the Taliban. It was not difficult because 9/11 had totally changed the atmosphere at the UN to produce a sense of solidarity with the United States, where Resolution 1368 authorizing military action against the Taliban passed with ease on September 12.

Iraq as the second stage of the war on terror

Blair initially aligned himself with Colin Powell and the State Department in resisting the inclusion of Iraq as the second stage of the new war on terror espoused by the United States. At the Iraq Inquiry Michael Boyce, Chief of the UK Defence Staff (CDS) 2001–2003 said that he told British officers stationed in Tampa, Florida, on Afghanistan business in late 2001 that they were not to engage in any contingency planning about Iraq. That would change in early 2002 (Boyce IIT 2009: 4). Shortly after Bush's axis of evil speech in January 2002 Blair asked his Joint Intelligence Committee (JIC) for a threat assessment for Iraq. Before this appeared, however, Blair's cabinet office presented an Iraq Options paper on March 8, 2002 to prepare the prime minister for an early April meeting with Bush at the Crawford ranch. Throughout 2002 Bush claimed that he had no Iraq war plans "on the table," but in December 2001 he had already asked General Tommy Franks to develop invasion plans. Franks prepared the Iraqi battlefield for ground troops by exploiting the southern NFZ to conduct increasingly aggressive air strikes. This Operation Southern Focus began in June 2002 with UK participation (Knights 2005: 255–260).

Generating a plausible Iraqi threat

The March 8 Iraq Options paper noted that, if Britain opted to participate in a full scale war against Iraq, it would need to contribute division level ground forces in addition to air and naval assets already in the region. To prepare for such a war would require a "media campaign to warn of the dangers that Saddam posed and to prepare public opinion both in the UK and abroad" (Paragraph 34). The only possible rationale for the UK to join in such a war was to inflate the threat posed by Saddam's alleged WMD programs, because self-defense did not apply and regime change was not an acceptable *casus belli*. The media campaign would thus have to show that Saddam was in breach of his disarmament obligations under the 1991 ceasefire agreement. Accordingly, John Williams, press secretary to the Foreign Secretary, was tasked with preparation of a media strategy to cover all circumstances including an invasion without UN authority (Williams Doc. 2002).

On March 11, 2002, without waiting for the JIC assessments, at a joint press conference with US Vice President Cheney at 10 Downing Street Blair confidently asserted: "That there is a threat from Saddam Hussein and the weapons of mass destruction there is no doubt at all." This was certainly not the view expressed four days later by the JIC, in its report of March 15, "The Status of Iraqi WMD Programmes," which pointed out that intelligence from Iraq was "sporadic and patchy" since Desert Fox drove inspectors out in December 1998. The JIC also noted that Security Council Resolution 687 had a fatal flaw, calling as it did for certification of the absence of WMD in Iraq as if such a thing was possible, i.e. the proof of a negative. At this stage the JIC was no help to the threat inflation exercise underway at No. 10. This would change as John Scarlett, then Chairman of the JIC, began to understand what the prime minister required.

On March 14, 2002 David Manning reported to Blair and his Chief of Staff that Condi Rice had warned him that Bush had no idea how to build support for the war or how to cope with "the morning after." On March 18 UK Ambassador to the United States, Christopher Meyer, reported to David Manning in Blair's office in London that he had told Paul Wolfowitz over Sunday lunch that the Blair government was working on a paper to make the case against Saddam strong enough "to take a critical mass of parliamentary and public opinion with us" (Meyer Doc. March 2002).

On March 22 Peter Ricketts (a former JIC chairman and at that time political director at the FCO) sent a memo to UK Foreign Secretary Jack Straw which reflected the March 15 JIC assessment that the WMD threat has not changed because of 9/11, and that claims of an WMD threat from Iraq were not persuasive. Ricketts expressed relief that Blair had

> decided to postpone publication of the unclassified document (an early draft of the September 24 WMD dossier). My meeting yesterday showed that there is more work to do to ensure that the figures are accurate and consistent with those of the US. But even the best surveys of Iraq's WMD will not show much advance in recent years ... they have not as far as we know been stepped up.

He went on to say that "we have to be convincing that the threat is so serious/imminent that it is worth sending our troops to die for" (Ricketts Doc. March 2002).

On the same day, MI5 (the UK equivalent of the American FBI) sent a memo to the JIC and the Home Office to the effect that Saddam posed no threat to the UK from either WMD or terrorist attacks – unless he felt the survival of his regime was at stake (Manningham-Buller Doc. 2002). Later, when testifying before the Iraq Inquiry on July 20, 2010, Eliza Manningham-Buller (head of MI5) confirmed that the threat to the UK increased dramatically as a result of the war against Iraq: "Our involvement in Iraq radicalized a whole generation of young people who saw our involvement in Iraq and Afghanistan as being an attack on them." "We gave Osama bin Laden his Iraqi jihad so that he was able to move into Iraq in a way that he was not before" (Manningham-Buller IIT July 2010).

On March 25, 2002, Jack Straw sent a memo to Blair repeating many of the points made by Manning and Ricketts, but also warning of the domestic risks in meeting with Bush in Crawford, Texas, because a majority of the Parliamentary Labour Party appeared to be against war with Iraq. He also cautioned that while Iraq posed a threat to its neighbors and therefore to international peace and security, that threat was no worse than the threat from Iran or North Korea, and that absent 9/11, no one would even be thinking of war with Iraq. He ended by worrying that even if regime change resulted from the war, there was no certainty that the replacement regime would be an improvement over Saddam, since Iraq had no history of democracy (Straw Doc. March 2002).

In Crawford on April 5 Blair committed British military support to Bush's war of regime change, which he confirmed in writing the following week: "if that (regime change) can't be done diplomatically, it has to be done militarily, Britain will be there" (Powell IIT 2010: 38). At the Crawford meeting Blair also explained to Bush how the UN could provide cover for the use of force. Plan A was to wrong-foot Saddam by making conditions for the return of UN inspectors so unacceptable that Saddam would refuse to allow the inspectors back in, and the United States and UK would then have their excuse to attack. In case Saddam was not so obliging, however, Plan B was being prepared, in effect to suggest that Iraqi WMD programs had been revived, putting Saddam in breach of Resolution 687. In the end, Plan B succeeded because the absence of Iraqi WMD was not universally accepted until the report of the Iraq Survey Group in 2004, when the war was well underway. In the year prior to the ground war the plan worked only too well.

The dossiers

To this end, Blair's staff produced two more WMD dossiers, the first of these appeared in September 2002 and the second in late January 2003. Over the summer of 2002 the JIC produced revised drafts of their WMD assessment, on August 21 and on September 9, which Tony Blair's staff fed into their dossier. The September 9 dossier draft included a new claim, namely that Saddam could use chemical and biological weapons "within 45 minutes" of an order.

Brian Jones, in 2002 the Head of the Nuclear Biological and Chemical Technical branch of the UK Defence Intelligence Staff (DIS), prepared a dossier on the global WMD threat for the UK Strategic Defence Review of 1998. He was not impressed with the way Tony Blair tried to educate the British public about WMD in 2002. Jones noticed that Blair preferred to use his own appointees rather than be briefed by long-standing government experts. This produced blinkered reviews because contributions from experts were curtailed. The DIS staff was asked to comment on reports, and then inputs were coordinated and filtered each step further removed from the center of excellence on the subject, with the result that in the search for efficiency status and rank were often confused with knowledge (Jones 2010: 49). This was especially true when intelligence was being used not to objectively assess threats, but to promote policy.

Jones was on vacation from late August to mid-September and on returning to his office on September 18 heard from his staff that the dossier drafts they had seen were not consistent with the available raw intelligence. DIS complaints were registered in the first half of September, but ignored. When Jones made inquiries of JIC members on September 19 he learned that MI6 had produced a new Report X provided by "a new source on trial" (i.e. would certainly need to be double checked and verified) which no one else, even in the intelligence community, was allowed to see. The gist of Report X was that Saddam had recently accelerated his production of chemical and biological weapons. Brian Jones and another colleague at DIS sent memos on September 19 and 20 respectively to the drafters of the dossier registering their concern that statements in the dossier were not supported by the intelligence. Specifically that it could not be said without doubt that Saddam had continued to produce chemical and biological weapons, and that the statement that WMD were ready for firing within forty-five minutes of an order had come from a single unreliable source and thus was not supportable (Jones 2010: 91–94).

As well as sins of commission there were also some serious omissions, for example no hint of a MI5 report in August 2002 warning that the buildup of US and UK forces in the Gulf would increase public hostility to Western interests. The WMD dossier was published on September 24 despite DIS and MI5 misgivings. "Iraq's Weapons of Mass Destruction: The Assessment of the British Government" was much more threatening than the March 15 JIC assessment. Gone were all the caveats and uncertainties. Iraq now posed a "current and serious threat to Britain." For Blair's purpose accuracy was not the main criterion. What was important was the effect the dossier had on parliament, which had been recalled a day early from their summer recess to consider it. Only later did it emerge that the DIS complaints had fallen on deaf ears.

A version of the dossier was also shared with UK allies in Europe, the more skeptical of whom came to London demanding more detail. Shortly after the dossier was published Brian Jones was invited to attend one such briefing by MI6 with his boss at DIS who feared he might be questioned by the group. Jones did not want to oblige, having no confidence in the dossier, but his superior insisted. At the meeting it transpired that the MI6 official designated to appear had refused to attend. He had no faith in the dossier either. Moreover the visiting delegation was apparently totally unconvinced by the presentation (Jones 2010: 96–98). In July 2003 (four months into the war) the JIC withdrew Report X (on which the dossier was based) as manifestly unreliable, but the damage was done. A week after the dossier was published Blair invited Bill Clinton to the Labour Party conference in Blackpool to help him face what he knew would be a skeptical – if not downright hostile – Labour Party over the possibility of war against Iraq. Clinton arrived with actor Kevin Spacey in tow and charmed the audience. His remarks on Iraq were nuanced and designed to please the crowd more than the prime minister:

Don't cross bridges we would rather not cross. Saddam needs to have one last chance. As an American and as a citizen of the world, I'm glad Tony Blair will be central to weighing the risk and making that call.

(Seldon *et al.* 2008: 118)

January 2003 dodgy dossier

The September dossier helped to bolster Blair's case that Saddam was in breach of his disarmament obligations. Nevertheless, even after the adoption of Resolution 1441 on November 8, 2002, the UK Attorney General continued to say that use of force would require explicit Security Council authorization. In London, Alastair Campbell, frustrated that parliament and the press were not yet on message, decided to produce another dossier to emphasize the Iraqi threat. As with the September dossier there was no mention of MI5 warnings of the risks to the West of a war against Iraq. There were at least three more of these in late 2002: on October 10 and 16, and December 13 (Omand ITT 2010: 37–40). The target for the new dossier was the press corps on Blair's flight to the Washington summit in late January, but the dossier was also posted on the FCO website and appeared in the subsequent Sunday newspapers. This time the intelligence agencies were asked for new material, but not asked to review the product. No need, because this – the infamous dodgy dossier – was pure spin, cobbled together by the "Coalition Information Centre" in the FCO, the ad hoc war press office established during the early phase of the war in Afghanistan, and revived to produce the new dossier. The text was manifestly not fact-checked and ten of its sixteen pages were direct cribs from an Internet copy of an un-attributed ten-year-old doctoral dissertation written by Ibrahim al-Marashi at the Monterey Institute of International Studies. Foreign Secretary Jack Straw and intelligence chief John Scarlett ('C') were both deeply embarrassed by the dossier which neither had seen before it was released (Kampfner 2003: 264–267). Robin Cook, whom Tony Blair sacked as Foreign Secretary at the beginning of his second term, called it a "spectacular own goal." On February 10, 2003 MI5 again warned Blair of the danger of increased radicalism among Muslim residents in UK should a war occur (Omand IIT 2010).

Striving for legality

Legal advice is available to the UK government from a number of sources. The prime minister relies primarily on advice from the Attorney General, a position held in Blair's second term (2001–2007) by Peter Goldsmith QC, a senior barrister but not an international lawyer. The FCO and the MOD also have teams of law officers. As the Iraq Inquiry has revealed, in the run up to the Iraq War not only Blair, but also foreign and defense ministers Jack Straw and Geoff Hoon received much advice from their law

officers who did not wait to be asked, when ministers made public statements suggesting they were planning illegal actions. Blair made it clear
that he did not want any written advice from Goldsmith until he was convinced the advice would be what he needed to go to war. From March
2002 until late February 2003, however, the lawyers consistently and
repeatedly told their political masters that Britain could not use force
against Saddam without explicit Security Council authorization.

The paper trail begins with a note from the FCO legal department,
attached to the Iraq Options paper presented to Blair on March 8, 2002,
which warned of the difficulties inherent in a war against Iraq, and drew
attention to significant differences between legal views in Washington and
London:

- In the UK's view a violation of Resolution 687 could revive the authorization to use force in Resolution 678 ... but ... it was for the Security
  Council to assess whether any such breach has occurred. The US view
  is different, maintaining that individual member states can make that
  assessment. *We are not aware of any other state which supports this view*
  (emphasis added).
- The UK invoked Resolution 1205 to revive 678 to justify participation
  in Desert Fox in December 1998, but our interpretation of 1205 was
  controversial.
- The NFZs established over northern and southern Iraq were not
  authorized by the Security Council.
- The US claim that the purpose of the NFZs was to enforce Iraqi compliance with resolutions 687 and 688. This view was not consistent with
  either 687 which does not deal with repression of the civilian population, or with 688 which was not adopted under Chapter VII of the UN
  Charter, and does not contain any provision for enforcement.

On March 28, 2002 Goldsmith reprimanded Hoon for saying in a BBC
interview with Jonathan Dimbleby that there was a clear basis for military
action against Saddam without further need of new UN authorization.
Goldsmith complained that Hoon's remarks put him – as the UK Attorney
General – in a difficult position since he had not yet been asked for legal
advice on the matter. He added that Resolution 687 adopted after the
Gulf War could not be revived without explicit authority of the Security
Council, citing advice given by previous law officers, Charlie Falconer and
John Morris, to the prime minister when Desert Fox was contemplated in
Iraq in 1997–1998:

> Charlie and I remain of the view that in the circumstances currently
> prevailing an essential precondition of the renewed use of force to
> compel compliance of the cease fire provisions is that the Security
> Council has stated that there has been a breach of the cease fire

conditions and that the Council considers the breach sufficiently grave to undermine the basis or effective operation of the cease fire.

(Goldsmith IIT 2010)

When Blair reported to his cabinet about the Crawford trip and the prospect of war in Iraq, Patricia Hewitt, whose constituency included a large Muslim community in Leicestershire, said:

> There will be a lot of tension among the Muslim communities in Britain if an attack on Iraq is seen as a unilateralist action. They would find it much easier to understand, and we should find it a lot easier to sell, if there was a specific agreement at the UN on the need for military action.

Blair's response was: "The time to debate the legal basis of our action is when we take that action." Robin Cook noted in his diary entry for that day that Blair displayed "a worryingly low priority for respect to international law" (Cook 2003: 135). And not only international law, Philippe Sands in his statement to the Iraq Inquiry notes that Para. 21 of the 2001 UK Ministerial Code of Conduct requires that the Attorney General be consulted "in good time" and "in full" before the government is committed to critical decisions involving legal considerations (Sands IIS 2010).

Goldsmith gives a green light for the air war

On June 1, 2002, Bush floated his new doctrine of pre-emptive attack at West Point. Later in the month Blair asked Goldsmith for advice about British participation in Operation Southern Focus, the air strikes designed by General Franks' CENTCOM to prepare the Iraqi battlefield for the ground war. Goldsmith gave a green light by referring back to the (dubious) advice his predecessor gave on Desert Fox in 1998. The publicly available record does not yet show how much Blair told Goldsmith about Operation Southern Focus, but whether he realized it or not – five months before Resolution 1441 was adopted in November 2002 – Goldsmith gave a green light for Britain to be part of the US war against Iraq, in the air at least. Goldsmith would certainly be aware that Bush's war plans were moving along on July 23 when he met with Blair at 10 Downing Street. Also present were Defence Minster Geoff Hoon, Foreign Secretary Jack Straw, Chief of the Defence Staff Admiral Boyce, Intelligence Chiefs John Scarlett and Richard Dearlove, as well as the Cabinet Secretary and various members of Blair's personal staff.

Dearlove told Blair that there was no imminent threat from Iraq that merited any military action and warned that in Washington intelligence assessments were being planned around the Bush schedule for war (i.e. more political than objective). Hoon reported that Operation Southern

Focus was providing "spikes of air activity" to provoke Saddam into action, and that the ground war would probably start in January 2003 (Rycroft Doc. July 23, 2002) Goldsmith still seemed to think at this stage that British participation in Bush's war could be averted, because he again warned Blair that the desire for regime change was not a legitimate basis for military action. The only three possible rationales were: self-defense, humanitarian intervention, or Security Council authorization. The first two were not applicable to Iraq and with respect to the third the UK could not rely on Resolution 1205 as it had in the case of Desert Fox in December 1998. Despite all the misgivings expressed, Blair instructed Rycroft (the minute-taker) to record the assumption that Britain would take part in any military action, but that before taking a firm decision the government would need details of the US plan (Rycroft IIT 2010).

A week later, on July 30, having seen the minutes of the July 23 meeting which did not correctly represent his own views, Goldsmith wrote to Blair, repeating at some length that military action without Security Council authorization would be "highly debatable" (Goldsmith Doc. July 30, 2002).

Meanwhile Jack Straw was also getting legal advice within the FCO. His chief law officer Michael Wood wrote to him on August 15, 2002, concerned that:

> "there appears to be an assumption that if military action were taken by the US we would not only support, but participate." Wood dismissed the "new doctrine of pre-emption" above and beyond anticipatory self-defense, as having no basis in international law. Nor of course was "regime change" a legal objective. In case Straw still had not got the message, Wood pointed out that "To act in flagrant disregard of the law would do lasting damage to the United Kingdom's international reputation (cf. Suez)" and warned that "military action outside the law leaves individual members of the armed forces potentially liable to charges of murder."
>
> (Wood Doc. August 2002)

Negotiating Resolution 1441

In discussions with George Bush, during 2001 and early 2002, Blair emphasized three priorities to help win public support for British participation in the war against Iraq: specific UN authority for the use of force; the UN to be in charge of post-war reconstruction; and a US commitment to revive the Middle East Peace Process (MEPP). US Secretary of State Colin Powell was sympathetic to this view, but it was a hard sell with Vice President Cheney and Defense Secretary Donald Rumsfeld, both of whom were disdainful of taking the UN route, no doubt fearing the process would take precious time and hold up the war. Nevertheless in the summer of 2002 Blair and Powell prevailed, and on September 12, 2002 in his annual speech to the UN General Assembly, Bush agreed to work through the UN on the Iraq issue:

> My nation will work with the United Nations Security Council to meet our common challenge. If Iraq's regime defies us again the world must move deliberately, decisively to hold Iraq to account. We will work with the Security Council for the necessary resolutions. But the purpose of the US should not be doubted. The Security Council resolutions will be enforced, the just demands of peace and security will be met, or action will be unavoidable and a regime which has lost its legitimacy will also lose its power.

Four days after Bush's UN speech, on September 16, Saddam indicated that he was willing to allow inspectors back into Iraq. Most of the UN Security Council wanted the inspectors to return as soon as possible. UNMOVIC had already been authorized under Resolution 1284 adopted on December 17, 1999. This was the last thing Bush and Blair wanted, however, until they had crafted the new Resolution with its tougher demands. They did not want UN inspectors returning to Iraq and finding no smoking gun just as Blair was about to publish his dossier inflating the WMD threat.

In Washington, three days later, on September 19, 2002, Bush released a National Security Strategy document, which outlined a new doctrine of preventive war, which would permit going to war against any regime that might pose a threat in the future. On the same day Colin Powell was asked at a House Committee on Foreign Affairs hearing what the United States would do if UNMOVIC inspectors were allowed into Iraq right away. Powell replied: "we would oppose it and if somebody tried to move the team in we would find ways to thwart it" (Morrison 2005). All of which reflects that the effort to disarm Saddam of his supposed stockpiles of WMD was just a smokescreen for regime change by force. Keeping the inspectors out made no sense if Blair and Bush truly believed Saddam had WMD arsenals to be discovered. Greenstock would later write: "the UN route over the winter of 2002–2003 was never more than an awkward diversion (from war planning) for the US administration" (Sands 2006: 196; Greenstock IIS 2009: 16).

Greenstock worked closely with John Negroponte, US ambassador to the UN, on the draft of the new resolution which Bush had agreed to seek. Their task was to find wording acceptable to those on the Security Council (France, Russia, and China) who were by now quite hostile to the Americans, and also to meet the wish of the Bush administration for tough conditions to be imposed on Iraq when the UN inspectors returned. The initial US draft Bush set the bar very high for Iraq, so that compliance would be well nigh impossible, providing the US excuse for war. Whereas Greenstock's understanding of the British position was that he should forge a resolution that would disarm Saddam of his WMD by effective new inspections, preferably short of war, but that if force was necessary it should be with the maximum international consensus.

Carne Ross, a former First Secretary at the UK mission to the UN, who drafted Resolution 1284, illuminated one aspect of 1441 that suggested that the new resolution was designed to give Iraq little chance to comply. Blair and Bush had considered 1284 not robust enough, so 1441 drastically shortened to sixty days the length of time UNMOVIC inspectors would be on the ground before having to report back to the Security Council (Article 5). Resolution 1248 stated that the head of UNMOVIC should report on Iraq's performance 120 days after the full system of ongoing monitoring and verification (OMV) has been established. OMV amounts to the baseline of knowledge of Iraq's capabilities and sites. Based on the UNSCOM experience it would take six to nine months to establish the new OMV. This means that inspectors should be on the ground at least ten months before being asked to report on Iraq's compliance (Ross IIS 2010: 3).

In October 2002, France proposed language for the new resolution that would require the Security Council to decide whether Iraq was in breach, and what action would follow, i.e. no automaticity from 1441 alone. To reconcile this view with the US desire for automaticity, the United States gave up language that would have made the use of military force automatic in the event of a breach, e.g. "to use all necessary means," while France gave up language that would have made it mandatory to adopt a second resolution before any force could be used.

Although 1441 passed 15–0 in the Security Council on November 8, the "explanations of vote" provided by the fifteen member states reflect a wide difference of interpretation, foreshadowing the diplomatic battles to come. The US position was the harshest:

> one way or another Iraq will be disarmed. If the Security Council fails to act decisively in the event of further Iraqi violations, this resolution does not constrain any Member State from acting to defend itself from the threat posed by Iraq.

The British view was softer:

> There is no automaticity in this resolution. If there is a further Iraq breach of its disarmament obligation, the matter will return to the Council for discussion as required in Paragraph 12. We would expect the Security Council to meet its responsibilities.

France, Russia, and China all took a different view from that of the United States and the UK. All three made individual explanations of their votes, but also made a joint statement as follows:

Resolution 1441 ... excludes any automaticity in the use of force. In this regard we register with satisfaction the declarations of the representatives of the United States and the United Kingdom confirming the understanding of their explanations of votes. ... In case of failure by Iraq to comply with its obligations the provisions of Paragraphs 4, 11 and 12 will apply. Such failure will be reported to the Security Council by the executive chairman of UNMOVIC or by the director general of the IAEA. It will be then for the Council to take a position on the basis of that report.

Of the ten non-permanent members of the Council, Mexico aligned firmly with Russia, France, and China, rather than the United States and the UK. "We reiterate the belief reflected in the agreed text that the possibility of the use of force is valid only as a last resort with prior explicit authorization required from the Security Council." Syria took a similar view. The other eight made rather bland statements, hoping for disarmament by peaceful means (Scott 2010: 953–964).

In September Goldsmith consulted John Scarlett to be quite sure that there was no intelligence suggesting that Iraq posed an imminent threat to Britain and was reassured there was no rationale for war on the grounds of self-defense (Goldsmith IIS 2011: 7). Goldsmith also congratulated Jack Straw and the prime minister for getting the United States back on to the UN route, but he was soon disillusioned. On October 4 Wood again chastised Straw for inappropriate public remarks, this time to the House of Commons Foreign Affairs Committee to the effect that a second UN resolution might not be necessary to authorize military action against Saddam (Wood IIT October 2002). Straw seemed rattled by this and on October 15 sent an urgent message to Wood, to ask two questions: first would the government or any individual service member be vulnerable in the UK or other courts to charges relating to unlawful use of force, and second, would the International Court of Justice (ICJ) in The Hague have any role? (McDonald Doc. October 2002).

Wood's reply was threefold. First, for the government to act contrary to legal advice would be a breach of the UK Ministerial Code which says clearly that ministers have to comply with the law, including international law. Second, to act unlawfully would have a negative effect on the UK's reputation internationally. And third, without sound legal backing the proposed action would have less domestic and international political support. If individual servicemen were accused of crimes of aggression they would more likely be tried at the International Criminal Court (ICC) rather than the ICJ. Wood sent his answer to 10 Downing Street as well as to Straw at the FCO. The response from the prime minister registered some alarm: "Why has this been put in writing" (Wood IIT 2010: 41). Meanwhile, Goldsmith, keeping track of the 1441 negotiations, telephoned Straw on October 18, 2002 noting that an early draft he had seen "did not provide legal authorization for the use of force" and reminding Straw "that the British government must be careful not to promise the US government that it can do things which the Attorney General considers to be unlawful" (Adams Doc. October 18, 2002). At this point Straw lost patience with Goldsmith and sent a message via the FCO lawyers on October 22, to say the FCO would not be consulting Goldsmith any more until the resolution was adopted and that further documentation would be provided for reference only (Goldsmith IIS 2011).

Interpreting Resolution 1441 back in London

After the resolution was adopted on November 8, Goldsmith telephoned Jonathan Powell (Blair's chief of staff) that the final draft 1441 did not provide a sound legal basis for the use of force against Iraq without explicit Security Council authorization (Brummell Doc. November 11, 2002). This prompted Jack Straw to telephone Goldsmith urging him to consider carefully the negotiating history before deciding whether or not 1441 authorized military action. By now everyone was becoming quite irritated with Goldsmith. On December 9 Jack Straw sent a message via the FCO lawyers that Goldsmith's advice was not welcome, or at least not yet. When Goldsmith explained to Blair's office on December 19 that 1441 still did not authorize military action, the assembled staff – Sally Morgan, Jonathan Powell, and David Manning – told him in effect: until you can give us a green light we do not want to hear from you (Goldsmith IIS 2011).

Into the New Year Goldsmith nevertheless continued to offer his increasingly unwelcome advice, and on January 14, 2003, handed Blair his initial interpretation of Resolution 1441, noting *inter alia* that:

1   "It is clear that 1441 contains no express authorization by the Security Council for the use of force. An early draft would have authorized states to 'use all necessary means to restore international peace and security in the area' but this wording was deleted during the negotiations."
2   However, the authorization to use force contained in Resolution 678 (1990) may revive where the Security Council has stated that there is a breach of cease fire conditions imposed by resolution 687. 1441 does not, however, revive the authorization to use force (in 678) in the absence of a further decision by the Security Council.

On January 24, 2003, Wood again reprimanded Straw for a statement he made in a meeting with Dick Cheney to the effect that: "Her Majesty's Government (HMG) would much prefer a second resolution. We would be fine if we got one. We would be OK if we tried and failed (a la Kosovo)." Peter Ricketts had already cautioned Blair against using the Kosovo option in early October (Ricketts Doc. October 2002). Wood also now cautioned

Straw, noting that the Kosovo operation was an action to avert an over-whelming humanitarian catastrophe as opposed to a pre-emptive war (Wood Doc. October 2003). Five days later Straw responded to this note with an extraordinary sentence: "I note your advice but I do not accept it" (Straw Doc. January 2003). This reply was copied to Goldsmith who responded to Straw on February 3, 2003, noting that the government's law officers must give advice they consider to be correct not the advice others may want to hear. (Interesting advice given the way Goldsmith changed his own advice two weeks later.)

The most unwelcome note to Blair from Goldsmith arrived on January 30, 2003 just before Blair left for Washington to meet Bush. In it Goldsmith wrote "I thought you would wish to know where I stand on the question of whether a further discussion of the Security Council is legally required in order to authorize the use of force against Iraq." Goldsmith's conclusion was unambiguous: "I remain of the view that the correct legal interpretation of resolution 1441 is that it does not authorize the use of military force without a further determination by the Security Council" (Goldsmith Doc. January 30, 2003). When Goldsmith's letter was made public for the Iraq Inquiry it included the handwritten reactions of the recipients in Blair's office. In the top left hand corner David Manning had scribbled: "clear advice from the Attorney on need for further Resolution." A more irritable note from Matthew Rycroft, Blair's private secretary: "Specifically we said we did not need further advice this week." On the left hand side in Blair's handwriting was scribbled: "I just don't understand this," an odd thing to say because Goldsmith had consistently advised that 1441 did not authorize the use of force.

The decision to seek a second resolution

In Washington on January 31, 2003, reflecting the warnings from Gold-smith, Blair told Bush he needed a second UN resolution. Bush agreed to go through the motions, but said that the United States would invade Iraq on or around March 10 with or without UN authorization, and regardless of whether UNMOVIC did or did not find any smoking gun. Blair made no objection to this statement, according to the Manning memo of January 31, 2003. The US team thought they had made 1441 so unacceptable to Saddam that he would not cooperate at all. Saddam, however, allowed UNMOVIC into Iraq and instead of finding a "smoking gun" the inspectors were reporting that Iraqi cooperation (if not perfect) was improving all the time. This was not good news for the war-mongers. They wanted more bad behavior from Saddam. David Manning's memo of the meeting reported three examples of the skullduggery that Bush was contemplating. The most extreme of which was to assassinate Saddam, a second was to bring forth a tame defector who would provide incriminating evidence, a third was to fly reconnaissance planes painted in UN colors and hope Saddam would shoot them down (Doward *et al.* 2009).

Blair was getting more and more frantic. On February 6 he introduced the concept of "the unreasonable veto" when he told Jeremy Paxman on BBC's *Newsnight* that if Saddam was judged to be in material breach of Resolution 687, and one of the P-5 vetoed military action, then Blair would feel free to act "outside that." Goldsmith told the Iraq Inquiry that Blair's remarks were incompatible with the legal advice he had given. It would be quite unlawful to act in the face of a Security Council veto (Goldsmith IIS 2011).

Jack Straw told the Iraq Inquiry that from February 14 until March 7 both in London and New York the UK worked hard to achieve a second resolution. On February 24 the United States, UK, and Spain produced a draft which laid out six benchmarks for Iraq to meet to avoid being in breach of its disarmament obligations. Straw claimed that the UK was willing to take "Yes" for an answer and abandon its war plans if and when Saddam complied (Straw IIT 2010). The same day France, Germany, and Russia tabled a separate memo on the UNMOVIC inspections stating that the conditions for using force against Saddam were not fulfilled (Sands 2006: 185). Given the degree to which the United States and the UK had alienated the rest of the P-5 in the negotiating of 1441, it was hardly surprising that few of the non-permanent members had any sympathy for another resolution if it gave a green light for military action. The other members of the Security Council judged that Saddam was beginning to cooperate and were in favor of giving UNMOVIC more time. Their preferred end result was disarmament and the lifting of sanctions, not war. Of the fifteen Security Council votes, the United States and the UK knew they could not count on votes from Russia, France, or China. Bulgaria and Spain caved in rather easily to US pressure, but Germany aligned unambiguously with France and Russia. Syria looked too difficult. So the focus was on the other six: Angola, Cameroon, Chile, Guinea, Mexico, and Pakistan.

Why a green light from Goldsmith despite no second resolution?

When, after several weeks of effort to seek the second resolution Greenstock reported back to London that there were still only four favorable votes: the United States, UK, Spain, and Bulgaria, Blair started to lean heavily on Goldsmith to come up with the "correct" advice. For twelve months Goldsmith and the FCO law officers had consistently advised Tony Blair and Jack Straw that joining the US war against Iraq would be unlawful without explicit authorization from the UN Security Council. Why then in early March did Goldsmith give Blair a green light to go to war? The answer came in two stages. The first was that Blair and Straw insisted that Goldsmith be briefed by those who negotiated 1441 so that he would be able to interpret the Resolution "correctly." The second stage came in mid March with requests from the Chief of the UK Defense Staff and from senior civil servants who wanted an unambiguous statement on legality before they could in good conscience send young men and women off to war.

The first effort to persuade Goldsmith to change his opinion was a meeting on January 23 in London with Jeremy Greenstock. As Goldsmith told the Iraq Inquiry, Greenstock made some good points "but he didn't quite get me there" (perhaps because Greenstock was not himself persuaded) (Goldsmith IIT 2010). On February 6, Jack Straw complained that Goldsmith was ignoring the negotiating history and pleaded for a conversation before Goldsmith sent his formal advice to No. 10 (McDonald Doc. 2003). A more powerful influence on Goldsmith's thinking was the set of briefings from Condoleeza Rice and the Bush administration lawyers in Washington on February 11. John Ashcroft, Alberto Gonzalez, Jim Haynes, and John Bellinger told Goldsmith that their instructions from the White House in September 2002 were to ensure that the language of Resolution 1441 must revive Resolution 678 which authorized the first Gulf War, and to ensure that there would be no need for further UN action before going to war against Saddam. John Bellinger would later tell a British official: "We had some trouble with your lawyer, but we got him there eventually" (Sands 2006: 196). But it was not the Americans who finally did the trick, because on March 7, 2003, the written advice that Goldsmith offered the prime minister was, as he put it, still "finely balanced," i.e. could be argued either way, with the implication that you might not want to take such a momentous step as full scale war on such a thin legal argument. Goldsmith now allowed for the possibility that 1441 could revive 678, but still said that the Security Council – rather than an individual member state – must decide whether Saddam was in material breach (Sands 2006: 328–342).

What finally put Goldsmith over the edge came at a meeting in Blair's office on March 11 attended by the Prime Minister and his deputy John Prescott as well as Cabinet Secretary Andrew Turnbull, several of Blair's kitchen cabinet, plus the Foreign Secretary, the Minister of Defence and the Chief of the Defence Staff. The latter two briefed the group on the military plans, in the course of which Boyce asked the Attorney General for a simple yes or no ruling on whether the war was legal. Andrew Turnbull did the same on behalf of the civil service. Juliet Wheldon, the Treasury Solicitor, had earlier asked Goldsmith for similar reassurance. At that point Goldsmith gave in and on March 14 sent Boyce and the civil servants his simple answer that the war would be legal. As he told the Chilcot inquiry "They deserved more, our troops deserved more, our civil servants who might be on line deserved more, than my saying there was a reasonable case" (Goldsmith IIT 2010: 171).

On March 13 Goldsmith had a number of meetings that the Iraq Inquiry explored in some detail. The first was a discussion with his colleague David Brummell to draft a minute explaining how Goldsmith had "come to a better view" of the legality of the war (Brummell Doc. March 2003). But Goldsmith knew that it was a thin case, so on the same day he hired an international lawyer (Christopher Greenwood) in case Britain was later sued for the crime of aggression in an international court. He then met with Jack Straw to say that he would prefer the cabinet to hear the more balanced view of his March 7 advice and answer any questions they might have. Straw discouraged him from such a reasonable action, warning of cabinet leaks. Goldsmith's last meeting of the day was with Charlie Falconer and Sally Morgan, two of Blair's closest aides, when Goldsmith relented on his insistence that the Security Council must define a material breach. His "better view" was now that the prime minister could do it.

On March 14 Jeremy Greenstock called Blair from New York to say there were still only four votes out of fifteen likely to vote for a second resolution. The other eleven all wanted the UNMOVIC inspectors to have more time before they could declare Saddam in material breach. This would have been a logical time for Blair to pause and call for a fundamental reassessment of the available intelligence on Iraqi WMD. But since the WMD issue was merely cover for Bush's war of regime change, the last thing Blair wanted to face was the reality that Saddam had already disarmed. The critical factor for Blair was that time was running out for the more than 45,000 British troops already on the ground in Kuwait poised to invade Iraq. The same pressure bore down on Goldsmith, who since the meeting on March 11 was aware that Bush could start the war at any minute. He could of course have ruled the war illegal, which would have meant standing down all the British troops. As Rodric Lyne observed at the Iraq Inquiry, the government was at a classic Grand Old Duke of York moment. It had marched its troops all the way up the hill, but did not want to march them all the way down again (Goldsmith IIT 2010).

As it happens Blair was offered the opportunity to march his troops down the hill on several occasions. Apparently more than once in early March Jack Straw sent Blair a handwritten note to suggest it was not too late to pull out. Charlie Falconer and Sally Morgan also repeatedly urged him to say "No" to Bush (Seldon *et al.* 2008: 163). And, as late as mid March, both George Bush and Donald Rumsfeld told Blair the United States could manage without Britain. On March 9 Bush called Blair to say the UK could drop out of the coalition, saying he did not want regime change in Britain. This horrified Blair whose main reason for putting British lives at risk in Iraq was to remain close to Bush, to keep the Special Relationship warm. His response to Bush was "I said I'm with you. I mean it." To add insult to injury on March 11, having heard from Geoff Hoon that Blair might lose a forthcoming parliamentary vote on Iraq, Rumsfeld called a press conference in Washington essentially to say he could manage without the Brits. British service chiefs were appalled. Having argued to Blair that if the UK was going to be part of the war it should play an important role in it, they did not want to be dumped before it began.

Conscious of the thinness of his case, on March 14 Goldsmith wanted to make sure that Tony Blair understood the enormity of what he was doing, so insisted that the prime minister give him written confirmation of "his unequivocal view" that Iraq had committed further material breaches since the last disarmament opportunity offered by 1441; essentially the trigger that was needed to revive Resolution 678. Goldsmith gave no guidance as to what a material breach would consist of and for such a momentous step the prime minister's response was remarkably casual. On March 15 he had his private secretary Mathew Rycroft send a note to Goldsmith's office confirming that it is indeed the "prime minister's unequivocal view' with no further explanation of the nature of the material breach of which Iraq was guilty (Goldsmith ITT 2010).

It later transpired that Blair had covered his tracks by getting a briefing from John Scarlett via David Manning on March 15 to the effect that:

> The JIC view is clear: Iraq possesses chemical and biological weapons, the means to deliver them and the capacity to re-establish production. The scale of the holdings is hard to quantify. It is undoubtedly much less than in 1991. Evidence points to a capability that is already militarily significant.
>
> (Hoon 2010 IIT)

This briefing seemed to be tailored for Blair, because it was at odds with a briefing Scarlett gave to Robin Cook on February 20, which confirmed Cook's own view that Saddam had no useable WMD (Cook 2003: 299–300).

On Sunday March 16, Blair, Bush, and Prime Minister Aznar of Spain met in the Azores to deliver one last ultimatum to Saddam before the war began. Just before the Azores "summit" French President Jacques Chirac repeated that France would vote against the resolution still on the table at the UN. This was a gift to Blair who was then able to persuade many British MPs that France had somehow blocked UN support for the war. France certainly did not want to vote for the war, but the French Ambassador in Washington, Jean-David Levitte, suggested they would not have been too comfortable voting against it either. He told CNN on March 16 that if the United States and the UK wanted to invade Iraq they would be wise not to force a vote, it would certainly be illegal to go to war if they lost the vote, but "it's a different situation if the US and UK use authority provided in prior resolutions" (Slavin 2003).

Goldsmith spent Sunday March 16, 2003 closeted in his office with eight other lawyers and senior civil servants drafting a document that could be presented to the Cabinet and the House of Lords on Monday March 17, and the House of Commons the following day. The resulting

337-word document purported to be a summary of the thirteen-page advice given to Blair on March 7, but it was nothing of the sort. All the caveats and uncertainties were removed and the war now proclaimed legal (Sands 2006: 342–344). At the cabinet meeting on March 17, Goldsmith was neither allowed to read the document nor to answer any questions about it (Short IIT 2010). On March 18 Blair secured approval for the war, after intense lobbying of skeptical Labour MPs and an eloquent (if not quite accurate) speech which condemned the French for obstructionism and hyped the threat from Iraq. Blair also promised that the UN would play a key rule in post-conflict Iraq, and the Bush administration would pursue the road map to a Middle East peace settlement (Blair 2003).

Conclusion: after hubris, nemesis

Even judged by his own criteria outlined in Chicago in April 1999, Blair's decision to take Britain into the Iraq War must be judged a mistake and the war itself an embarrassing failure. The case for war was so unsound that Blair had to inflate the threat and lean heavily on his Attorney General to change his advice. Nor were all diplomatic means exhausted before the invasion began. A majority of the UN Security Council favored giving UNMOVIC more time to conduct inspections before declaring Saddam in breach of Resolution 687. Blair might argue, and his aides certainly did on his behalf, that one reason Britain went to war to oust Saddam was that, with US military power available, it could be done. But it could only be done at huge cost to Britain's reputation, and to the reputation of Britain's armed forces. Nor did Bush and Blair prepare for the long term. By abdicating responsibility for post-conflict reconstruction to Donald Rumsfeld and the Pentagon, there was no serious effort to build infrastructure or develop civil institutions. The result was not a working democracy in Iraq, but rather the prospect of a long running civil war. And no British national interest was served by the war. Blair would say that sticking close to the United States is always in British national interest. But Britain was not threatened by Iraq in 2003, and has been far more vulnerable to global terrorism since the war, just as MI5 predicted.

Tony Blair himself has achieved quasi pariah status and no longer spends much time in the UK. In 2010 when his memoir *A Journey* was published, book signings had to be cancelled for fear of riots and when he first testified before the Iraq Inquiry he had to be smuggled in through a back door. Whenever he does appear, crowds gather to chastise him for taking Britain into an illegal war which has not only cost too many British lives, but also lowered Britain's standing in all the international organizations on which her security and prosperity depends. Nevertheless, as the Iraq Inquiry transcripts show, while the fullest responsibility for the war lies with Blair, there were others in government service who failed in their duty of restraint.

With respect to the intelligence establishment, the DIS did an admirable job in gathering and analyzing data. In addition MI5 repeatedly warned Blair of the risks to British security if he invaded Iraq. But other intelligence agencies, in particular MI6 and the JIC, too often seem to have been manipulated by the Downing Street policy-makers. As David Omand, intelligence coordinator in the cabinet office 2002–2005, admitted to the Iraq Inquiry on January 10, 2010, Blair and his advisers became a dangerously self-referential group. Omand likened the manipulation of the 1441 text to the concept of Zugzwang in chess, whereby you force your opponent into a position where every subsequent move makes their position worse: "the diplomats thought they had done that to Saddam with 1441 ... but the biter was bit" forcing the United States and the UK into an impossible military timetable (Omand IIT 2010: 55–57).

At the FCO the lawyers served the country well, consistently advising the prime minister that he had no legal authority to use military force in Iraq, and in some cases resigning when they were ignored. The Foreign Secretary himself, however, proved a very weak reed indeed. His early notes to Blair revealed an awareness that the war would be a disaster for Britain and that regime change in Iraq was no guarantee of an improvement over Saddam. But loyalty to Blair clouded Jack Straw's judgment and he stayed in post, knowing that he could have stopped the war by resigning. Robin Cook, his predecessor, did resign because he opposed the war, but he had already been demoted to Leader of the House at the beginning of Blair's second term so his resignation – though magnificent oratory – did not carry as much weight.

The MOD and CDS were remiss in not pointing out to Blair that the armed forces were not properly equipped to fight in the desert and in any case were severely overstretched by fighting in both Afghanistan and Iraq at the same time. It was thus impossible to deliver what was promised and they knew it. Had Hoon made the Attorney General aware of the risks to British troops due to inadequate equipment, perhaps instead of merely looking after the interests of his client (the prime minister) Peter Goldsmith would have served the national interest better by sticking to his principles and his initial advice, that without Security Council authority the war was illegal. As for the parliamentarians, those who voted for the war were too easily swayed by Blair's rhetoric. Fewer of them would have voted for the war without the promises of UN involvement and the US pursuit of peace in the Middle East.

The war did little to strengthen the much-vaunted Special Relationship. In his first foreign policy speech at the Lord Mayor's banquet in London on November 11, 1997, Blair proclaimed: "When Britain and America work together there is little we cannot achieve ... by virtue of our geography, our history and the strengths of our people, Britain is a global player." But the wars in Iraq and Afghanistan show that neither the United States nor the UK had *much* idea what to do beyond the use of military force. For all the "new" policies and surges, they could not rebuild the civil society because the invading powers were all so woefully ignorant of the local cultures. In the United States few in any case ever saw the relationship with Britain as special, and American critics of the Iraq War saw Blair's support of Bush as positively toxic (Brzezinski 2004).

Finally, the war underscored a major difference between the United States and the UK in attitudes toward the rule of law. Respect for international law is vital for small countries like the UK, but superpowers like the United States are less dependent on the behavior of others. In December 2003 Bush himself questioned the whole concept of international law: "International Law? I'd better call my lawyer ... I don't know what you're talking about by international law" (Sands 2006: 205). This narrative suggests that British governments care deeply about international law, even if Blair and his Attorney General flouted it in the end. The lesson for future UK governments should be to forge its most important relationships with like-minded states that have a healthy respect for the UN Charter and the Geneva Conventions. In effect this means stronger ties with the European Union and working toward the best possible relationship between a united EU and the United States.

References

Ames, R. and Norton-Taylor, R. (2010) "Memo shows 2002 plan to sell Iraq invasion to UK media," *Guardian*, December 11.

Blair, T. (2003) Speech in the House of Commons, March 18.

Blair, T. (2010) *A Journey*, London: Hutchinson.

Blix, H. (2004) *Disarming Iraq*, London: Bloomsbury.

Brzezinski, B. (2004) "America's policy blunders were compounded by Britain," *Financial Times* (London), August 6, p. 17.

Cook, R. (2003) *Point of Departure*, London: Simon & Schuster.

Doward, J., Hinsliff, G., and Townsend, M. (2009) "Confidential memo reveals US plan to provoke and invasion of Iraq," *Observer* (London), June 21, p. 5.

Grice, A (1998) "Blair sends carrier to Gulf" *Independent*, December 21.

Jones, B. (2010) *Failing Intelligence*, London: Biteback Publishing.

Kampfner, J. (2003) *Blair's Wars*, London: Simon & Schuster.

Kettle, M. (2010) "The real problem was Blair's policy towards America, not Iraq", *Guardian*, January 28.

Knights, M (2005) *Cradle of Conflict*, Annapolis: Naval Institute Press.

Meyer, C. (2005) *DC Confidential*, London: Orion Publishing Co.

Morrison, D. (2005) "How regime change was dressed up as disarmament," *Labour and Trade Union Review*, December.

Powell, J. (2010) *The New Machiavelli*, London: Bodley Head.

Rice, C. (2000) "Promoting the national interest," *Foreign Affairs*, January–February.

Ritter, S. (1999) *Endgame: Solving the Iraq Crisis*, London: Simon & Schuster.

Sands, P. (2006) *Lawless World*, London: Penguin.

Sands, P. (2010) "A very British conceit," *New York Review of Books*, September 30.

Scott, C. (2010) "Postscript on 'The serious consequences of word games': The signaling game around the 'final opportunity' for Iraq in Security Council Resolution 1441," *German Law Review*, 11: 943–964.

Seldon, A., Collins, D., and Snowdon, P. (2008) *Blair Unbound*, London: Penguin.

Slavin, B. (2003) "Allies say France makes consensus impossible," *USA Today*, March 16.

Iraq inquiry

(All documents accessed at www.iraqinquiry.co.uk)
Transcripts of evidence noted as IIT
Statements by witness noted as IIS
Blair, T.
IIS, January 29, 2010
IIT, January 29, 2010
IIS, January 14, 2011
IIT, January 14, 2011
Boyce, M.
IIT, December 3, 2009
Campbell, A.
January 12, 2010
Goldsmith, P.
IIT, January 27, 2010
IIS, January 4, 2011
Greenstock, J
IIS, November 27, 2009
IIT, November 27, 2009
Hoon, G.
IIT, January 19, 2010
Manningham-Buller, E.
IIT, July 20, 2010
Meyer, C.
IIT, November 26, 2009
Omand, D.
IIT, January 20, 2010
Powell, J.
IIT, January 18, 2010
Ricketts, P. Patey, W., and Webb, S.
IIT, November 24, 2009
Ross, C.
IIT, July 12, 2010
IIS, July 12, 2010
Rycroft, M.
IIT, September 10, 2010
Sands, P.
IIS (letter to Chilcot), September 10, 2010
Sawers, J.
IIT, December 10, 2009 and December 16, 2009
Short, C.

IIT, February 2, 2010
Straw, J.
IIT, January 21, 2010 and February 8, 2010
Tebbit, K.
IIT, December 3, 2009 and February 3, 2010
Wall, S.
ITT, January 19, 2011
Wilmshurst, E.
IIT, January 26, 2010
IIS, January 18, 2010
Wood, M.
IIT, November 24, 2010 and January 26, 2010

Declassified documents

2000

October 20, 2000
Alan Goulty, FCO Middle East and North Africa Department to Tom McKane
   Cabinet Office to John Sawers No 10, Simon Webb MOD and Margaret Vowles
   DFID

2001

February 12, 2001
David Brummell to Tom McKane
"Iraq: No Fly Zones"
February 15, 2001
Tom McKane to John Sawers
"Iraq" (Containment and the need for smarter sanctions)
April 6, 2001
Tom McKane (MOD) to John Sawers
"Iraq" (Containment and NFZs)
September 18, 2001
Tom McKane, Cabinet Office to David Manning
"Iraq Stocktake"
December 3, 2001
Simon McDonald (PPS) to Jack Straw FCO to David Manning
"Iraq Options"

2002

March 2002

March 8, 2002
Overseas and Defence Secretariat Cabinet Office
1. "Iraq Options paper"
2. "Iraq Legal Background" (FCO document attached)

March 14, 2002
David Manning to Tony Blair and Jonathan Powell
"Your trip to the US"
March 16, 2002
Joint Intelligence Committee (JIC)
"Status of Iraqi WMD Programmes"
March 17, 2002
Tony Blair to Jonathan Powell
"Iraq: Three Thoughts"
March 18, 2002
Ambassador Christopher Meyer to Davod Manning
"Iraq and Afghanistan: Conversation with Wolfowitz"
March 22, 2002
Peter Ricketts to Jack Straw (Foreign Secrretary)
"Iraq: Advice for the Prime Minister"
Eliza Manningham-Buller to John Gieve, Home Office
"Iraq: Possible Terrorist Response to a US Attack"
March 25, 2002
Jack Straw to Tony Blair
"Crawford/Iraq"
March 26, 2002
From Michael Wood (FCO lawyer) to Jack Straw's private secretary (Simon Mac-
    Donald)
March 28, 2002
Letter from Peter Goldsmith to Geoff Hoon (Minister of Defence)

April 2002

April 5–7, 2002
Extracts DIPTEL 73 0f 101727Z, April 2002
"The Prime Minister's Meeting with President Bush 5–7 April"

July 2002

July 8, 2002
Jack Straw to Tony Blair
"Iraq: Contingency Planning"
July 19, 2002
Jonathan Powell to Tony Blair and David Manning
July 23, 2002
Matthew Rycroft to David Manning *et al.* S 195/02
"Iraq: Prime Minister's Meeting, 23 July"
July 30, 2002
Peter Goldsmith to Tony Blair

August 2002

August 15, 2002
Michael Wood to Stephen Wright in Jack Straw's office

September 2002

September 4, 2002
John Wiliams, "Iraq Media Strategy"
September 9, 2002
JIC assessment
"Iraqi Use of Chemical and Biolocal Weapons – Possible Scenarios"
September 24, 2002
Simon McDonald to Michael Wood
Note of telephone call between Jack Straw and Peter Goldsmith on September 23

October 2002

October 3, 2002
Peter Ricketts to Jack Straw's Private Secretary, David Manning and Jeremy Greenstock
"Iraq: Resolutions: The Kosovo Option"
October 4, 2002
Michael Wood to Simon McDonald, Jack Straw's private secretary
October 15, 2002
Simon McDonald to Michael Wood
"Iraq"
Michael Wood to Simon McDonald
"Iraq"
October 17, 2002
Michael Wood to Simon McDonald *et al.*
On the Kosovo precedent
October 18, 2002
Mark Sedwill to Peter Ricketts
"Iraq: Foreign Secretary's Conversation with the Attorney General"
Cathy Adams
"Iraq: Record of Attorney General's telephone conversation with the Foreign Secretary 18 October"
October 22, 2002
Cathy Adams (AG office)
"Iraq: meeting with Prime Minister 22 October"

November 2002

November 11, 2002
David Brummell:
"Note of Telephone Conversation Between the Attorney General and Jonathan Powell"
November 12, 2002
David Brummell
"Iraq: Note of Telephone Conversation between the Foreign Secretary and the Attorney General on Tuesday 12 November 2002"

December 2002

December 9, 2002
Michael Woods (FCO) to Cathy Adams (AG's office)
"Iraq: Security Council Resolution 1441 (2002)"
December 19, 2002
David Brummell to Jonathan Powell, Sally Morgan, David Manning and Peter
  Goldsmith
"Iraq: Note of Meeting at No 10 Downing Street 4.00pm 19 December 2002"

2003

January 2003

January 14, 2003
Peter Goldsmith to Tony Blair
Draft: Iraq: Interpretation of Resolution 1441
January 15, 2003
Note of Blair meeting with Chiefs of Staff
January 22, 2003
Matthew Rycroft to David Manning and Jonathan Powell
"Iraq: Meeting with Jeremy Greenstock"
January 24, 2003
Michael Wood to various senior FCO officials
"Iraq: Legal Basis for Use of Force"
January 29, 2003
Jack Straw to Michael Wood
"Iraq: Legal Basis for the Use of Force"
January 30, 2003
Peter Goldsmith to Tony Blair
"Iraq"
January 31, 2003
David Manning memo to participants of 30 January meeting in Washington DC
  excerpted in Sands (2006: 272–274)

February 2003

February 3, 2003
Peter Goldsmith to Jack Straw
Letter objecting to Straw's January 29 letter to Michael Wood
February 6, 2003
Simon McDonald (for Jack Straw) to Peter Goldsmith
Straw's response to Goldsmiths opinion about an Iraq second resolution
February 12, 2003
Peter Goldsmith to Tony Blair
Iraq: Interpretation of Resolution 1441
February 19, 2003
"JIC assessment: Southern Iraq: What's in Store?"

March 2003

March 5, 2003
Iraq Planning Unit
"Planning for the UK's Role in Iraq After Saddam"
Kevin Tebbit to Andrew Turnbull
Iraq post-conflict issues
March 7, 2003
Peter Goldsmith advice to Tony Blair
Appendix in Sands Book
March 10, 2003
Excerpt report of visit to Kuwait by General Sir Mike Jackson
Complains of lack of desert clothing, negative impact on morale of troops
March 11, 2003
Matthew Rycroft to Simon McDonald
"Iraq: Legal and Military Aspects"
Questions at meeting about simple yes or no answer to Question "is the war legal?"
March 13, 2003
David Brummel to Peter Goldsmith
"Iraq: Legal Basis for Use of Force: Note of discussion with Attorney General
    Thursday 13 March 2003"
March 17, 2003
Simon McDonald Note for the Record
"Iraq: Meeting with the Attorney General"
Report on meeting between Peter Goldsmith, Jack Straw, Michael Wood, Iain
    McLeod, Patrick David on March 13, schedule meeting for 16th to produce
    document for March 17 and 18
March 19, 2003
Jack Straw and Geoff Hoon to Tony Blair
"Iraq: UK military contribution to post-conflict Iraq"
On the need to draw down UK troops to a third of invasion strength

April 2003

JIC assessment April 16, 2003
"Iraq: the initial landscape post Saddam"

10 In pursuit of primacy

Why the United States invaded Iraq

Jane K. Cramer and Edward C. Duggan

> The United States did not go to war in Iraq solely because of WMD. In my view, I doubt it was even a principle cause.
>
> Former CIA Director George Tenet (2007: 321)

Why did the United States invade Iraq? Was it one of the first preventive wars in history against weapons of mass destruction as it has been described (Lake 2010)? In this chapter we evaluate the hypotheses analyzed by the other chapters in this volume and then proffer our own hypothesis. We believe it can be shown that this war was very likely not primarily about WMD, as George Tenet conceded in his memoir and thus should not be considered a preventive war. We also find that too much emphasis has been placed on neoconservative ideology, especially the idea that this war was idealistically motivated by a desire to transform the Middle East region democratically. Instead, central to our argument is the finding that the top leaders, Vice President Dick Cheney, Secretary of Defense Donald Rumsfeld and President George W. Bush were not persuaded by the neoconservatives *after* 9/11 to invade Iraq. We show evidence demonstrating these leaders already wanted to pursue regime change in Iraq upon taking office (and earlier), and argue 9/11 gave them the "window of opportunity" they needed to pursue this policy. This finding then leads us to reverse the dominant narrative that the neoconservatives were the instigators of this invasion. While it is true that the neoconservatives had been publicly pressing for regime change in Iraq for years, we find it is likely they were appointed to their high level advisory positions because they advocated a policy the top leaders agreed with and wanted to pursue.

This refocus on the top leaders also undercuts the Israel lobby theory. There is no doubt that the majority of the most vocal and visible neoconservatives have always been, for various reasons, especially concerned with the security of Israel. It is also true that the neoconservatives and the Israel lobby helped to sell the Iraq invasion to the Congress and the public after 9/11. Nonetheless, the top leaders—Cheney, Rumsfeld and Bush— were not neoconservatives themselves nor were they persuaded by the neoconservatives or the Israel lobby to pursue the Iraq invasion. Similarly, there is no known substantial evidence of special interests in oil demanding this invasion. Ultimately, we argue that to understand this invasion, the shared ideology of these top leaders needs to be discerned. Some have argued that these top leaders should be viewed as "assertive nationalists." We find this categorization is essentially correct, but we argue that based on the three decades of history of the two top decision-makers, Cheney and Rumsfeld, both of whom President Bush favored and relied upon during this decision, the label of US primacists better captures their profoundly bold strategic vision. The history of Cheney and Rumsfeld and their shared ideology is now much better understood than it was when the "first draft" of the history of this Iraq decision was written (Packer 2005; Ricks 2006; Mearsheimer and Walt 2007). Many scholars then characterized these leaders as realists, reluctant to intervene militarily. Instead these leaders should be viewed as primacists who strongly favored assertive military action to promote US hegemony, especially in this geopolitically important oil-rich region.

A preventive war aimed at eliminating weapons of mass destruction?

Did the United States invade Iraq to end a WMD threat posed by Saddam Hussein? Was this the first preventive war in history? Robert Jervis writes, "There is little reason to doubt that Bush and his colleagues sincerely believed that Saddam had active WMD programs." Jervis also argues that this was the judgment of American intelligence, that this intelligence judgment was not the result of political pressures, and that other countries who opposed the war concurred in this intelligence assessment. Jervis buttresses his claims by adding that the "frantic search" for WMD after the invasion, along with leaders' evident distress in not finding any WMD, are further proof that leaders believed Saddam had active weapons programs. We contend there is solid evidence that directly counters each of these claims.

We find there is little question the administration, in collusion with the British, fabricated the imminent WMD threat entirely—it was "made from whole cloth." We show below why we think this story has become clear beyond a reasonable doubt (Prados and Ames 2010; Powers 2007, 2010; Armstrong 2010; Isikoff and Corn 2006). If so, the last remaining question is whether the Bush leaders, even with no evidence of active programs or evidence of an imminent threat of any kind, still feared Saddam as a highly dangerous *future* threat; a threat they needed to eliminate even if he was currently disarmed. If this was true, the war was a preventive war aimed at a *possible* future threat. While it appears impossible to prove or disprove whether or not leaders sincerely feared a *possible* future threat, we put forward two compelling arguments drawing on circumstantial evidence that make it highly likely that WMD was not a sincere motive. Instead, it appears WMD was merely an instrumental argument used to mobilize the public for a regime change policy motivated by other reasons—US primacy reasons—predominantly unrelated to WMD as we explain in later sections of this chapter.

The details of the Bush administration's intentional threat manipulation and inflation are now well-documented and have been analyzed from many angles. The most important starting place for summarizing this episode is to recognize that American intelligence overall did not find Saddam Hussein to be worrisome in early 2002 even though President Bush declared Iraq to be part of an "axis of evil" in his January 29, 2002 State of the Union speech. President Bush made the broad allegations that Iraq was supporting terror, and "plot[ting] to develop anthrax and nerve gas and nuclear weapons for over a decade." Despite these seemingly alarming claims by President Bush, in March 2002 Iraq was not even listed by American intelligence as among the five most pressing "near-term concerns" of US interests (Isikoff and Corn 2006: 26). Both US and British intelligence agreed that Saddam had been successfully restrained, even if they were not certain Saddam was fully disarmed. In other words, in early 2002, both nations supposed Iraq might have "residual" amounts of chemical and biological weapons, but neither thought Iraq had actual nuclear programs at all, and there was no technical or "hard" evidence of active programs of any kind. No intelligence assessments in early 2002 argued Saddam had a growing arsenal. In a now publicly available British memo of March 22, 2002 by Peter Ricketts, the Political Director of the UK Foreign and Commonwealth Office, which was sent to Jack Straw, UK Foreign Secretary, to provide advice to the prime minister, the problem with justifying the invasion using the "THREAT" was specifically outlined. Ricketts wrote:

> But even the best survey of Iraq's WMD programmes will not show much advance in recent years on the nuclear, missile or CW/BW fronts: the programmes are extremely worrying but have not, as far as we know, been stepped up.

In other words, it was very clear to the top leaders that there was no evidence that Saddam posed a growing, imminent threat.

The inner circle of the Bush administration may have believed in early 2002 that Iraq had active WMD programs (based on their own assumptions of his intentions and raw intelligence rumors), but it is interesting to notice that President Bush did not actually say anything about active programs in his early 2002 speech. He very vaguely said it was true sometime in the past decade or so. Bush's speech writer, David Frum, has described writing this "axis of evil" speech as a means of making a case for war against Iraq. If President Bush or his advisers truly believed Saddam

Hussein had active WMD programs, they most likely would have pressed to say so in as strong terms as they possibly could in this speech in order to make the case for war. Not only did they fail to specifically claim Saddam Hussein had active programs then, they also did not request a national intelligence estimate (NIE) on Iraq in this period. A new, comprehensive intelligence estimate of Iraq would have been the usual way for the administration to make its case with other lawmakers about an alleged imminent national security threat. It cannot be said the administration was focused on other things as it was making many other specific plans for war against Iraq in the first eight months of 2002. Therefore, logically, if the administration thought Saddam had active WMD programs, a comprehensive intelligence review would have helped the leaders make their case with other lawmakers and make a better plan for the invasion militarily.

Instead, no new comprehensive intelligence assessment on Iraq happened until September 2002, and even then the Bush administration did not request it. The review came about after Vice President Cheney argued publicly that Saddam was a growing threat, declaring most certainly: "We now know that Saddam has resumed his efforts to acquire nuclear weapons. … Many of us are convinced that Saddam will acquire nuclear weapons fairly soon" (Prados 2004: 21). At this time, CIA Director George Tenet orally briefed a secret session of the Senate intelligence committee on the latest intelligence on Iraq saying the agency had concluded Saddam was rebuilding his nuclear program, that they estimated he had 550 sites where WMD were stored, and that Saddam had developed a significant unmanned aerial vehicle (UAV) capability that could deliver biological or chemical agents. Democratic Senators asked to see the national intelligence estimate (NIE) on Iraq, but Tenet conceded no NIE had been prepared—there was no written report to review. The stunned Democrats requested that Tenet assemble an NIE on Iraq, but the CIA director told the Senators that his people were too busy with other matters. Days later, the CIA finally agreed to produce an actual NIE on Iraq after four Senators wrote a letter demanding that Bush and the CIA show the intelligence committee the full and best information justifying the proposed war (Isikoff and Corn 2006: 42).

Tenet's clear resistance to producing an actual official NIE on Iraq is evidence that he knew his agency lacked the evidence required to support the intelligence claims he was making orally in support of the administration's public claims. The CIA did compile what has been described as a hasty NIE on Iraq in the month of September that found with "high confidence" that Iraq did have worrisome active weapons programs. The case against Iraq as an imminent threat was based on three "erroneous" findings overall: a faulty analysis about a shipment of aluminum tubes, defector reports of mobile biological warfare labs, and one fabricated report that Iraq was trying to buy uranium "yellowcake" from Niger.

In brief, the argument about the aluminum tubes was based on an analysis from a single CIA analyst in the summer of 2001, Joe Turner, about a shipment of 60,000 aluminum tubes Iraq had been *openly* procuring from international suppliers. Turner tenaciously argued that the *only* suitable use for the aluminum tubes was for centrifuges for enriching uranium. While Turner had some experience as a weapons procurement analyst, he held only a bachelor's degree in mechanical engineering. Samples of the aluminum tubes were sent to the Department of Energy (DOE) scientists who were specialists in uranium enrichment. These experts concluded the tubes were not the right size and shape for nuclear enrichment, but found they were very similar to tubes Iraq had previously openly obtained to build conventional rocket launchers. In addition to the experts at DOE, the State Department's intelligence agency also fully investigated this important allegation about Iraq and found the tubes were not likely for centrifuges, but did match tubes for rocket launchers. These expert analysts thought the aluminum tubes question had been resolved in 2001, but somehow Turner's analysis of the tubes showed up in the NIE as a major CIA finding, while the dissenting opinion by the State Department was buried in a footnote sixty pages later in the report, and the analysis by the DOE experts was not included at all.

The frightening claim that Iraq had mobile labs for the production of biological weapons was based on reports from an Iraqi defector to Germany by the codename Curveball. The Germans passed along many reports from Curveball to the US Defense Intelligence Agency, and these reports became key building blocks in the case against Iraq. US intelligence agencies knew there was no hard, physical evidence to support these claims, and they knew that such defector reports were inherently unreliable since many defectors had strong motives to fabricate frightening information (either to provoke the United States to go against Saddam, which many of them wanted, or to personally be a valuable "asset" to intelligence, and thereby gain protection and money, or all of the above). By December 2002 the German intelligence chief was repeatedly warning the United States that Curveball's claims had never been corroborated and many officials thought he was a fabricator. Despite repeated warnings, Colin Powell based his most specific hair-raising claims about mobile biological weapons labs in his speech before the UN in early 2003 on the uncorroborated, highly dubious reports of Curveball.

The claim that Iraq was trying to procure yellowcake uranium from Niger was based on crudely faked documents, so crude that Tenet twice blocked President Bush from making the yellowcake claim in the fall of 2002. Nonetheless, the yellowcake story made it into the NIE in October. President Bush included this claim in his January 2003 State of the Union speech under the suspicious attribution "The British government has learned that Saddam Hussein recently sought significant quantities of uranium from Africa" even though US intelligence had told the White House repeatedly the story was not a credible one. These became the infamous "sixteen words" that many point to as clearly demonstrating intentional threat inflation because it was well-known US intelligence did not agree with this most serious claim. Colin Powell knew this claim was not credible and refused to repeat this uranium story in front of the UN just eight days later.

Democratic Senators who read the October NIE on Iraq found it to be skewed, and they were furious about the discrepancy between the secret NIE and the public "white paper" which was supposed to be the declassified summary of the NIE. The white paper on Iraq did not include *any* of the dissenting opinions found in the NIE; instead it conveyed unanimity and certainty. According to recently released documents, the white paper was not based on the NIE at all as it is almost identical to a report written in July 2002 before the NIE was even underway (Prados 2008). The CIA author of the white paper, Paul Pillar, was under a lot of pressure because he had made comments about how Saddam had no links to terrorism. He had heard that Paul Wolfowitz wanted him fired. Pillar has since said that he regrets writing the white paper. He has said he believes it wasn't really intelligence analysis. "In retrospect, we shouldn't have done it at all.... The white paper was policy advocacy" (Isikoff and Corn 2006: 139).

In early October 2002, Democrats were pointing out as openly as they could that the secret NIE actually contradicted claims the President was making publicly. To counter this, National Security Adviser Condoleezza Rice called CIA Director George Tenet and asked him, "Would you please call a reporter at the *New York Times* and say there really is no difference—no inconsistency from what the President's saying and what Democrats are saying [is in the NIE]." Tenet did make the call and said, "There is no inconsistency between our view of Saddam's growing threat and the view expressed by the President" (Isikoff and Corn 2006: 142–143). Senators were enraged by this statement because this statement contradicted important CIA testimony they had just been hearing; Tenet was contradicting his agency's own more nuanced findings. Tenet fails to mention this important phone call to the *New York Times* in his memoirs, but in a 2007 interview with Tim Russert, he admitted the call was a mistake:

> Well, it is, it is, it is, Tim, and all you can do after the fact is look at people and say, "I wish I hadn't done that. It was a mistake to do that." I can't take it—you know, I can't do it any other way but to be honest with you about the fact I made a mistake.

According to Tenet, mistakes were made, but instead of mistakes, the evidence points to political pressure forcing the intelligence community to support its preferred policies.

Other countries who opposed the war did not concur with US intelligence that Saddam had active WMD programs or was an imminent threat as Jervis asserts. France, Germany, and Russia all believed it was possible that Iraq had chemical and biological weapons stocks, but unlike the

October NIE, the foreign intelligence agencies did not have any certainty or "high confidence" about the existence of WMD. For this reason, the foreign intelligence agencies wanted to wait to see the results of the UN inspections. Furthermore, Russia and France were very skeptical of the most important assertion by the Americans: that Iraq had reconstituted its nuclear weapons program. French secret agents wrote in September 2002, "Saddam's Iraq does not represent any kind of nuclear threat at this time." French intelligence officials also said that American claims of Iraqi nukes are a "phony threat." Russian President Putin was also unimpressed by the American assertions of WMD. He said:

> Fears are one thing, hard facts are another. Russia does not have in its possession any trustworthy data that supports the existence of nuclear weapons or any weapons of mass destruction in Iraq and we have not received any such information from our partners yet. This fact has also been supported by the information sent by the CIA to the US Congress.
>
> (White 2002)

Also demonstrating that foreign countries did not concur with US intelligence before the war is the fact that the British Foreign Secretary Robin Cook resigned from Blair's cabinet on March 17, 2003, just before the war, after looking at the latest intelligence. He stated:

> Iraq probably has no weapons of mass destruction in the commonly understood sense of the term—namely a credible device capable of being delivered against a strategic city target.... It probably still has biological toxins and battlefield munitions, but it has had them since the 1980s.
>
> (Coughlin 2006: 297)

Foreign intelligence services did not agree with anything except the *possibility* that residual chemical and biological weapons were likely to be found, and active programs were possible since Saddam had such programs in the past—but foreign countries wanted current proof.

Foreign intelligence services wanted to use UN inspections to find some evidence of current Iraqi WMD before going along with an invasion. On September 17, 2002, Iraq announced it would readmit UN inspectors without conditions. Despite this new opportunity to find Iraqi WMD, the American intelligence community refused to help UN inspectors with identifying alleged sites in Iraq. Between late November and mid-March 2003, UN inspectors made 700 separate visits to 500 sites. The head of the Iraq Inspection Unit of the IAEA, Jacques Baute, begged the US and British governments for any information they had on WMD so the inspectors could better investigate any suspected sites. They especially wanted information about the alleged reconstituted nuclear weapons program. All Baute was given was the location of about three dozen suspected sites (even though George Tenet had told the Senate there were likely 550 WMD sites). Baute was told these three dozen were "the best" in the database, but they turned up nothing.

Jervis argues the "frantic search" for weapons after the invasion helps demonstrate top leaders sincerely believed WMD would be found. However, the administration's refusal to cooperate with the search for WMD before the war contravenes this argument. Logically, it would have helped the Bush administration's case against Iraq tremendously to find WMD before the war—Saddam would then have been in "material breach" of the UN resolutions requiring Iraqi disarmament. If the top Bush leaders thought active programs existed, they should have been aiding the search for WMD to discover some proof of WMD. Instead, the US obstructed the inspections; many people argue they obstructed the inspections and "rushed to war" while the fig leaf of possible WMD existed because they knew over time nothing would be found. Further, there is little evidence of a true "frantic search" after the invasion at all. Units were tasked with searching for WMD after the invasion, but according to the chief of Army Intelligence at the time of the invasion, General James Marks, no intelligence was given to the invading army in order to secure WMD stocks at all. Marks says, "They ostensibly cared, but their give-a-shit level was really low" (Goodman 2008: 246). Overall, the search for WMDs after the invasion, however frantic or not, is far less revealing than the refusal to even help the UN look for WMDs before the war. If the Bush administration had believed there were active WMD programs, they would have helped the inspectors try to discover a "material breach" instead of refusing to cooperate with them.

Jervis cites the "evident distress" of leaders as they found out after the invasion that there were no WMD as evidence the leaders truly expected to find WMD. The record on this point is difficult to assess. For example, Colin Powell was reportedly distressed, but he "took it like a soldier ... but it was a blow" when George Tenet would telephone to say his agency was formally withdrawing another pillar of the UN speech. On the other hand, Tenet's memoirs do not reveal any genuine surprise about finding out the CIA got everything wrong. Overall, it appears that many leaders both inside and outside President Bush's inner circle were not at all surprised to find no active programs, but many did expect to uncover residual weapons capabilities.

Even if it can be agreed that Bush administration leaders exaggerated the "imminent threat" from Iraq, many analysts argue these top leaders were sincerely motivated to invade Iraq to head off a *possible*, and in their view *likely*, WMD threat from Iraq. While this possible motivation cannot be completely disproved, powerful circumstantial evidence points to the WMD threat argument being a political mobilization strategy rather than a real primary reason for the invasion.

First, as Michael Lind points out in his chapter, the neoconservatives (he includes Cheney and Rumsfeld in this category), are a group of recidivist threat inflators who have repeatedly accused the CIA of underestimating national security threats in order to justify tougher policies and higher defense budgets than the CIA intelligence estimates sustained. Beginning in the 1970s, under the Ford administration, with Rumsfeld as Secretary of Defense and Cheney as White House Chief of Staff, CIA Director George H. W. Bush allowed a group of outside experts known as "Team B" to second-guess all of the CIA's conclusions about the Soviets. This "experiment" in intelligence analysis led to wildly exaggerated estimates of Soviet military power and intentions. These "findings" were leaked and then publicized by the Committee on the Present Danger, ultimately making President Carter appear weak and ushering in the election of President Ronald Reagan who abandoned détente and instituted the highest peacetime defense budgets of the Cold War. Even though each of Team B's findings was found to be completely wrong and even ridiculously exaggerated, the veterans of the Team B exercise went on to both laud this episode and attempt to repeat this winning political strategy numerous times after their victorious political reign in the 1980s.

For example, in the 1990s, many former Team B participants formed the Project for the New American Century (modeled on the Committee on the Present Danger) and these defense intellectuals repeatedly exaggerated the threat from China and Iraq, using inflated threat claims to politically justify higher defense budgets and hard-line foreign policies. In one nearly precisely parallel episode to Team B, Donald Rumsfeld led a panel of distinguished outsiders to re-evaluate the findings of the CIA that the likely threat from international ballistic missiles after the Cold War was remote. Proponents of missile defense programs had been extremely upset with CIA estimates. The findings of the Rumsfeld Report satisfied the proponents of missile defense because the report made the missile threat sound possibly imminent and dire. Similar to Team B, the Rumsfeld Report used worst-case analysis to make general speculations about what could possibly happen with no definite conclusions about what was actually occurring or likely to happen. This report, along with some coincidental test missile launches by Iran and North Korea, helped pressure the Democrats to increase funding for missile defense programs.

The threat inflation strategies of Team B and the Rumsfeld Report directly match the intelligence manipulation by Cheney, Rumsfeld and the Pentagon's Office of Special Plans before the Iraq War. These leaders insisted on creating their own intelligence findings—challenging and opposing the CIA's findings. Their special intelligence, much of it directly from Ahmed Chalabi's INC, was specially massaged to justify policies preferred in advance of the intelligence process. Dire threat inflation claims about Iraq's possible, but wholly unproven, WMD were used to politically mobilize others behind their preferred policy of regime change.

In addition to the broad pattern of repeated threat inflation episodes, Cheney's experience as Secretary of Defense during the first Gulf War working to justify rolling back Saddam Hussein from Kuwait likely left a lasting impression. The George H. W. Bush administration presented multiple rationales for the American troop deployment including defending vital US oil interests, defending Saudi Arabia, liberating Kuwait, protecting the US economy, and confronting aggression to help establish a "New World Order." In October 1990 Robert Teeter, the chief pollster of the administration, lamented that too many messages were flying around. In early November, Cheney, who had been monitoring the public debate closely, became concerned that the campaign for war was failing (Woodward 1991: 315, 323). Hill and Knowlton, a public relations firm hired by the Kuwaiti government, had conducted millions of dollars worth of polling and media research. They determined that the winning theme for war "was the fact that Saddam Hussein was a madman who had committed atrocities even against his own people, and had tremendous power to do further damage, and he needed to be stopped" (Alfonsi 2006: 127). In the remaining months before the invasion the George H. W. Bush administration successfully emphasized biological and chemical weapons, along with an imminent threat of Saddam the madman possibly acquiring nuclear weapons quickly. Using these WMD arguments, the administration successfully gathered enough public support to sway a skeptical Congress to authorize Desert Storm. This lesson of how best to rally public support was certainly clear to Cheney.

Taken together, both the abundant evidence that the intelligence was manipulated and inflated to justify regime change in Iraq despite no imminent need for disarmament as claimed, along with the fact that Cheney and Rumsfeld had decades of experience with employing successful threat inflation to rally support for their preferred policies, including rallying support in the first Gulf War, leads to the evident conclusion that the Iraq War was not likely aimed at preventing a WMD threat, but was a regime change motivated by other reasons.

A war caused by 9/11 and the adoption of the neoconservative vision of transforming the Middle East by spreading democracy?

The leading hypothesis among scholars for why the United States invaded Iraq is that US leaders ultimately decided to adopt a bold idealistic strategic vision of transforming the Middle East by spreading democracy—starting with Iraq. As Colin Dueck contends, the Bush administration came to see the overthrow of Saddam Hussein and the establishment of democracy in Iraq as the first major step of a larger project of "muscular Wilsonianism." The neoconservatives who proposed this vision sought not only to depose Saddam Hussein but also to undermine the other autocratic regimes in the Middle East—unpopular regimes such as Saudi Arabia, Syria, Iran and Egypt that directly and indirectly supported terrorism. It is contended the neoconservatives sincerely advocated, and the top leadership genuinely adopted, the guiding principle that establishing a democratic Iraq would trigger a cascade of democratic dominoes in the region (Mearsheimer and Walt 2007: 255–257).

This explanation for the invasion, Dueck specifically delineates:

> prior to 9/11 the dominant theme in both the strategic thinking and the actual strategic behavior of the Bush team was not so much "primacy" as "realism." Initially, Bush and his advisors made their skepticism regarding nation building and humanitarian intervention abundantly clear.

According to this view, the top leaders of Cheney, Rumsfeld and Bush were "realists" prior to 9/11 who were conservative about using military force generally, and especially scornful of using military force internationally for idealistic goals as had President Clinton. Dueck describes President Bush before 9/11: "His instincts seemed to be hard-nosed, nationalistic and pragmatic, rather than hugely ambitious and idealistic." According to Andrew Flibbert, "some observers feared an American turn toward isolationism under the new president." These ideational accounts find that Bush leaders were realists and not idealistic before 9/11, and they were not intent on regime change in Iraq in early 2001.

In this explanation for the invasion, the critical turning point for the top leaders was 9/11. Dueck explains:

> The terrorists simply opened up a window of opportunity for advocates of alternative grand strategies to come forward and make their case ... this new strategy — epitomized by the war against Iraq—was both more aggressive, and in many ways more idealistic, than Bush's previous approach. It tapped into longstanding, classical liberal assumptions within the United States as to how to meet foreign threats.

Similarly, Flibbert argues the neoconservative advisers persuaded the top leadership after 9/11, "The war occurred because powerful actors were persuaded by the logic of a specific set of ideas, which deemed war a necessary response to the attacks of September 11." According to many scholars, key evidence demonstrating the official adoption of this Wilsonian vision is the 2002 National Security Strategy (NSS) that stated that the United States had a "moment of opportunity to extend the benefits of freedom across the globe ... [the United States] will actively work to bring the hope of democracy, development, free markets and free trade to every corner of the world" (e.g. Monten 2005: 112). This NSS came to be known as the "Bush Doctrine." Advocates of this strategy claimed it was both the moral as well as the necessary course to take after 9/11 because it offered the best long-term remedy for fully defeating anti-American terrorism emanating from the region.

What evidence should we see based on this hypothesis? First, we should see some kind of debate take place within the administration after 9/11 where the neoconservative advisers play a new and important role in shaping policy. Second, we should likely see the top officials make a decision to invade based on those ideas after being persuaded by the neoconservative advisers. Third we should also see evidence that the top officials have internalized the Wilsonian arguments for regime change, and are attempting to implement a Wilsonian vision rather than just using Wilsonian-type justifications for the invasion to gain public approval. Fourth, even if evidence of persuasion is lacking after 9/11, we should not see that the top leaders were already planning and looking for an opportunity to overthrow Saddam Hussein when they took office in 2001 and in the eight months of the Bush administration prior to 9/11. If Cheney, Rumsfeld and Bush did not need to be persuaded by the neoconservatives after 9/11 because they already wanted to invade Iraq prior to 9/11, then it would appear this narrative is fatally flawed.

In a recently released collection of national security documents from both the United States and Britain entitled "The Iraq War, Part II: Was There Even a Decision?" (Prados and Ames 2010) the point is clearly made that what is most notable about the records of the decision-making process is the absence of any debate about whether to invade Iraq within the Bush administration. It appears the decision had already been made and no alternative to invasion was seriously considered. Rumsfeld confirmed in his memoirs the findings of this study, "While the president and I had many discussions about the war preparations, I do not recall his ever asking me if I thought going to war with Iraq was the right decision" (Prados 2011). Further, there is no evidence that the neoconservatives persuaded the top officials. It is interesting to notice that Paul Wolfowitz, an alleged key neoconservative persuader, preferred a strategy of creating a covertly supported Iraqi National Congress (INC) enclave in Southern Iraq and using it as a base to overthrow Saddam. This idea was well-known before 9/11 and ridiculed and rejected by the military, the CIA, the State Department and the White House. After 9/11, his continuing insistence on working with the INC was still not welcome—and was in part rejected for clearly appearing undemocratic as the INC was not popular among the Iraqis. Additionally, the Wilsonian ideas of spreading democracy are absent from the documents used for planning the invasion. The documents make frequent reference to a "stable, law abiding Iraq" that will be necessary in order to preclude the possibility of an authoritarian regime restarting a WMD program, but visions of actually spreading democracy are notably absent.

Instead of earnestly debating or discussing how to spread democracy the emphasis in most of the documents seems to be on the need for finding a justification to sell the invasion plan to the American and British publics and to the UN. As one British document makes clear, "A legal justification for invasion would be needed" and that "none currently exists" (Overseas and Defence Secretariat, Cabinet Office 2002). These documents exhibit little to no evidence that the top leaders had internalized Wilsonian ideals or these ideals led to a decision to invade. In fact it appears the first time that Bush articulates the plan or idea of spreading democracy throughout the Middle East is on February 28, 2003 at the American Enterprise Institute; this is long after the decision to invade had been made over a year earlier. Based on the available documents of the decision-making process, a considerable number at this point, it appears the narrative of "neoconservative persuasion" and the importance of the idealistic vision of spreading democracy is simply another curious incident of a dog that doesn't bark. Analysts who originally argued this narrative was true had to rely on the available public accounts of the decision. These accounts were primarily based on what appears to have been neoconservative "spin" about the decision-making process using candid interviews with prominent neoconservatives such as Richard Perle, Robert Kagan and Kenneth Adelman as the main evidence (e.g. Packer 2005; Ricks 2006) along with Bush's rhetorical explanations for why he adopted the Bush Doctrine.

Of course absence of evidence of neoconservative persuasion or discussion of Wilsonian ideals is not wholly satisfying evidence of absence. However, if it can be shown that the top leaders of Cheney, Rumsfeld and Bush already strongly desired to invade Iraq before taking office and while in office prior to 9/11, then arguments for the importance of the neoconservatives are completely suspect, and most likely without merit at all. We argue that with close examination of the available evidence, it can be shown that in the case of each of these top leaders there was already a strong desire to remove Saddam Hussein before taking office, and strong military actions were being taken by them to pursue this policy in the first eight months of 2001. In the final section of this chapter we trace the ideology that appears to have driven these leaders and it was not Wilsonian idealism.

In the case of Vice President Cheney, who has been widely recognized as the most important decision-maker behind the invasion of Iraq, much has been made of his many public statements throughout the 1990s which appear to confirm that he strongly supported President George H. W. Bush's decision not to overthrow Saddam during the first Gulf War. We argue very little weight can be placed on these public protestations because it was critically important for Cheney politically to remain loyal to his former boss, President George Bush Sr. In fact Cheney always remained loyal to Bush Sr. who was repeatedly criticized for not having gone all the way to Baghdad. It appears Cheney's loyalty was well rewarded. According to a July 2000 *New York Times* article, Cheney privately expressed a desire for the Vice Presidency to Brent Scowcroft, Scowcroft mentioned it to Bush Sr. and then Bush Sr. met repeatedly with his son to discuss the appointment of his running mate (Bruni and Schmitt 2000). It is highly unlikely Cheney would have even been considered if he had publicly broken with Bush Sr. over Iraq as others had.

Most scholars accept Cheney's public statements because little can be found out about Cheney's private beliefs; he is enigmatic, many say highly secretive, about his private views. However, a few private statements and some key public statements indicate Cheney was intent on removing Saddam from power as early as 1991 and definitely long before 9/11. Much more significant than the few available statements are Cheney's strong actions in pursuit of removing Saddam Hussein long before 9/11 for what appears to be US primacist reasons and not for Wilsonian ideals.

First, while Cheney publicly defended the decision to stop US troops from conquering Baghdad in 1991 during the first Persian Gulf War, it has come to light Cheney privately urged George H. W. Bush to finish off Saddam Hussein at that time (Unger 2007: 182). In line with the goal of removing Saddam Hussein, in June of 1997, Cheney met the leader of the INC, Ahmed Chalabi, who was pushing a plan to create an insurgency to overthrow Saddam. According to Francis Brooke, a public relations representative for Chalabi, "Cheney was in philosophical agreement with his plan." When Cheney was chosen as Vice President, Chalabi was very happy with the decision, saying, "This will be good for us" (Foer and Ackerman 2003). During the 2000 presidential campaign Cheney often talked about a "humble" foreign policy in line with candidate Bush's declared policy stance, but occasionally Cheney would use much more aggressive rhetoric. In particular, during the Vice Presidential debate, Cheney said a Bush administration might "have to take military action to forcibly remove Saddam from power" (CATO Daily Dispatch 2000). In addition to this clear indication that Cheney was at least thinking about removing Saddam Hussein militarily, another account published in the *Wall Street Journal* in 2002 discussed comments that the Vice President shared privately with a group of friends after the 2000 election. Cheney reportedly said that the "new White House team may have a rare historic opportunity to right a wrong committed during a previous term—the mistake of leaving Saddam Hussein in place atop the Iraqi government" (Robbins and Cummings 2002).

Confirming that these few statements accurately reveal Cheney's actual preference for removing Saddam Hussein are the actions Cheney took. In early 2001, just after assuming the Vice Presidency, Cheney immediately fought the State Department to gain funding for Ahmed Chalabi's INC. The INC then worked to provide intelligence on Iraq for both Rumsfeld's and Cheney's offices (Foyer and Ackerman 2003; Hoyle 2008: 198). Also, upon taking office, Cheney convened weekly staff meetings where toppling Iraq was nearly always the chief goal on the agenda. According to Assistant Secretary of State for Near Eastern Affairs, Edward Walker, Cheney was showing increasing frustration at the lack of options for Iraq. Walker says:

> Everything that had been tried before didn't work. By a system of elimination — sanctions won't stop him, bombing won't stop him, and so on — you come down to the last resort: Then we'll have to take him out.
>
> (Foyer and Ackerman 2003)

These direct actions in early 2001 demonstrate a strong desire to remove Saddam Hussein before 9/11.

Likely even more significant than planning meetings is the fact that Cheney lobbied for and personally appointed so many outspoken advocates of regime change in Iraq as high-level advisers in the Bush administration. Cheney helped appoint thirteen out of the eighteen members of the Project for the New American Century who had signed the original public letter urging President Clinton to overthrow Saddam Hussein in 1998. According to Barton Gellman, one of Cheney's biographers, Cheney operated by the motto "personnel is policy" (Gellman 2008: 35). Cheney had served at the highest levels of the executive branch in two earlier administrations and he was keenly aware that whomever he appointed to key posts would have a large impact on the policies the administration pursued. Therefore it is highly unlikely, in light of the fact of how openly and vehemently these neoconservatives advocated for overthrowing Saddam Hussein during the 1990s, that he would appoint so many of these advocates to key posts while not supporting the policy himself. Cheney did not casually or accidentally make the PNAC appointments across time; on the contrary, while the 2000 election was still being contested in Florida, Cheney was carefully maneuvering and pressing to get these outspoken advocates of regime change into very important positions in the administration.

Cheney lobbied strongly for one open advocate of regime change— Donald Rumsfeld—who was appointed to be Secretary of Defense. And then, Cheney and Rumsfeld together appointed perhaps the most famous advocate for overthrowing Saddam Hussein in order to create a democracy in Iraq, Paul Wolfowitz, as Undersecretary of Defense. Cheney created a powerful dual position for Scooter Libby as Special Assistant to the President and as Chief of Staff for the Office of the Vice President; Libby is considered, along with Wolfowitz, to have been one of the strongest neoconservative advocates for invading Iraq prior to 9/11 (Mann 2004a). Other famous neoconservative appointments by Cheney included: John Bolton as special assistant Undersecretary of State for Arms Control and International Security; David Wurmser as Bolton's chief assistant; Robert Zoellick as US Trade Representative; and Zalmay Khalilzad as head of the Pentagon transition team. Working with Rumsfeld, other neoconservative appointments included: Elliot Abrams, Douglas Feith, Richard Perle and Abram Schulsky.

All of these appointments are perhaps the best evidence that Cheney strongly desired regime change in Iraq upon taking office in 2001. One senior official in the Bush administration described him: "Cheney was the detail guy. And Cheney doesn't care how many people hate him. He's the senior guy who had his hands on the steering wheel" (Mayer 2008: 7). In January 2004, soon after the successful invasion of Iraq, at a moment when Cheney was perhaps most proud of the decision to invade, he reveled in his artful management practices, "Am I the evil genius in the corner that nobody ever sees come out of his hole? It's a nice way to operate, actually" (Unger 2007: 314). The evidence suggests Cheney was not convinced by his advisers after 9/11 but rather strongly desired to pursue regime change in Iraq at least upon taking office in 2001.

Although Cheney appointed the allegedly ideologically driven neoconservatives to positions of power, there is no evidence that Cheney shared or embraced the Wilsonian vision of these advisers before or after 9/11. Instead there is strong evidence that Cheney was firmly rooted in the realpolitik of oil and power politics. Prior to assuming office under George W. Bush, Cheney served as CEO of Halliburton (an oil and gasfield services corporation). Cheney openly advocated ignoring the importance of supporting democracy and doing business with dictatorships in the pursuit of oil. Cheney, in a speech in 1998, responded to criticism for doing business with unsavory dictatorships, "You've got to go where the oil is. I don't think about it very much" (Bruno and Vallette 2001). In another speech in 1999 as Halliburton CEO, Cheney made it clear where foreign oil companies needed to go to find oil. He said:

> While many regions of the world offer great oil opportunities, the Middle East with two thirds of the world's oil and the lowest cost is still where the prize ultimately lies, even though companies are anxious for greater access there, progress continues to be slow.
>
> (Cheney 1999)

Upon taking office, Cheney remained focused on gaining access to Middle Eastern oil fields. He convened a National Energy Development Project Group (NEDPG), and while most of what was discussed is still secret, it is known that along with other participants, Cheney looked at maps of Iraq and examined a list of contracts signed by foreign oil companies with Saddam Hussein. Cheney appears to have been intent on overthrowing Saddam Hussein prior to 9/11, and given the absence of Wilsonian concerns and the strong evidence of his focus on energy security and access to oil reserves in the Middle East, oil very likely played a pre-eminent role in his motives (McClellan 2008: 145).

In the case of Secretary of Defense Rumsfeld, there is no doubt he strongly supported regime change in Iraq before taking office and pursued this policy while in office prior to 9/11. Rumsfeld is not widely considered a neoconservative, but he was a co-signer of the Project for the New American Century (PNAC) letter to President Clinton calling for ousting Saddam Hussein in 1998. And of course, along with Cheney, Rumsfeld appointed the ardent neoconservatives such as Paul Wolfowitz, Douglas Feith and Richard Perle to high-level positions in the administration. However, the very best evidence confirming Rumsfeld's absolute preoccupation with Iraq comes from notes recorded on September 11, 2001 after the terrorist attacks. According to aide Stephen Cambone's notes about a conversation he had with Rumsfeld, Rumsfeld wanted the "best info fast. Judge whether good enough hit S.H. [Saddam Hussein] at same time. Not only UBL [Osama bin Laden].... Need to move swiftly.... Go massive. Sweep it all up. Things related and not" (Bamford 2004: 285). This note is smoking-gun evidence that Rumsfeld did not need to be convinced by the neoconservatives after 9/11 to invade Iraq. Rumsfeld was ready to "Go massive" and he even knew hitting Saddam Hussein was probably not related to the events of 9/11 or connected to Osama Bin Laden. Just a few days later, on September 19, 2001, in one session with his Pentagon staff, Rumsfeld discussed attacking Iraq, and according to one account: "There was no flowery talk of inculcating democracy in the heart of the Middle East. Rumsfeld was advocating a demonstration of American power" (Gordon and Trainor 2007: 21). It is clear Rumsfeld was committed to an invasion but there is no significant evidence he was interested in a Wilsonian vision for the Middle East after 9/11.

It is now widely believed that Rumsfeld was ideologically driven to "transform" the US military into a high-tech military force that was more usable than the large troop-centered force the Pentagon preferred (Herspring 2008). It appears Rumsfeld merged this goal of "proving transformation" with the goal of invading Iraq. In the words of Rumsfeld, on September 10, 2001, the transformation of the military was "a matter of life and death, ultimately, every American's" (Rumsfeld 2001). Allegedly, for Rumsfeld, targeting Iraq represented an opportunity to accelerate and prove the utility of this military transformation. Rumsfeld felt war in Afghanistan did not offer an opportunity to powerfully demonstrate new US military technologies and tactics. According to Richard Clarke, on September 11 Rumsfeld said, "There aren't any good targets in Afghanistan. And there are lots of good targets in Iraq" (Leung 2004). The record is unequivocal; Rumsfeld was anxious to find a way to target Iraq and was not convinced by the neoconservatives after 9/11 to invade Iraq.

President George W. Bush is a more ambiguous case than Rumsfeld. Like Cheney, Bush maintained a public persona that claimed to be reticent about using military force. While running for office, he repeatedly quipped he wanted to pursue a "humble" foreign policy. However, many scattered accounts of his more candid moments disaffirm this political rhetoric. In 1999 candidate Bush divulged emphatically to Mike Herskowitz, his ghostwriter for his autobiography, his desire to invade for political gain. According to Herskowitz, Bush said:

> One of the keys to being seen as a great leader is to be seen as a commander in chief. My father had all this political capital built up when drove the Iraqis out of Kuwait, and he wasted it. If I have a chance to invade ... if I had that much capital, I'm not going to waste it. I'm going to get everything passed that I want to get passed, and I'm going to have a successful presidency.
>
> (Baker 2009: 423)

In another account of July 1999, the director of the movie *Three Kings*, David O. Russell, ran into Bush and told him that he had made a movie that was critical of his father's legacy in the Gulf War. Bush responded, "Then I guess I'm going to have to finish the job, aren't I" (Gumbell 2004). On November 18, 1999, in an interview with the BBC, Bush said: "No one had envisioned Saddam, at least at that point in history, no one envisioned him still standing – it's time to finish the task" (Keane 2003). Also in late 1999, Richard Perle emerged from a meeting with Bush in which the candidate had assured him that Saddam must go.

Publicly, during the Republican primary debates on December 2, 1999, Bush said that if Saddam Hussein started to develop weapons of mass destruction he would "take 'em out." The whole sentence and the use of " 'em" left confusion as to whether Bush was referring to the weapons or Saddam. The next morning after the debate when asked by a reporter about how he could get rid of the Texas-accented "em" for them which sounded too much like "him," Bush reveled in the ambiguity and the message it sent, saying, "That's for Saddam to figure out" (Bruni 1999).

Apparently, there was no ambiguity about whether he would take out Saddam when he spoke with some groups and individuals. According to the publisher for *The Arab American* newspaper, Osama Siblani, on May 17, 2000, in front of a group of Republicans at a Michigan hotel, Bush said that he would take out Saddam (Goodman 2005). Bush spent some time courting the Arab American vote, particularly in Michigan. He had repeated meetings with a Muslim leader in Detroit, Sayed Hassan al-Qazwini, the head of one of the largest mosques in the nation. In an interview with the *New York Times*, al-Qazwini said that Bush made six or seven statements before and after the campaign that he would take out Saddam (Stevenson 2004). Also, in the spring of 2000, Bush adviser Stephen Hadley reassured GOP policy-makers that Bush's main policy would be removing Saddam (Unger 2007: 174–175). From these various reports, it appears that even before Bush was elected he quietly and repeatedly expressed that he had a strong intent to depose Saddam Hussein.

Soon after the election, on December 29, 2000, George W. Bush met for two hours with President Clinton to discuss the issues that Bush would face as President. Clinton outlined the major foreign policy priorities discussing the Pakistan/India nuclear conflict, the Israeli/Palestinian conflict, North Korea and lastly Iraq and Saddam. Bush responded by saying, "Thanks for your advice, Mr. President, but I think you've got your priorities wrong. I'm putting Saddam at the top of the list" (Moore 2004: 6–7).

Once in office, in mid-February 2001, David Frum, a speech writer for Bush, interviewed the president for a book he was writing. His notes show that Bush demonstrated "his focus on the danger presented by Iran (and) his determination to dig Saddam Hussein out of power in Iraq" (Frum 2003: 26). On March 15, 2001, Saudi Ambassador Prince Bandar said that the no-fly zones were hurting Saddam and Bush made a telling response that indicates he was not interested in halfway measures: "If there is any military action, then it has to be decisive. That can finalize the issue. The Iraqi opposition is useless and not effective." (Risen 2006: 183–84)

During this same period of early 2001, according to several Bush administration insiders, including former Treasury Secretary Paul O'Neill and former counter-terrorism czar Richard Clarke, we now know in detail how Bush, Cheney, Rumsfeld, Rice and other key leaders demonstrated that they were focused on Iraq from the very beginning of the administration, even in the very first NSC meeting (Suskind 2004: 70–86). Also demonstrating through significant military actions the high priority of their Iraq plans before 9/11 is the fact that the administration greatly escalated the bombing campaign against Saddam Hussein in February of 2001, by bombing outside of the no-fly zone for the first time since Operation Desert Fox in 1998 (CNN 2001). According to Paul O'Neill, in February 2001 Rumsfeld was "focused on how an incident might cause escalated tensions—like the shooting down of an American plane in the regular engagements between US fighters and Iraqi antiaircraft batteries—and what US responses to such an occurrence might be" (Suskind 2004: 96). Some have viewed this escalation in bombing as a deliberate effort to provoke Saddam Hussein into some type of action which could be used to justify a military action to remove him. In addition to the stepped up bombing, in July of 2001 Bush approved thirty projects (without consulting Congress) worth $700 million in Kuwait that would help prepare the US bases in the country for a possible invasion of Iraq (Chatterjee 2009: 79).

Similar to Rumsfeld, right after 9/11, on September 12, President Bush clearly demonstrated his determination to pursue Saddam Hussein. President Bush confronted Richard Clarke and demanded that Clarke look for evidence that Saddam was behind the terror attack. According to Clarke, Bush said: "I want you, as soon as you can, to go back over everything,

everything. ... See if Saddam did this." Clarke responded, "But Mr. President, al-Qaeda did this." To which Bush replied, "I know, I know, but ... see if Saddam was involved. Just look. I want to know any shred." Clarke then insisted that the CIA, FBI and White House already concluded that there were no links to Saddam. But then, as Clarke exited the room, Bush "testily" said again, "Look into Iraq, Saddam" (Clarke 2004: 32). Further confirming that President Bush's mind was already set on pursuing Saddam, later that week, on September 17, Bush signed a top-secret document authorizing a plan to go to war against Afghanistan and he also authorized the Pentagon to start planning the invasion of Iraq (Kessler 2003). All of this evidence strongly suggests that it was not necessary for the neoconservatives to persuade Bush after 9/11 to invade Iraq—Bush was already determined to act to remove Saddam Hussein.

Much of the confusion about Bush's intentions in this period comes from his rejection of the specific neoconservative plan for Iraq that Paul Wolfowitz and other neoconservatives were pushing Bush to support in the days right after 9/11. As mentioned above, Wolfowitz and others wanted to pursue an "enclave strategy" in which the United States would take over the southern oil fields of Iraq, turn them over to the Iraqi opposition (INC) and use this foothold to take over the rest of the country (Woodward 2004: 22). This plan had been pushed by the INC in 1998 and had been mocked then by Central Command head Anthony Zinni in congressional testimony as a "Bay of Goats" (Lang 2004). On the morning of September 15, 2001, Bush sent out a message to his closest advisers that he was rejecting the Wolfowitz/INC plan and that there should be no more talk of Iraq (Woodward 2002: 85). But on that same day, Bush assured the Chairman of the Joint Chiefs of Staff, Hugh Shelton, that in spite of rejecting Wolfowitz's risky plan, he was determined to invade Iraq. He said, "We will get this guy, but at a time and place of our choosing" (Gordon and Trainor 2007: 17). The rejection of the "enclave strategy" by Cheney and Bush has been mistakenly interpreted by scholars as proof of an overall reluctance by the senior leaders to invade Iraq, but we now know this was not the case (Mearsheimer and Walt 2007: 229–262).

Cheney, Rumsfeld and Bush were not persuaded by the neoconservatives after 9/11 to pursue an idealistic muscular Wilsonian vision. The record indicates they did not even make a decision after 9/11; they apparently had already made up their minds so they did not need to deliberate or debate. Instead they discussed war preparations and strategies for convincing the public and Congress, with no planning for how to make democracy take shape in Iraq.

A war for the Israel lobby?

The Israel lobby hypothesis contends that following 9/11, neoconservatives within the Bush administration, along with the larger "Israel Lobby," persuaded Bush administration leaders, Congress, and the American public to launch an invasion of Iraq that they believed was in the security interests of both the United States and Israel (Mearsheimer and Walt 2007: 229–262). As we argue above, Cheney, Rumsfeld and Bush were not convinced to invade after 9/11 by the neoconservatives or anyone else because they were intent on ousting Saddam Hussein long before. Thus, while we generally agree that the Israel lobby is highly influential in many US foreign policy decisions, we believe that in this Iraq invasion case the lobby was at most important to selling the invasion to Congress and the American people; it was not at all integral to convincing the top Bush administration leaders.

Thus, we concur with most of Jerome Slater's analysis; we especially concur with two of his main arguments. First, it appears there is no evidence in this case that the lobby tried to convince or prevailed over the President and the executive branch. Second, and most important, is Slater's point that while the policies preferred by the lobby and those adopted by the government converged, the *goals* of the Bush leaders substantially differed from those of the neoconservatives and the Israel lobby. This is a very important point we expand upon in this section.

This point also speaks to Michael Lind's arguments in this volume and elsewhere where he emphatically argues that with the exception of its strategy in the Middle East, there is nothing inherently "Jewish" about neoconservative ideology. He argues neoconservatism is a non-ethnic ideological crusade for democracy in pursuit of American hegemony, to which he adds that Donald Rumsfeld and Dick Cheney are full-fledged neocons. We find this argument surprising and incongruous, and we believe Lind's thinking has evolved substantially on this point. Lind is a non-Jewish former neoconservative, so he has been widely regarded as an expert insider on neoconservative ideology and strategems. In April 2003, Lind wrote a short but widely cited piece explaining "The weird men behind George W. Bush's war." In this piece he explained the influence of the "neoconservative defense intellectuals" and described them as the key players who devised the Iraq invasion with the main purpose being to begin to make the Middle East safe for Israel. He emphasized the importance of Wolfowitz, Libby, Perle and others, while calling Donald Rumsfeld an "elderly figurehead" and discussing Cheney simply as providing the "stroke of luck" that brought the neoconservatives to power. In this 2003 piece he emphasized the neoconservatives' connections with the Israel lobby, and their far-right Likud strain of Zionism.

In a February 2004 article "A Tragedy of Errors," Lind again explains how the ideology of the neoconservatives led to the Iraq War. He begins the article by describing their ideology in terms of "neoconservative bingo," and how one could read any essay or book by a neoconservative and discover the same clichés of "The China Threat," "The Global Democratic Revolution," "Down With the Appeasers!" and much more, with the free space in the center of the bingo card being something like "The Pal-estinian People Do Not Exist" (Lind 2004). In this article he gave more regard to Rumsfeld and Cheney, describing them as full-fledged neocon-servatives, and arguing that it was not necessary to invent a different cat-egory for them such as "nationalist conservative" or "Western conservative" because there was nothing particularly "Jewish" about neoconservative views on foreign policy—again, except neoconservative Middle East strat-egy. Lind explains that the overall global strategy of the neocons is simply a misguided crusade in the name of democracy; at the same time, Lind explains that neoconservatism has been hijacked by elite American sup-porters of the Likud, both Jewish and non-Jewish. He attests that "there are neoconservatives, including Jewish neoconservatives, who don't share a love affair with the Likud, but if they said so in public their careers in the movement would end" (Lind 2004).

In this volume, Lind again describes neoconservative strategy, this time adding the question: why was idiosyncratic neoconservative strategy suc-cessful in shaping US foreign policy after 9/11? He here argues that neoconservative strategy actually fits well into "the post-Cold War U.S. foreign policy consensus in favor of a US grand strategy of hegemony." Thus, while all neoconservatives supported US hegemony, not all sup-porters of American hegemony were neoconservatives. We agree. We argue here that Lind does not follow the logic of his own argument far enough. In short, were Cheney, Rumsfeld (and Bush) truly full-fledged neoconservatives even so far as supporting the neoconservative Middle East strategy? Or, as we argue, did they fully support the neoconservative goal of aggressively pursuing American hegemony while not sharing in the goal of spreading democracy or invading Iraq as part of a strategy of making the Middle East safe for Israel? In short, as Slater argues, we explain here how the policy of aggressively invading Iraq converged between the neoconservatives and the top leaders of Cheney, Rumsfeld and Bush—but the *goals* of these two groups differed substantially. In this section, we go so far as to argue that the neoconservatives and the Israel lobby were "used" to publicly sell the invasion, while the plans and prior-ities of the neoconservatives were sidelined during the war by the top Bush leaders.

As the neoconservatives repeatedly explained, they saw the invasion of Iraq as the first step toward transforming the Middle East. Central to their plan for Iraq was flooding the market with privatized Iraqi oil, thereby undermining Middle East oil producers such as Saudi Arabia, Iran, other OPEC members and even Russia. Bringing oil prices down would benefit the US economy and punish Saudi Arabia and Iran, countries that had supported terrorism against the United States and Israel. The neoconser-vatives' plan was made clear in December 2002 when, backed by Paul Wol-fowitz, Elliot Abrams created a plan for the United States to take direct control of Iraqi oil fields and exclude the UN from any decision-making about the oil (Dettmer 2002). Ahmed Chalabi, who had promised to give Americans a "first shot" at Iraqi oil and to extend a pipeline from Mosul in Iraq to Haifa in Israel, was entrusted to carry out Abram's plan. We now know these plans began to take shape in October 2002 when Chalabi attended meetings with three US oil companies and discussed the future of Iraqi oil (Beaumont and Islam 2002; Cholmondeley 2002).

While Chalabi and neoconservatives in the Pentagon were planning out the future of Iraqi oil, the State Department was formulating a very different plan for Iraqi oil. Less than one month after 9/11 a group of Iraqi exiles and Arab experts began to meet at the State Department to plan for a post-Saddam Iraq. The State Department's *The Future of Iraq Project* has since been declassified (Hassen 2006). The State Department's plan for oil differed dramatically from the plan being devised by neoconservatives within the Pentagon. The State Department plan called for formally keeping Iraq's oil nationalized, keeping Iraq in OPEC, using Iraqi oil technicians, and working within the UN. These plans aimed substantially at stability for prices and for OPEC.

In the months leading up to the invasion, the policy debate over oil had not been decided. The State Department and the oil industry were becoming increasingly alarmed about the neoconservative's oil plan and Chalabi's open advocacy for it. In the eyes of the mainstream oil industry, an aggressive oil grab by the United States might lead to a destabilization of the oil market and a delegitimizing of the Iraq invasion. This was argued in an independent report put out on January 23, 2003 by the Council on Foreign Relations and the Baker Institute entitled *Guiding Principles for U.S. Post-Conflict Policy in Iraq*. The report cautioned against taking direct control of Iraqi oil, saying, "A heavy American hand will only convince them (the Iraqis), and the rest of the world, that the operation in Iraq was carried out for imperialist rather than disarmament reasons. It is in American interests to discourage such misperceptions" (Baker 2003). Such cautions may have contributed to Bush telling his aides in January 2003 that he admired Chalabi but would not appoint him to head the Iraqi government, and in February 2003 Cheney ordering the Pentagon to curb their support for Chalabi (Landay and Strobel 2003).

The neoconservatives persisted in their support for Chalabi, who had promised to create an Israel-friendly government in Iraq and could be counted on to implement the neoconservatives' oil plan. To publicly counter the State Department plan the Heritage Foundation published the neoconservatives' plan for oil spelled out in a 2002 report posted on their website on March 5, 2003 entitled *The Road to Economic Recovery in Post-War Iraq* (Cohen and Driscoll 2002).

The State Department plan triumphed over the neoconservatives' plan, and this helps demonstrate that Cheney, Rumsfeld and Bush did not allow the neoconservatives and the Israel lobby to dominate US foreign policy even from the inception of the invasion. In fact, Bush appointed Phillip

Carroll, the former chief of Shell Oil, to oversee the Iraqi oil business. Carroll executed much of the oil industries' preferred plans for Iraqi oil. Revealingly, when L. Paul Bremer, the head of the Coalition Provisional Authority, ordered the de-Ba'athification of all government ministries in Iraq, Carroll refused to comply with Bremer's order because removing the Ba'athist oil technocrats would have hindered the Iraqi oil business. In the end, the Baker plan (aligned with US oil industry interests) was implemented in its entirety. The US official policy was to use Production Sharing Agreements (PSAs) that legally left the ownership of the oil in Iraqi government hands while attempting to ensure new long-term multinational oil corporation profits (Muttitt 2005). Had the neoconservatives been in control of US policy in the Middle East, the Iraq oil policy would have favored undermining oil profits rather than sustaining them.

Plans for Iraq's oil were just a piece of the neoconservatives' plan, which along with Iraq, targeted Saudi Arabia, Syria, Egypt, Iran and other countries in the Middle East. For example, in the immediate aftermath of 9/11, the neoconservatives attempted to turn US policy against Saudi Arabia. They condemned Saudi Arabia in media articles and policy papers, pointing out that Saudi Arabia financially supported Al Qaeda and was home to 15 of the 19 hijackers. On July 10, 2002, Richard Perle, a leading neoconservative, invited Laurent Murawiec of the RAND Corporation to speak at the Defense Policy Review Board, a prestigious body of advisers to the Pentagon. Murawiec called Saudi Arabia "the kernel of evil, the prime mover, the most dangerous opponent" in the Middle East (Ricks 2002). The Bush administration then took great pains to apologize to the Saudis. Colin Powell called the Saudi Foreign Minister to make amends and Donald Rumsfeld made it clear that the presentation by Murawiec "did not represent the views of the government, it didn't represent the views of the Defense Policy Review Board" (Burkeman 2002). The Bush administration never pressured Saudi Arabia to democratize. In 2007 Bush signaled his support for Saudi Arabia by offering to sell them twenty billion dollars in sophisticated weapons, against the wishes of Israeli hawks (Lappin 2007). In May 2008, in a highly controversial move, Bush further pledged to help build up the Saudi nuclear energy program (Markey 2008). The Bush administration's support for the House of Saud directly opposed the neoconservatives' agenda.

Syria, also long targeted by neoconservatives, was another main enemy of Israel much discussed in the now-famous 1996 neoconservative strategy for the Middle East sent to newly elected Benjamin Netanyahu entitled *A Clean Break* (Perle *et al.* 1996). Just a few weeks after the successful invasion of Iraq, Wolfowitz confidently told the press, "There will have to be change in Syria" (Vulliamy 2003). But despite the aggressive neoconservative rhetoric, Bush did not militarily pressure Syria at all. Similarly, the neoconservatives and the Israel lobby campaigned for an attack on Iran, coordinating their political campaign through think tanks, conservative publications and legislative action in Congress (Mearsheimer and Walt 2007: 291–294). Again, Bush never went further than backing these ideas with his own aggressive rhetoric.

It appears the Bush administration essentially ignored neoconservative plans for Iraqi oil policy and for reshaping the Middle East. Table 10.1 shows how the neoconservatives repeatedly lost to the plans of the top leaders, whom we describe as US primacists, who are closely allied with the oil industry. Like the neoconservatives, the primacists aggressively pursue US hegemony, but they do not share the goals of the neoconservatives in the Middle East nor do they share the ideological goal of spreading democracy.

After numerous policy defeats neoconservatives realized that they had been used to sell the war publicly but were marginalized when it came to the creation of the Middle East policy. In 2006 prominent neoconservatives broke with the administration and resoundingly attacked Bush's policies. In *Vanity Fair*, the neoconservatives spoke of having been "used." David Frum summarized their feelings:

> I always believed as a speechwriter that if you could persuade the president to commit himself to certain words, he would feel himself committed to the ideas that underlay those words. And the big shock to me has been that, although the president said the words, he just did not absorb the ideas. And that is the root of, maybe, everything.
>
> (Rose 2006)

Most observers interpreted these neoconservative remarks as a self-serving attempt to distance themselves from what turned out to be a disastrous invasion. Perhaps the invasion would have been even more costly and disastrous had the neoconservatives' policies been followed, but their lament that their ideas were ignored seems to be well-founded.

Table 10.1 The neoconservative scorecard

Goals	Primacists and oil industry	Neoconservatives	Actual outcome
Invade Iraq	Yes	Yes	Yes
De-Bathification of Iraq Oil Ministry	No	Yes	No
Chalabi as head of Iraq	No	Yes	No
Iraq leaves OPEC	No	Yes	No
Privatize the oil	Partial	Full	Partial
Bomb Syria	No	Yes	No
Threaten Saudi Arabia	No	Yes	No
$20 billion in arms to Saudi Arabia	Yes	No	Yes
Saudi nuclear energy	Yes	No	Yes
Bomb Iran	No	Yes	No

Geopolitics: war for oil?

The geopolitical hypothesis argues that the United States invaded Iraq for a clear national interest in maintaining the free flow of Persian Gulf oil to protect US economic interests and the stability of the world economy. The most prominent admission of this motive came from Alan Greenspan, who in August of 2007 caused much controversy by saying in his political memoir, *The Age of Turbulence*, "I am saddened that it is politically inconvenient to acknowledge what everyone knows: Iraq is largely about oil" (Greenspan 2007: 463). Greenspan acknowledged what some analysts and many anti-war activists had been saying: the United States invaded Iraq to better control or "manage" the second largest oil reserves in the world by removing Saddam Hussein. In this section, we present both some key pieces of the abundant evidence supporting this hypothesis, as well as the strong arguments many scholars make against this possible motive for invasion. In the end we find that oil was very likely a primary, necessary reason for the war; if Iraq had no oil, there would not have been an invasion. In our final section of this chapter we explain how we find oil to likely not be a sufficient reason for the war, as it was not the only goal, just an obvious critical factor in the pursuit of the broader ideological ambition of achieving US primacy as perceived by Cheney, Rumsfeld and Bush.

The best evidence for the importance of the geopolitical hypothesis, in addition to much that has been presented in the chapters by Michael Klare and John Duffield, are the many speeches and reports in which the top Bush leaders and other leaders repeatedly claim that Saddam Hussein was the main obstacle to maintaining an adequate oil supply for the United States and the West. Most well-known is Cheney's August 1999 speech at the London Institute of Petroleum in which he presented in detail a widely-shared rationale for radically changing the Middle East situation, with Iraq central to that change (Cheney 1999). Cheney said that in order to meet world oil demand and continue economic growth, fifty million more barrels of oil a day were needed by 2010. Cheney warned of a massive energy crisis unless international oil companies gained access to the increasingly nationalized Middle Eastern oil fields. Cheney contended that the nationalized oil companies lacked the competence and expertise to meet growing demand, and if production was not increased, demand would soon exceed supply. Oil prices would then rise rapidly and economic growth would likely significantly stall.

Other leaders echoed Cheney's concerns. Senator Richard Lugar and former CIA Director James Woolsey warned of an impending energy crisis in *Foreign Affairs* (Lugar and Woolsey 1999). Lugar and Woolsey stated that non-Middle East oil production would peak in 1999, after which OPEC would increasingly control US energy.

US oil prices rose significantly during the 2000 presidential campaign. Candidate George W. Bush repeatedly conveyed the same impending energy crisis message. For example, in Saginaw, Michigan, on September 29, 2000, Bush said, "oil consumption is increasing. Our production is dropping. Our imports are skyrocketing. As a result, America, more than ever, is at the mercy of foreign governments and cartels—at the mercy of big foreign oil." Bush said the first step to increasing production would be to rebuild American influence in the Persian Gulf. He specifically mentioned Iraqi oil, "one of our worst international enemies is gaining more and more control over America's economic future" (Bush 2000).

Upon taking office in 2001 the Bush administration made increasing energy supplies a top priority, just as they had promised. Cheney immediately commissioned a report by the James Baker Institute to study the United States' energy future. In April 2001, the Baker Report contained the same message:

> The United States remains a prisoner of its energy dilemma, suffering on a recurring basis from negative consequences of sporadic energy shortages. These consequences can include recession, social dislocation of the poorest Americans, and at the extremes, a need for military intervention.... Iraq remains a destabilizing influence to U.S. allies in the Middle East, as well as to regional and global order, and to the flow of oil to international markets from the Middle East. Saddam Hussein has also demonstrated a willingness to threaten to use the oil weapon and to use his own export program to manipulate oil markets.

According to this report on the United States' energy future, Iraq was a destabilizing influence and a central problem for the world economy. Energy shortages could have the consequence of creating "a need for military intervention" (Baker Report 2001: 34, 42).

Also in early 2001, Cheney convened a closed-door group to handle the growing energy crisis, the National Energy Development Project Group (NEDPG). The NEDPG report stated that rising oil demand and diminishing supplies would strain the market and empower Persian Gulf suppliers (Cheney *et al.* 2001). As the Chair of the NEDPG, Cheney met with leaders from the Persian Gulf and with heads of major multinational oil corporations to discuss the United States' future energy policy, but much of what happened among this group is unknown. Judicial Watch filed a Freedom of Information Act lawsuit and the Commerce Department turned over seven pages of documents from the NEDPG (Judicial Watch 2002). The documents were maps of oil fields of Saudi Arabia, Iraq and the UAE, along with a list of all prospective oil projects for each of the countries. The two pages of oil projects planned for Iraq were titled "Foreign Suitors of Iraqi Oil" and listed various foreign national oil companies with US and British oil companies noticeably absent. Without context, it is impossible to know how important these documents truly were to the NEDPG but the documents clearly show that the NEDPG had taken notice of the United States being locked out of the Iraqi oil market.

Altogether, these reports and speeches point to widespread awareness of the possibility of supply shortages and rising oil prices. It was also well-known that Iraq represented one of the last major oil supply frontiers since it had little oil exploration since the 1970s. The US Department of Energy estimated that Iraq possibly had reserves of 400 billion barrels, possibly the largest reserves in the world, potentially dwarfing Saudi Arabia's 260 billion barrels (Paul 2002). Oil experts concurred: foreign oil companies with high technology could significantly increase Iraqi oil production and mitigate the potential crisis. The repeated emphasis by Cheney, Bush and other leaders of an impending oil crisis, with a focus on Iraq as central to this crisis, is compelling evidence for the geopolitical hypothesis. But recognition of an energy dilemma does not necessitate an invasion of Iraq as a solution.

Many scholars flatly reject the geopolitical hypothesis and argue oil was not central to the invasion decision. First, many argue logically that it was clear the costs of an invasion would outweigh the economic benefits. Second, they support this view by pointing to realist political leaders, who were known to have prioritized US oil interests in the past, who spoke out against the invasion. They also argue that generally oil interests much prefer stability over the uncertainty of war.

Supporting the argument that this invasion was not about oil is the fact that prominent realist scholars vociferously argued in the fall of 2002 that the cost-benefit analysis heavily weighed against an invasion of Iraq, particularly a unilateral invasion. There was widespread expert agreement that an invasion would be costly, with no easy exit strategy. It was argued repeatedly that because of high costs and no imminent threat from Iraq, an invasion of Iraq did not meet the criteria for being in the United States' vital interests. Most prominently, many realist scholars and other scholars of international security affairs explained this view in an advertisement on the op-ed page of the *New York Times* on September 26, 2002. The thirty-three scholars stated: "Military force should be used only when it advances U.S. national interests. War with Iraq does not meet this standard" (Art *et al.* 2002). Despite the academic consensus that the costs would clearly outweigh the benefits, it is of course still possible Bush administration leaders made a different calculation and invaded for geopolitical reasons.

Buttressing scholars' views that the war was not for geopolitical interests is the noted fact that a number of prominent realist policy-makers were outspoken critics of the invasion plan. Unlike the realist scholars, the realist policy-makers were not unambiguously opposed to an invasion. For example, scholars have often pointed to Brent Scowcroft, Bush Senior's National Security Advisor and loyal friend, as an example of a realist policy-maker opposed to an invasion. Scowcroft wrote a much-noticed op-ed entitled "Don't Attack Saddam" published on August 15, 2002 in the

Wall Street Journal. Scowcroft energetically challenged the *immediate* need for an invasion (Scowcroft 2002). However, while it appeared Scowcroft opposed invasion broadly, what Scowcroft actually carefully argued was that unless the United States obtained international support, an invasion would likely destabilize the security of the region and jeopardize the war on terror.

Scowcroft offered a different strategy for arranging an internationally legitimate invasion. He said that the United States should propose no-notice inspections and, if Saddam rejected them, this would create a legitimate *casus belli* for invasion. We now know this was precisely Britain's preferred approach to achieving legal legitimacy for the invasion plan.

Another prominent realist, Henry Kissinger, had similar criticisms of the push for an invasion of Iraq. While it superficially appeared he opposed an invasion, he actually argued the administration was pursuing a faulty campaign to sell the invasion; he thought the United States should insist on stringent inspections of Iraq and then use non-compliance as an excuse to invade, so "The case for military intervention then will have been made in the context of seeking a common approach" (Kissinger 2002b). Overall, Kissinger vigorously supported an invasion. In a January 13, 2002 *Washington Post* op-ed, Kissinger gave his reasons for endorsing an invasion: "The challenge of Iraq is essentially geopolitical. Iraq's policy is implacably hostile to the United States and to certain neighboring countries" (Kissinger 2002a). Scowcroft, Kissinger and even Secretary of State Colin Powell had reservations about a unilateral invasion, but clearly understood and appreciated the compelling geopolitical reasons for an invasion if costs could be limited through multilateral action.

While most scholars find there is very little direct evidence that the war was waged for the purpose of taking control of Iraq's oil, it is also clear that an impending world oil shortage was a pressing concern for the top leaders in the Bush administration and others. Realist scholars and policy-makers loudly contended that the risks to the oil market would be great if the United States invaded, particularly if it invaded without international legitimacy and support. But the cost-benefit analysis of an invasion might have been different for the top leaders of the Bush administration, especially if Cheney, Rumsfeld and Bush calculated the invasion would be swift and easy because of their confidence in high-tech US military capabilities.

In the end, we argue that Cheney, Rumsfeld and Bush were US primacists and not realists, so their calculations about costs and benefits were likely not congruent with realist calculations at all. While a unilateral invasion of Iraq held some risks, for them a unilateral invasion also offered great rewards. If the United States was successful, it would not have to share the spoils of victory with a broader coalition. For them, there was also no reason the United States should share the spoils since no other country in the coalition would bring significant military capability to the table. For a primacist, the costs of a coalition likely outweighed the benefits. Asserting

American military strength in the Middle East over perhaps the largest oil reserves in the world fits neatly into an ideology of US primacy. However, while Iraq clearly represented a potential bonanza for US oil companies if the invasion was successful, without more direct evidence that actual oil interests lobbied for an invasion, the specific role oil interests played is unknown. The most that can be demonstrated is that Cheney, Rumsfeld and Bush were ardent believers that access to inexpensive oil was a key factor in US primacy, and the steadfast pursuit of US primacy was an ideology they shared.

A war to assert US primacy?

> A couple of years ago I asked Rumsfeld to comment on accusations that the Jewish lobby maneuvered the administration into war. "I suppose the implication of that is the President and the Vice President and myself and Colin Powell just fell off a turnip truck to take these jobs," he said.
>
> (Goldberg 2007)

In this chapter we have shown that Cheney, Rumsfeld and Bush were not convinced by the neoconservatives but were intent on removing Saddam Hussein from power long before 9/11. In some ways President Bush was fresh "off a turnip truck" in terms of being new to foreign policy decision-making, but he trusted Cheney and Rumsfeld on this decision. Cheney and Rumsfeld had nearly three decades of experience at the highest levels of public service. They had developed and shared a clear ideology that guided their foreign policy preferences. Some have argued that they were primarily driven to use their power as public officials to make tens, even hundreds, of millions of dollars in the weapons and oil industries for themselves and their supporters. We find that their goals appear to be much broader and more ideological than solely the pursuit of personal power or the enrichment of their supporters.

Suspicions about their goals arise because they did not publicly "sell" their goal of US primacy in clear terms. The main problem they faced was that the ideology they embraced was not moralistic but hard-nosed. Some have called it an "assertive nationalist" ideology, connoting a vision of aggressively pursuing the national interest (Daalder and Lindsay 2003). While this is in essence accurate, their vision appears to have been even grander; they wanted to achieve nothing less than full, unquestioned US primacy. For three decades they emphasized and further developed ideas captured by key phrases they frequently employed such as achieving "maximum flexibility" for the president and full "freedom of action" for the United States militarily. Throughout their careers they focused on what they perceived as two crucial ingredients for achieving US primacy: first that the US president needed to be unencumbered in the pursuit of US foreign policy goals (free from interference by Congress, the UN, the public and the press) and second the United States must have by far the most technologically advanced and superior military force in the world. For them, achieving US primacy would be the best way to further US national interests. While an exhaustive study of Cheney and Rumsfeld's multifaceted pursuit of their ideology is not possible here, a brief recounting of some of the most telling episodes reveals their unstinting dedication to these goals.

Rumsfeld and Cheney first came to power in the 1970s during the period of the fallout from Vietnam and Watergate. At this time, Congress was attempting to assert itself in the realm of foreign policy, especially with the new law of the War Powers Act that set limits on the President's ability to send troops abroad indefinitely. Congress was also doing multiple investigations of the secret conduct of past presidents, especially CIA activities overthrowing foreign governments and waging wars without informing Congress. Cheney and Rumsfeld both encouraged President Ford to defy Congress and resist congressional oversight in numerous ways. For example, on May 25, 1975, Cheney, Chief of Staff to President Ford, advised Ford to prosecute the reporter Seymour Hersh for treason for detailing a submarine program spying on the Soviets in an article in the *New York Times*. He wanted to make an example of Hersh in order to weaken the Church and Pike congressional investigations. His advice was overruled by other less hard-line members of the Ford administration (Savage 2007). Apparently, Cheney's uncompromising ideology in favor of a sovereign presidency able to employ hard power unilaterally was frequently on display behind closed doors. As a close adviser and speech writer to Ford, Robert Hartmann noted about Cheney: "Whenever his private ideology was exposed, he appeared somewhat to the right of Ford, Rumsfeld or, for that matter, Genghis Khan" (Mann 2004a: 64). Cheney would later say in 2005 that he saw the 1970s as "the nadir of the modern presidency in terms of authority and legitimacy" and that restoring the power of the executive "has been a continuing theme, if you will, in terms of my career" (Walsh 2006).

Also during this period of détente, which many thought was the end of the Cold War with the Soviet Union, reduced defense spending was widely expected. Cheney and Rumsfeld were determined to lead the country in the opposite direction and strengthen the military substantially by increasing the defense budget and creating a more high-tech force. In particular, Rumsfeld embraced a new vision for the military called the Revolution in Military Affairs (RMA). In February 1975, analysts closely associated with the Pentagon and the RAND Corporation, especially Albert Wohlstetter and Andrew Marshall, the founders of the RMA concept, wrote a classified plan that outlined the beginning of military transformation. The report envisioned remotely piloted vehicles, precision guided missiles, satellite technology, new radar technology, and a Global Positioning System all integrated into one ultra high-tech military system. According to Wohlstetter, the new system would give the president a variety of non-nuclear "strategic response options" to a Soviet invasion of Europe, or other contingencies (Kaplan 2008: 12–15). In his last year as Secretary of Defense under Ford, Rumsfeld worked to secure a nine-billion dollar defense budget increase; he managed this even during this period of relative economic austerity. It was the first real defense increase in constant dollars since 1967, and was no small feat at the time.

In the 1980s, Cheney served as a Congressman from Wyoming, but he still prioritized protecting and enhancing the power of the president and increasing the power of the military through larger budgets, especially high-tech programs. For example, on November 18, 1980, after James Baker was appointed to be White House of Chief of Staff for Reagan, Baker consulted with Cheney who had served as Chief of Staff under Ford. At the meeting, Cheney took the opportunity to push for more executive power in foreign policy and overturning the War Powers Act. Baker's notes say, "Pres. Seriously weakened in recent yrs. Restore power & auth to Exec Branch—Need stronger ldr'ship. Get rid of War Powers Act-restore independent rights." The passage was marked with two double lines and six asterisks and in the margin Baker wrote, "Central theme we ought to push" (Savage 2007: 43).

Later in the 1980s, Cheney again attempted to strengthen the control of the executive over foreign policy when he wrote the minority report of the Iran Contra Affair. His report declared the entire investigation of Reagan's administration unconstitutional. After turning in the report in November 1987 Cheney publicly gave a lengthy summary of his ideology:

> If you go back to the early 1970s coming out of the war in Vietnam and Watergate, Congress moved very aggressively to assert the notion that it was important to place limits on presidential power and authority, so that future Presidents would not abuse Presidential power the way it was alleged Lyndon Johnson had in the war in Southeast Asia or Richard Nixon had in connection with Watergate. The result of that was a series of legislative enactments: The War Powers Act in 1973 that limits the president's ability to commit troops overseas. The Turkish Arms embargo in 1974 that shut off the flow of arms to a key NATO ally. The Clark Amendment in 1975 that shut down what up till then had been a very successful effort to support Jonas Savimbi in covert action in Angola. He's still there today and making significant military gains. But when Ronald Reagan came to power in 1980 many of us who were his supporters believed that he offered us the opportunity to correct the imbalance that had developed in the 70s between Congress and the President in the area of foreign policy and national security matters. I believe that it's absolutely essential that you recognize the President as the pre-eminent authority in foreign policy. That

in the world we live in with all its inherent danger that it's impossible to talk about a reasonable national security policy, foreign policy that's carried out by 535 Secretaries of State up there on Capitol Hill.

(Cheney 1987)

Congressman Cheney also consistently supported proposals to strengthen the military by backing increases in the defense budget. He fully supported funding for a newer generation of chemical weapons, the multiple warhead MX missile, the Strategic Defense Initiative and other RMA programs. Serving under President George Bush Sr. as Secretary of Defense, Cheney described himself, "As a member of Congress (I) voted for every single defense program – I never saw a defense program I didn't like" (Chatterjee 2009: 37).

While Rumsfeld spent most of the 1980s involved in private business he also stayed involved in foreign policy. He worked as an envoy to the Middle East for the Reagan administration where he met with Iraqi officials including Saddam Hussein. According to declassified documents from November 1983, Rumsfeld was aware of Iraq's "almost daily" use of chemical weapons, and despite this knowledge, Rumsfeld had a very positive meeting with Saddam Hussein on December 21, 1983. Later that day he also had a meeting with Saddam's assistant, Tariq Aziz, where Rumsfeld mentioned chemical weapons but also made it clear that the United States wanted to end the war and offered "our willingness to do more" (Battle 2003). Rumsfeld's repeated negotiations with Iraq reveal a hard-power ideology, devoid of moral scruples.

Also in the 1980s, President Reagan, without consulting Congress and through a secret executive order, started a new Continuity of Government (COG) program. The program ignored the constitutional line of succession to the presidency. In the exercise, after the death of the president and vice president, the presidency would fall to a cabinet member and not the Speaker of the House and then the president *pro tempore* of the Senate as specified by Federal Law. Further, the program did not plan to reconstitute Congress on the basis that this would lead to confusion and might take valuable time from responding to the crisis. In short, Rumsfeld and Cheney took part in a top-secret annual exercise that simulated complete presidential control of government in a crisis. Once a year during the Reagan presidency they would lead two of three teams that would be taken to separate undisclosed locations and engage in a simulated response to a Soviet attack. Perhaps most importantly, the teams would act as all-powerful executives taking control of government and not consulting with Congress. In the hours after 9/11, Cheney enacted many of the provisions in the COG plan, ordering the president not to return to Washington and sending various public officials off to undisclosed locations (Mann 2004b).

In the 1990s, as Secretary of Defense under George H. W. Bush, Cheney attempted to strengthen the presidency during the Persian Gulf crisis. After President George H. W. Bush made the decision to send troops to Saudi Arabia and confront Saddam, he began to face continuous congressional criticism for not consulting Congress about using force. After much debate, Bush ultimately decided to seek congressional approval for the decision to intervene in Kuwait. Cheney forcefully disagreed with asking for Congressional approval, saying, "In the end they don't accept responsibility for tough decisions up there" (Alfonsi 2006: 152). Bush overruled his Secretary of Defense but the incident illustrates how Cheney did not want to legitimize the role of Congress in foreign policy.

After the Cold War, Cheney also fought hard against the whole notion of a "peace dividend," repeating the phrase, "There is no peace dividend. The dividend of military spending has been 40 years of peace" (Marullo 1993: 192). In an effort to stop the movement for a peace dividend and a post-Cold War demobilization, Cheney and Powell decided they needed to justify their overarching plan for maintaining vast US military superiority. In early 1992, Powell gave Congressional testimony endorsing a new "base force" plan. Powell told members of the House Armed Services Committee that the United States required "sufficient power" to "deter any challenger from ever dreaming of challenging us on the world stage" (Armstrong 2002). Cheney also took steps to create a new defense doctrine that would codify a clear rationale for the large defense budget he thought necessary to maintain in the post-Cold War world. Cheney authorized Paul Wolfowitz to manage a group project to write up a new Defense Planning Guidance (DPG) drafted by various authors throughout the Pentagon in full consultation with the Chairman of the Joint Chiefs of Staff, Colin Powell (Burr 2008).

The DPG was leaked to the *New York Times* on March 7, 1992 (Tyler 1992). The radical plan caused a political firestorm as it called for US military primacy over every strategic region on the planet. It stated that US strategy

> requires that we endeavor to prevent any hostile power from dominating a region whose resources would, under consolidated control, be sufficient to generate global power. These regions include Western Europe, East Asia, the territory of the former Soviet Union, and Southwest Asia.

Echoing the words of Colin Powell the plan said the United States would assure dominance of the strategic regions by showing both allies and enemies "that they need not aspire to a greater role or pursue a more aggressive posture to protect their legitimate interests." The plan even included Japan and Germany in the list of potential future rivals. It also said that the United States would reserve the right to act unilaterally to protect not only our interests, but those of our allies or friends, or those which could seriously unsettle international relations. Various types of US interests may be involved in such instances: access to vital raw materials, primarily Persian Gulf oil; proliferation of weapons of mass destruction and ballistic missiles; threats to US citizens from terrorism or regional or local conflict; and threats to US society from narcotics trafficking.

American allies such as Germany and Japan and Congressmen in the United States openly criticized the document. Presidential candidate Bill Clinton's spokesman George Stephanopoulos called it an excuse for huge defense budgets (Dorrien 2004: 41).

The draft DPG leaked in 1992 was widely perceived as a radical neoconservative document that was not endorsed by the high officials in the George H. W. Bush administration. Dick Cheney sought to distance himself from the document publicly while heartily endorsing it privately. Pentagon spokesman Pete Williams claimed that Cheney and Wolfowitz had not read it. Numerous other Pentagon officials stepped forward to say that the report represented the views of one man: Paul Wolfowitz. The campaign to scapegoat Wolfowitz for the unpopular plan was successful and the press dubbed the DPG as the "Wolfowitz Doctrine." However, recently released classified documents show that the document was based on Powell's "base force" plan and was drafted with the full consultation of Cheney and many other high Pentagon officials (Burr 2008).

In the days after the leak, Wolfowitz and others worried that the plan would be dropped altogether. But in spite of the controversy, Cheney was very happy with the document, telling Zalmay Khalilzad, one of the main authors, "You have discovered a new rationale for our role in the world" (Hoyle 2008: 50). Cheney tasked Wolfowitz and Libby to work through more drafts. Wolfowitz and Libby had to report back to Cheney who made sure that none of the hard-line principles of world primacy and presidential authority were undermined. On May 19, 1992 Wolfowitz sent a memo to Cheney reassuring him that the new draft of the DPG "is still a rather hard-hitting document which retains the substance you liked in the February 18th draft" (Burr 2008). The May 19 memo also included copies of the DPG that had received input from David Addington, Cheney's lawyer who zealously worked for presidential supremacy over foreign policy (Savage 2007).

The final copy of the DPG was closely overseen by Cheney and actively endorsed by Colin Powell. It was released publicly in January 1993, the same month that Clinton was inaugurated. The new document held the same principles as the originally leaked DPG. For example, it endorsed precluding rivals from key regions but left out language about Japan and Germany. It claimed the United States would still assert the right to act unilaterally, justified by the fact that "even when a broad potential coalition exists, leadership will be necessary to realize it." It also endorsed the idea of presidential control over foreign policy saying, "A future president will need options, allowing him to lead and where the international reaction proves sluggish or inadequate, to act independently to protect our critical interests." The new document also repeatedly endorsed the concept of the RMA, stating, "The Gulf War made clear the early promise of this revolution, emphasizing the importance of recent breakthroughs in low observable, information gathering and processing, precision strike, and other key technologies." Softening the clear assertion of a strategy of US primacy was language endorsing democratic allies, collective security, international treaties and institutions; this language had largely been absent from the leaked document.

While President Clinton shelved the DPG in 1993, Cheney and Rumsfeld continued advocating the DPG's strategy for US primacy primarily with the help of the Project for the New American Century (PNAC). While Cheney only signed on to the "Statement of Principles" of PNAC, which stated the need for American leadership in the world and a strengthening of US military forces, Rumsfeld was much more active in this primarily neoconservative group. The central document for PNAC was a detailed analysis of US defense objectives titled *Rebuilding America's Defenses*. This report states it was built directly on the DPG and quotes Cheney when he was answering the critics of the DPG, "We can either sustain the armed forces we require and remain in a position to help shape things for the better or we can throw that advantage away" (Donnelly *et al.* 2000: ii). But *Rebuilding America's Defenses* goes further than the DPG, expanding in detail about strategic objectives particularly in respect to the Persian Gulf. When discussing the Gulf there is no flowery talk of democracy or inflated threats of WMD, just blunt admissions of the need for a US military presence in a region of vital importance. Although not stated outright, the region being home to two thirds of the world's known oil reserves must contribute to the region's "vital importance." The document states:

> Indeed the United States has for decades sought a more permanent role in Gulf Regional Security. While the unresolved conflict with Iraq provides the immediate justification, the need for a substantial American force presence in the Gulf transcends the issue of the regime of Saddam Hussein.
>
> (Donnelly *et al.* 2000: 14)

On the Revolution in Military Affairs, the document greatly laments the lack of money going into research and development in new technologies. The report says:

> Further, the process of transformation, even if it brings revolutionary change, is likely to be a long one, absent some catastrophic and

catalyzing event – like a new Pearl Harbor. Domestic politics and industrial policy will shape the pace and content of transformation as much as the requirements of current missions.

(Donnelly *et al.* 2000: 51)

Many people have noticed that after 9/11, both Cheney and Rumsfeld seized on the new Pearl Harbor to "Go Massive" and achieve goals unrelated to 9/11, but clearly outlined in this incredibly blunt strategy document.

This sketch of Cheney and Rumsfeld outlines how they have had a long-standing goal of asserting US hard power in the world to establish US primacy as others have now shown in much greater detail (Warshaw 2009; Chatterjee 2009; Gellman 2008; Herspring 2008; Kaplan 2008; Savage 2007). Scholars still point to the quote by Richard Haass, a member of the State Department at the time of the invasion, who claims not to know why the United States invaded: "it still isn't possible to be sure, and this remains the most remarkable thing about the Iraq war." We believe the apparent mystery of this invasion is not as mysterious as many of the architects of this war would like the world to believe. We think a gradual consensus is forming among scholars of the war that Cheney, and to a lesser degree Rumsfeld, were the primary individuals whom Bush trusted. These three leaders together shared the desire to forcefully remove Saddam Hussein, they made the decision, and they made the key appointments of the talented advisers who crafted the arguments to sell the war to the American people. We have shown that President Bush was a zealous participant in the decision to invade, but he was likely not a primary architect to the extent the much more seasoned Cheney and Rumsfeld were. We find that the recently released documents proving intentional intelligence manipulation (especially from the British Iraq Inquiry, see Chapter 9), combined with the long career paths of Cheney and Rumsfeld and the actions of these top leaders before and after 9/11, belie the perception that the administration was swept up by events and acted out of misguided notions of imminent threats, Iraqi connections to Al Qaeda, or crusading idealism. The United States did not emotionally stumble into war because of 9/11. On the contrary, the top leaders took a calculated risk to achieve their goals of US primacy, including proving the effectiveness of the revolution in military affairs, and strengthening the power of the president.

One of the main goals of this chapter has been to show that the neoconservatives were not the primary movers behind the invasion even though they had been noisily lobbying for regime change for over a decade since the first Persian Gulf War. Instead we find that Cheney and Rumsfeld also desired an invasion of Iraq, but for different reasons and with different goals in mind. But why does it matter which leaders were the primary movers and what the goals of the invasion were? What are the stakes in this debate? Can the lessons that are drawn from the Iraq invasion be used in the future to avoid other US wars?

Possibly. For example, if the United States went to war due to bad intelligence then scholars should focus on suggestions for improving the CIA, other intelligence bodies or international inspections. If the United States waged a preventive war against WMD, then scholars need to try to understand how to head off preventive wars through better bargaining or diplomacy. If neoconservative ideology tragically misled US leaders into thinking they could spread democracy with military force, then lessons about the difficulty of spreading democracy may be all that is needed to prevent future endeavors. Or if the United States went to war on behalf of Israel because of a powerful domestic lobby, exposing this lobby may be a remedy. But if the United States went to war in order to achieve US primacy then scholars need to expose and critique this ideology. If this ideology is based on tragic "myths" that other empires have disastrously embraced—then where do these pernicious myths come from? (Snyder 1991). In the final analysis, this invasion was far too easily consummated by a very few leaders in the executive branch, with absolutely impotent congressional oversight. If the United States wants to be a peaceful democratic nation and avoid disastrous wars in the future, one primary lesson from this episode is that war needs to become politically, democratically, more difficult to wage. This is a tall order, but a good start may be at least to return to what Cheney would consider "the dark days of the 1970s" when Congress held meaningful investigations of executive branch wrongdoing and the media worked independently to inform the public by exposing the truth.

References

Alfonsi, C. (2006) *Circle in the Sand: Why We Went Back to Iraq*, New York: Doubleday.

Armstrong, D. (2002) "Dick Cheney's Song of America," *Harper Magazine*, October, 305: 1829.

Armstrong, F. (2010) "The CIA and WMDs: The Damning Evidence," *The New York Review of Books*, August 19.

Art, R. J. *et al.* (2002) "War with Iraq is not in America's National Interest," *New York Times*, September 26, Online. Available at: file://C:/DOCUME~1/GTF/LOCALS~1/Temp/26%20September%202002%20ScholarNYT%20Advertisement.htm (accessed May 10, 2010).

Baker, J. A. (2001) *Strategic Energy Policy Challenges for the 21st Century*, Independent Task Force on Strategic Energy Policy, Online. Available at: www.ratical.org/ratville//CAH/linkscopy/energycfr.pdf (accessed June 7, 2010).

Baker, J. A. (2003) *Guiding Principles for U.S. Post-Conflict Policy in Iraq*, January 23, Online. Available at: www.cfr.org/content/publications/attachments/Post-War_Iraq.pdf (accessed May 14, 2010).

Baker, R. (2009) *Family of Secrets: The Bush Dynasty, the Powerful Forces that Put it in the White House, and What their Influence Means for America*, New York: Bloomsbury.

Bamford, J. (2004) *A Pretext for War: 9/11, Iraq, and the Abuse of America's Intelligence Agencies*, New York: Anchor Books.

Battle, J. (2003) "Shaking Hands with Saddam Hussein: The U.S. Tilts toward Iraq, 1980–1984" *National Security Archive*, February 25. Available at: www.gwu.edu/~nsarchiv/NSAEBB/NSAEBB82 (accessed June 3, 2010).

Beaumont, P. and Islam, F. (2002) "Carve-up of Oil Riches Begins: U.S. Plans to Ditch Industry Rivals and Force End of OPEC," *Guardian*, November 3: 16.

Bruni, F. (1999) "Bush Has Tough Words and Rough Enunciation for Iraqi Chief," *New York Times*, December 3, Online. Available at: http://query.nytimes.com/gst/fullpage.html?res=9503EFDD153EF937A35751C1A96F958260 (accessed May 4, 2010).

Bruni, F. and Schmitt, E. (2000) "The 2000 Campaign: The Bush Connection; Looking for Just the Right Fit, Bush Finds it in Dad's Cabinet," *New York Times*, July 25, Online. Available at: www.nytimes.com/2000/07/25/us/2000-campaign-bush-connection-looking-for-just-right-fit-bush-finds-it-dad-s.html (accessed June 4, 2010).

Bruno, K. and Vallette, J. (2001) "Cheney and Halliburton: Go Where the Oil Is," *Multinational Monitor*, May, 22: 5.

Burkeman, O. (2002) "US Apologizes to 'Enemy' Saudis. Coalition Powell Disowns Briefing at Pentagon," *Guardian*, August 7: 5.

Burr, W. (2008) "The Making of Cheney Regional Defense Strategy, 1991–1992," *National Security Archive*, George Washington University, February 26, Online. Available at: www.gwu.edu/~nsarchiv/nukevault/ebb245 (accessed February 1, 2011).

Bush G. W. (2000) "A Comprehensive National Energy Policy," Saginaw, Michigan, *CNN Transcripts*, September 29, Online. Available at: http://transcripts.cnn.com/TRANSCRIPTS/0009/29/se.01.html (accessed May 2, 2010).

Cato Daily Dispatch (2000) Online. Available at: www.cato.org/dispatch/10–06–00d.html (accessed May 15, 2011).

Chatterjee, P. (2009) *Halliburton's Army: How a Well-Connected Texas Oil Company Revolutionized the Way America Makes War*, New York: Nation Books.

Cheney D. (1987) "Dick Cheney on the Iran Contra Controversy," *Issues Facing the Nation*, November 19, Online. Available at: www.youtube.com/watch?v=4_3he1Rm6cI (accessed February 5, 2011).

Cheney, D. (1999) "Full Text of Dick Cheney's Speech at IP Autumn Lunch," Institute of Petroleum, Autumn, Online. Available at: http://web.archive.org/web/20000414054656/www.petroleum.co.uk/speeches.htm (accessed May 21, 2010).

Cheney, D. *et al.* (2001) The National Energy Development Group, *National Energy Policy*, Washington DC: U.S. Government Printing Office.

Cholmondeley, T. (2002) "Over a Barrel," *Guardian*, November 22: 23.

Clarke, R. (2004) *Against All Enemies: Inside America's War on Terror*, New York: Free Press.

Cohen, A. and Driscoll Jr., G. P. (2002) "The Road to Economic Prosperity for a Post Saddam Iraq," *The Heritage Foundation*, September 25, Online. Available at: www.heritage.org/Research/MiddleEast/bg1594.cfm (accessed May 25, 2010).

Coughlin, C. (2006) *American Ally: Tony Blair and the War on Terror*, New York: HarperCollins.

CNN (2001) "Two Iraqis Killed in U.S./U.K. Bombing of Iraq," February 17,

Online. Available at: www.ccmep.org/usbombingwatch/2001.htm#2/22/01 (accessed May 15, 2010).

Daalder, I. and Lindsay, J. (2003) *America Unbound: The Bush Revolution in Foreign Policy*, Washington, DC: Brookings Institution Press.

Dettmer, J. (2002) "Iraqi Oil Strategy Divides State, White House," *Insight on the News*, December 24, Online. Available at: http://findarticles.com/p/articles/mi_m1571/is_1_19/ai_95914207/?tag=content;coll (accessed May 9, 2010).

Donnelly, T. *et al.* (2000) "Rebuilding America's Defenses," *Project for the New American Century*, Online. Available at: www.newamericancentury.org/RebuildingAmericasDefenses.pdf (accessed February 1, 2011).

Dorrien, G. (2004) *Imperial Designs: Neoconservatism and the Pax Americana*, New York: Routledge.

Foyer, F. and Ackerman, S. (2003) "The Radical: What Dick Cheney Really Believes," *The New Republic*, December 1, Online. Available at: www.tnr.com/article/the-radical (accessed May 20, 2010).

Frum, D. (2003) *The Right Man: The Surprise Presidency of George W. Bush*, New York: Random House.

Gellman, B. (2008) *Angler: The Cheney Vice Presidency*, New York: Penguin Press.

Goldberg, J. (2007) "The Usual Suspect," *The New Republic*, October 1, Online. Available at: www.tnr.com/article/the-usual-suspect (accessed February 1, 2011).

Goodman, A. (2005) "Interview of Osama Siblani," *Democracy Now*, March 11, Online. Available at: www.democracynow.org/2005/3/11/arab_american_publisher_says_bush_told (accessed May 15, 2010).

Goodman, M. A. (2008) *Failure of Intelligence: The Decline and Fall of the CIA*, New York: Rowman and Littlefield Publishers.

Gordon, M. R. and Trainor, B. E. (2007) *Cobra II: The Inside Story of the Invasion and Occupation of Iraq*, New York: Vintage Books.

Greenspan, A. (2007) *The Age of Turbulence: Adventures in a New World*, New York: Penguin Press.

Gumbell, A. (2004) "Back to the Future," *Independent*, May 28, Online. Available at: www.independent.co.uk/arts-entertainment/films/features/back-to-the-future-551642.html (accessed February 3, 2011).

Hassen, F. (2006) "The Future of Iraq Project," Department of State, *National Security Archive*, September 1, Online. Available at: www.gwu.edu/~nsarchiv/NSAEBB/NSAEBB198/index.htm (accessed May 21, 2010).

Herspring, D. (2008) *Rumsfeld's Wars: The Arrogance of Power*, Lawrence: Kansas University Publishers.

Hoyle, R. (2008) *Going to War: How Misinformation, Disinformation, and Arrogance Led America into Iraq*, New York: Thomas Dunne.

Isikoff, M. and Corn, D. (2006) *Hubris: The Inside Story of Spin, Scandal, and the Selling of the Iraq War*, New York: Crown.

Judicial Watch (2002) "Maps and Charts of Iraqi Oil Fields," March 5, Online. Available at: www.judicialwatch.org/story/2002/mar/maps-and-charts-iraqi-oilfields (accessed May 12, 2010).

Kaplan, F. (2008) *Daydream Believers: How a Few Grand Ideas Wrecked American Power*, Hoboken: Wiley.

Keane, F. (2003) "The Road to War," in Downing, M. and Beck, S. (eds.) *The Battle for Iraq: BBC News Correspondents on the War Against Saddam*, London: Johns Hopkins University Press.

Kessler, G. (2003) "U.S. Position on Iraq Has Puzzling Past," *The Washington Post,* January 12, Online. Available at: www.washingtonpost.com/ac2/wp-dyn/A43909–2003Jan11?language=printer (accessed May 17, 2010).

Kissinger H. (2002a) "Phase II and Iraq," *The Washington Post,* January 13.

Kissinger, H. (2002b) "Steps on the Way to Ousting Saddam from Iraq," *The Washington Post,* August 12.

Lake, D. A. (2010) "Two Cheers for Bargaining Theory: Assessing Rationalist Explanations of the Iraq War," *International Security,* 35: 7–52.

Landay, J. S. and Strobel, W. P. (2003) "Pentagon Civilians' Lack of Planning Contributed to Chaos in Iraq," *Knight Ridder,* July 12, Online. Available at: www.commondreams.org/headlines03/0712–05.htm (accessed June 4, 2010).

Lang, P. W. (2004) "Drinking the Kool-Aid," *Middle East Policy,* 11: 2, 39–60.

Lappin, Y. (2007) "Saudi Arms Deal Problematic," *Ynet News,* July 31, Online. Available at: www.ynetnews.com/articles/0,7340,L-3432163,00.html (accessed April 12, 2010).

Leung, R. (2004) "Clarke's Take on Terror," *CBS News,* March 21, Online. Available at: www.cbsnews.com/stories/2004/03/19/60minutes/main607356.shtml (accessed May 15, 2010).

Lind, M. (2003) "The Weird Men behind George W. Bush's War," *NewStatesman,* April 7, Online. Available at: www.newstatesman.com/200304070003 (accessed February 1, 2011).

Lind, M. (2004) "A Tragedy of Errors," *The Nation,* February 5, Online. Available at: www.thenation.com/article/tragedy-errors (accessed February 1, 2011).

Lugar, R. and Woolsey, J. (1999) "The New Petroleum," *Foreign Affairs* 78: 1.

McClellan, S. (2008) *What Happened: Inside the Bush White House and Washington's Culture of Deception,* New York: Public Affairs.

Mann, J. (2004a) *Rise of the Vulcans: The History of Bush's War Cabinet,* New York: Viking Press.

Mann, J. (2004b) "The Armageddon Plan," *Atlantic Magazine,* March, Online. Available at: www.theatlantic.com/past/docs/issues/2004/03/mann.htm (accessed February 5, 2011).

Markey, E. J. (2008) "Why is Bush Helping Saudi Arabia Build Nukes," *Wall Street Journal,* June 10: A15.

Marullo, S. (1993) *Ending the Cold War at Home,* New York: Lexington Books.

Mayer, J. (2008) *The Dark Side: The Inside Story of How the War on Terror Turned into a War on American Ideals,* New York: Doubleday.

Mearsheimer, J. J. and Walt, S. M. (2007) *The Israel Lobby and U.S. Foreign Policy,* New York: Farrar, Straus and Giroux.

Monten, J. (2005) "The Roots of the Bush Doctrine: Power, Nationalism and Democracy Promotion in U.S. Strategy," *International Security* 29: 112–156.

Moore, J. (2004) *Bush's War for Reelection: Iraq, the White House and the People,* New York: Wiley.

Muttitt, G. (2005) "Crude Designs," *Platform,* November, Online. Available at: www.neweconomics.org/publications/crude-designs (accessed May 7, 2010).

Overseas and Defence Secretariat, Cabinet Office (2002) Iraq Options Paper, Downing Street Documents, *National Security Archive,* March 8, Online. Available at: www.gwu.edu/~nsarchiv/NSAEBB/NSAEBB328/II-Doc01.pdf (accessed December 5, 2010).

Packer, G. (2005) *The Assassins' Gate: America in Iraq,* New York: Farrar, Straus and Giroux.

Paul, J. A. (2002) "Oil in Iraq: The Heart of the Crisis," *Global Policy Forum*, December, Online. Available at: www.globalpolicy.org/security/oil/2002/12heart.htm (accessed May 4, 2010).

Perle, R. *et al.* (1996) *Clean Break: A New Strategy for Securing the Realm*, Online. Available at: www.iasps.org/strat1.htm (accessed April 14, 2010).

Powers, T. (2007) "What Tenet Knew," *The New York Review of Books*, July 19.

Powers, T. (2010) "How They Got Their Bloody Way," *The New York Review of Books*, May 27.

Prados, J. (2004) *Hoodwinked: The Documents that Reveal how Bush Sold us a War*, New York: The New Press.

Prados, J. (2008) PR Push for Iraq War Preceded Intelligence Findings, *National Security Archive Briefing Book No. 254*, August 22. Available at: www.gwu. edu/~nsarchiv/NSAEBB/NSAEBB254/index.htm (accessed December 5, 2010).

Prados, J. (2011) "Rumsfeld Confirms Archive Analysis," *The National Security Archive*, February 8, Online. Available at: http://nsarchive.wordpress. com/2011/02/08/rumsfeld-confirms-archive-analysis (accessed February 12, 2011).

Prados, J. and Ames, C. (2010) "Iraq War Part II: Was There Even a Decision?" *National Security Archive Electronic Briefing Book 328*, Online. Available at: www. gwu.edu/~nsarchiv/NSAEBB/NSAEBB328/index.htm (accessed February 5, 2011).

Ricks, T. (2002) "Briefing Depicted Saudis as Enemies," *Washington Post*, August 6: A01.

Ricks, T. (2006) *Fiasco: The American Military Adventure in Iraq*, New York: Penguin Press.

Risen, J. (2006) *State of War: The Secret History of the CIA and the Bush Administration*, New York: Simon & Schuster.

Robbins, C. A. and Cummings, J. A. (2002) "How Bush Decided That Hussein Must Be Ousted from Atop Iraq," *Wall Street Journal*, June 14: 1.

Rose, D. (2006) "Neo Culpa," *Vanity Fair*, November 3, Online. Available at: www. vanityfair.com/politics/features/2006/12/neocons200612?currentPage=2 (accessed May 3, 2010).

Rumsfeld, D. (2001) "Bureaucracy to Battlefield," U.S. Department of Defense, September 10, Online. Available at: www.defense.gov/speeches/speech. aspx?speechid=430 (accessed May 2, 2010).

Savage, C. (2007) *Takeover: The Return of the Imperial Presidency and the Subversion of American Democracy*, New York: Back Bay.

Scowcroft, B. (2002) "Don't Attack Saddam," *Wall Street Journal*, August 15: 12.

Stevenson, R. W. (2004) "Bush Disputes Ex-officials Claim that War with Iraq was Early Administration Goal," *New York Times*, January 13.

Suskind, R. (2004) *The Price of Loyalty: George W. Bush, the White House, and the Education of Paul O'Neill*, New York: Simon & Schuster.

Tenet, G. (2007) *At the Center of the Storm: My Years at the CIA*, New York: HarperCollins.

Tyler, P. E. (1992) "U.S. Strategy Calls for Insuring No Rival Develops," March 8. Available at: www.nytimes.com/1992/03/08/world/us-strategy-plan-calls-for-insuring-no-rivals-develop.html (accessed May 7, 2010).

Unger, C. (2007) *The Fall of the House of Bush*, New York: Scribner.

Vulliamy, E. (2003) "Bush Ready to Fight War on Two Fronts," *Observer*, April 13, Online. Available at: www.guardian.co.uk/world/2003/apr/13/iraq.georgebush (accessed May 2, 2010).

Walsh, K. T. (2006) "The Cheney Factor," *U.S. News and World Reports*, January 15, Online. Available at: www.usnews.com/usnews/news/articles/060123/23cheney_2.htm (accessed February 3, 2011).

Warshaw, S. A. (2009) *The Co-Presidency of Bush and Cheney*, Stanford: Stanford University Press.

White, M. (2002) "Putin Demands Proof over Iraqi Weapons," *Guardian*, October 12, Online. Available at: www.guardian.co.uk/uk/2002/oct/12/russia.politics (accessed May 5, 2010).

Woodward, B. (1991) *The Commanders*, New York: Simon & Schuster.

Woodward, B. (2002) *Bush At War*, New York: Simon & Schuster.

Woodward, B. (2004) *Plan of Attack*, New York: Simon & Schuster.

Index

19607570R00151

Printed in Great Britain
by Amazon